REA

ACPL ITEM
DISCARDED

Y0-BST-935

1-16-76

CAMBRIDGE GED PROGRAM

INTERPRETATION OF LITERARY MATERIALS

Preparation for the High School Equivalency Examination

COMPLETELY REVISED AND ENLARGED

by Marilyn Manley, M.A.

Director, Curriculum Resource Center, Regional Opportunities Program of the City University of New York
Developer of GED Literature Curriculum for the Public Service Careers Program of the City University of New York

CAMBRIDGE BOOK COMPANY
488 Madison Avenue, New York, N.Y. 10022

 A NEW YORK TIMES COMPANY

Copyright © 1974, 1970, 1968, by Cambridge Book Company, A Division of the New York Times Media Company, Inc. All rights reserved. No part of this work covered by the copyrights hereon may be reproduced or used in any form or by any means—graphic, electronic, or mechanical, including photocopying, recording, or information storage and retrieval systems—without written permission of the publisher. Manufactured in the United States of America.

PREFACE TO REVISED EDITION

One of the most important features of this Revised Edition of Interpretation of Literary Materials is the inclusion of a new section on Reading Comprehension Skills as they apply to the interpretation of Literature. Recognizing that the techniques needed for reading and understanding literary passages may differ greatly from the skills required to interpret science and social studies material, the author has identified for the student—and treated under separate headings—the different skills needed for the comprehension and interpretation of essays, plays, fiction, and poetry. A wealth of exercise material gives the student ample practice in determining main idea or theme within each particular kind of literary category, and matching as closely as possible the types of questions most frequently asked on the High School Equivalency Examination. Additional material suggests techniques and gives practice in verifying supporting details from the text—another type of question often given on the GED Examination.

A second important feature of this Revised Edition is the classification and labeling of each multiple-choice question in the Diagnostic and Simulated Tests according to the principal reading skill required in order to arrive at the correct answer. If you have trouble with a particular type of question, turn to the section of the book which teaches that skill for additional explanation and practice (see Introduction, page 1).

Interpretation of Literary Materials has one purpose: to help you pass the "Interpretation of Literary Materials" section of the General Educational Development (GED) Test, commonly called the High School Equivalency Examination. This test makes it possible each year for hundreds of thousands of men and women who have left school without completing their studies to get a high school diploma or its equivalent.

This book is not just another question-and-answer book. It has been written with one examination in mind—the "Interpretation of Literary Materials" section of the GED Test. It is a carefully structured combination of instructional material and drill in the interpretation of literary forms and devices. Everything in this book reflects the latest developments in the GED Literature examination. Instructional material and questions are designed to teach you the special skills necessary for reading and understanding prose, poetry, and drama. All practice exercises and tests contain the same kinds of questions that appear on the actual GED Literature test, and have fully explained answers. A special feature is the complete two-hour Simulated GED Literature Examination, a test which closely follows the content, form, and level of difficulty of the official test.

In order to be equally well prepared for the other four sections of the High School Equivalency Examination, you will want to study the other books in the Cambridge GED Program. Each reflects the latest developments in the official GED Examination, and provides thorough, in-depth instruction in each specific subject area of the test. They are:

Correctness and Effectiveness of Expression.   This volume provides you with instruction and drill in the fundamentals of English, including spelling, grammar and usage, and punctuation. Hundreds of practice exercises strengthen your skills in these areas. A two-hour Simulated GED English Usage Examination is included. New edition is completely revised and reorganized.

Interpretation of Reading Materials in the Natural Sciences.   This volume contains a carefully prepared series of reading exercises in biology, chemistry, physics, and earth science. It also includes a glossary of important scientific terms, and a two-hour Simulated GED Science Examination. Revised edition. All answers identified and labeled according to reading skill involved.

Interpretation of Reading Materials in the Social Studies.   This volume presents a structured combination of instruction and drill in United States and world history, economics, and other important social studies areas. Included are glossaries, a special section on interpreting maps and graphs, a chart of Highlights of United States Presidential Administrations, and a two-hour Simulated GED Social Studies Examination. Revised edition contains a section on Reading Comprehension and Vocabulary Skills. All answers are labeled according to reading skill involved.

General Mathematical Ability.   This specialized text provides you with comprehensive instruction and numerous practice exercises in many areas of mathematics, including fractions, algebra, geometry, and modern mathematics. It also includes a two-hour Simulated GED Mathematics Examination. New edition includes additional testing sections.

You may wish to supplement your study with an additional volume that treats all five subject areas of the test concisely with new material. Although it does not contain the more detailed coverage and explanations included in the five individual books described above, it will be especially useful for extra practice:

Preparation for the High School Equivalency Examination (GED). This volume reflects the latest developments in the GED Test and provides instruction and drill in all five subject areas of the examination: English Usage, Social Studies, Science, Literature, and Mathematics. It contains a full ten-hour Simulated GED Test. Revised edition contains an enlarged Reading Comprehension section. All answers are labeled according to reading skill involved.

Many special features make each book a unique study tool for the examination. Each of the books contains a Diagnostic Test designed to pinpoint those areas in which you need further study. In addition, each volume contains instructional material and practice exercises with explanatory answers. These give you the practice essential for doing well on the Examination. And finally, each book, as described above, concludes with the unique "Simulated GED Test." This test—patterned as closely as possible on the official examination or the section of it covered in that book—is designed to give you additional review and a "feel" for the real thing. It can be of major assistance to you in raising your score. For information on where to take the GED Test, check with your local high school or county or state department of education. A complete listing of state policies and addresses is included in the Appendix of *Preparation for the High School Equivalency Examination.*

ACKNOWLEDGMENTS

Brandt & Brandt: From "The Quiet Man" by Maurice Walsh. Copyright 1933 by Curtis Publishing Company. Copyright renewed © 1960 by Maurice Walsh. From *The Corn Is Green,* by Emlyn Williams. Copyright 1941 by Emlyn Williams. Reprinted by permission of Brandt & Brandt.

James Brown Associates, Inc.: From *An Almanac for Moderns,* by Donald Culross Peattie. Reprinted by permission of Noel R. Peattie and his agent, James Brown Associates, Inc. Copyright © 1935 by Donald Culrose Peattie.

Collins-Knowlton-Wing, Inc.: From *H. M. S. Titanic,* by Hanson W. Baldwin. Copyright 1933 by Harper & Row, Publishers Incorporated; copyright renewed 1961. Reprinted by permission of Collins-Knowlton-Wing, Inc.

Thomas Y. Crowell, Inc.: From *Cheaper by the Dozen,* by Frank B. Gilbreth, Jr. and Ernestine Gilbreth Carey. Copyright © 1963, 1948 by Frank B. Gilbreth, Jr. and Ernestine Gilbreth Carey. Reprinted by permission of Thomas Y. Crowell Company, Inc., New York, publishers.

Frank Marshall Davis: "Four Glimpses of Night," by Frank Marshall Davis. Reprinted by permission of Frank Marshall Davis.

J. M. Dent & Sons Ltd.: "Do Not Go Gentle into That Good Night," by Dylan

Thomas. From *The Collected Poems of Dylan Thomas*. Reprinted by permission of J. M. Dent & Sons Ltd. and the Trustees for the Copyrights of the late Dylan Thomas.

Dodd, Mead and Company: "A Ballade of Suicide," from *The Collected Poems of G. K. Chesterton*. Copyright 1911, 1923, 1932. "My Financial Career," from *Literary Lapses*, by Stephen Leacock. Reprinted by permission of Dodd, Mead & Company.

Doubleday & Company, Inc.: From *Mary, Mary,* by Jean Kerr. Copyright © 1960, 1961, 1963 by Jean Kerr. From "When I Heard the Learn'd Astronomer" by Walt Whitman from the book *Leaves of Grass*. Reprinted by permission of Doubleday & Company.

Norma Millay Ellis: "Love Is Not All," by Edna St. Vincent Millay. From Sonnet XCIX. *Collected Poems*. Harper & Row. Copyright 1931, 1958 by Edna St. Vincent Millay, and Norma Millay Ellis. Reprinted by permission of Norma Millay Ellis.

Harcourt, Brace & World, Inc.: "in Just-," "my specialty is living," and "what if a much of a which of a wind," from *Poems 1923–1954*, by E. E. Cummings. "Theft," from *Flowering Judas and Other Stories*, by Katherine Anne Porter. Reprinted by permission of Harcourt, Brace & World, Inc.

Harper & Row, Publishers: "The Lost Boy," by Thomas Wolfe. From pp. 39, 40, 41–42 "The Lost Boy" in *The Hills Beyond* by Thomas Wolfe. Copyright 1937 by Maxwell Perkins; renewed 1965 by Paul Gitlin. Reprinted by permission of Harper & Row, Publishers.

Harvard University Press: "Hope is the thing with feathers," "The Lightning Is a Yellow Fork," and "I Never Saw a Moor" by Emily Dickinson. Reprinted by permission of the publishers and the Trustees of Amherst College from Thomas H. Johnson, Editor, *The Poems of Emily Dickinson,* Cambridge, Mass.: The Belknap Press of Harvard University Press, Copyright 1951, 1955, by the President and Fellows of Harvard College.

Hayden Book Company, Inc.: From *The Dictionary and the Language,* by R. R. Lodwig and E. F. Barrett. Copyright © 1967. Reprinted by permission of Hayden Book Company, Inc.

Hill & Wang, Inc.: "Coffee Break," from *Simple's Uncle Sam* by Langston Hughes. Copyright © 1965 by Langston Hughes. Reprinted by permisson of Hill & Wang, Inc.

Holt, Rinehart & Winston, Inc.: From "The Ballad of William Sycamore" from *Ballads and Poems* by Stephen Vincent Benét. Copyright 1931 by Stephen Vincent Benét. Copyright © 1969 by Rosemary Carr Benét. From "Mending Wall," from *The Poetry of Robert Frost,* edited by Edward Connery Lathem. Copyright 1930, 1939, © 1969 by Holt, Rinehart and Winston, Inc. Copyright © 1958 by Robert Frost. Copyright © 1967 by Lesley Frost Ballantine. From "With Rue My Heart is Laden"—Authorized Edition—from *The Collected Poems of A. E. Housman.* Copyright 1939, 1940, © 1965 by Holt, Rinehart and Winston, Inc. Copyright © 1967, 1968 by Robert E. Symons. Reprinted by permission of Holt, Rinehart and Winston, Inc.

Houghton Mifflin Company: "Lilacs" and "Wind and Silver" by Amy Lowell, from *The Complete Poetical Works of Amy Lowell.* Copyright 1955 by Houghton Mifflin Company. Reprinted by permission of Houghton Mifflin Company.

Sir Julian Huxley: From "An Essay on Bird-Mind," from *Essays of a Biologist,* by Sir Julian Huxley. Originally published in the United States by Alfred A. Knopf, Inc. Reprinted by permission of Sir Julian Huxley.

Intext Press: From "The Jade Goddess" by Lin Yutang. Copyright 1948, 1951, 1952 by Lin Yutang. Reprinted from *Famous Chinese Short Stories* by Lin Yutang by permission of the John Day Company, Inc., an Intext Publisher.

Alfred A. Knopf, Inc.:   From *The Immoralist,* by André Gide, translated by Dorothy Bussy. Copyright 1930 and renewed 1958 by Alfred A. Knopf, Inc. "Dreams," from *The Dream Keeper,* by Langston Hughes, "Island," by Langston Hughes, from *Selected Poems,* by Langston Hughes. Copyright 1952 by Langston Hughes. From "The Garden Party," by Katherine Mansfield. From the *Short Stories of Katherine Mansfield.* Copyright 1920, 1922, 1923, 1924, 1926, 1937 by Alfred A. Knopf, Inc. "My Oedipus Complex," by Frank O'Connor. Copyright 1950 by Frank O'Connor. Reprinted from *The Stories of Frank O'Connor.* Reprinted by permission of Alfred A. Knopf, Inc.

Little, Brown and Company: "It Sifts from Leaden Sieves," "The Sea said 'Come' to the Brook," "There is no frigate like a book," from *The Complete Poems of Emily Dickinson* edited by Thomas H. Johnson. Copyright 1914, 1942 by Martha Dickinson Bianchi. Reprinted by permission of Little, Brown and Company.

Liveright Publishing Corporation: "Fear," by Hart Crane, from *The Complete Poems and Selected Letters and Prose of Hart Crane* by Hart Crane. Permission by Liveright, Publishers, New York. Copyright 1933, 1958, 1966 by Liveright Publishing Corporation.

Macmillan Publishing Co., Inc.:   "Factory Windows Are Always Broken" by Vachel Lindsay. Copyright © 1914 by Macmillan Publishing Co., Inc. Renewed 1942 by Elizabeth C. Lindsay. "A Birthday" by Christina Rossetti. Reprinted by permission of Macmillan Publishing Co., Inc.

New Directions Publishing Corporation: "Do Not Go Gentle into That Good Night," by Dylan Thomas. From Dylan Thomas *The Collected Poems of Dylan Thomas.* Copyright 1952 by Dylan Thomas. From *Cat on a Hot Tin Roof* by Tennessee Williams. Copyright 1955 by Tennessee Williams. Reprinted by permission of New Directions Publishing Corporation.

The New York Times: From "The Harp in the Air Still Sings" by Sean O'Casey. Copyright © 1959 by The New York Times. From "Thoughts on the Brotherhood of Men" by Eric Hoffer. Copyright © 1959 by Eric Hoffer. Reprinted by permission.

Harold Ober Associates, Inc.:   From "Death in the Woods," by Sherwood Anderson. Reprinted by permission of Harold Ober Associates Incorporated. Copyright 1926 by The American Mercury, Inc. Copyright renewed 1953 by Eleanor Copenhaver Anderson. Taken from Sherwood Anderson, "Death in the Woods," *American Mercury,* September 1926.

Sonia Brownell Orwell and Secker & Warburg: From "A Hanging" by George

Orwell. Copyright © 1950 by Sonia Brownell Orwell. Reprinted by permission of A. M. Heath & Company Ltd.

A. D. Peters & Company: "My Oedipus Complex," by Frank O'Connor. From *The Stories of Frank O'Connor.* "Departing Guests" and "Dreams," from *Delight,* by J. D. Priestley. Reprinted by permission of A. D. Peters & Company.

Random House, Inc.: From *Tea and Sympathy* by Robert Anderson. Copyright © 1953 by Robert Anderson. From "The Bear," by William Faulkner. Copyright 1942 by Curtis Publishing Company. Copyright 1942 by William Faulkner. Reprinted from *Go Down, Moses,* by William Faulkner. "Speech on Receiving the Nobel Prize," by William Faulkner, from *The Faulkner Reader.* Copyright 1954 by William Faulkner. "Wash," by William Faulkner, from *Collected Stories of William Faulkner.* Copyright 1934, renewed 1962 by William Faulkner. From *A Clearing in the Woods,* by Arthur Laurents. Copyright © 1957 by Arthur Laurents. From *A Hatful of Rain* by Michael Gazzo. Copyright © 1956 by Michael Gazzo. From *A Moon for the Misbegotten* by Eugene O'Neill. Copyright © 1952 by Eugene O'Neill. From *The Corn Is Green,* by Emlyn Williams. Copyright © 1941 by Emlyn Williams. Reprinted by permission of Random House, Inc.

St. Martin's Press: "Sight," by Wilfrid Wilson Gibson, from *Collected Poems,* by Wilfrid Wilson Gibson. Reprinted by permission of St. Martin's Press, and Macmillan & Company, Ltd., London, Michael Gibson, Executor.

Charles Scribner's Sons: From *The Old Man and the Sea,* by Ernest Hemingway. Reprinted with the permission of Charles Scribner's Sons from *The Old Man and the Sea.* Copyright 1952 by Ernest Hemingway. From "Circus at Dawn" is reprinted with the permission of Charles Scribner's Sons from *From Death to Morning* by Thomas Wolfe. Copyright 1934, 1935 by Modern Monthly, Inc.

Simon & Schuster, Inc: From *Baby and Child Care* by Benjamin Spock, M.D. Copyright 1957 by Benjamin Spock. Reprinted by permission of Pocket Books, a division of Simon & Schuster, Inc. From *Madame Bovary,* by Gustave Flaubert. Translated by Eleanor Marx-Aveling. Copyright 1942, 1953. Reprinted by permission of Simon & Schuster, Inc.

Helen W. Thurber: From "The Case Against Women" in *Let Your Mind Alone,* published by Harper & Row. Originally printed in *The New Yorker.* Copyright © 1937 by James Thurber. Copyright © 1965 by Helen W. Thurber and Rosemary Thurber Sauers. Reprinted by permission of Helen W. Thurber.

The Viking Press, Inc.: From "A Little Cloud," by James Joyce. From *Dubliners* by James Joyce. Originally published by B. W. Huebsch, Inc. in 1916. Copyright © 1967 by the Estate of James Joyce. All rights reserved. From *The Pearl* by John Steinbeck. Copyright 1945 by John Steinbeck. From "Flight" from *The Long Valley* by John Steinbeck. Copyright © 1966 by John Steinbeck. Reprinted by permission of Viking Press, Inc.

Walker and Company: From *Daffodils Are Dangerous: The Poisonous Plants in Your Garden* by Hubert Creekmore, published by Walker and Company, Inc. Copyright © 1966 by Hubert Creekmore. Reprinted by the permission of Walker and Company.

CONTENTS

INTRODUCTION

In most states, an adult who achieves a satisfactory score on the High School Equivalency Examination is eligible to receive a High School Equivalency Diploma or Certificate. This is the legal equivalent of a diploma issued by a local high school. As such, it serves the same purpose as a high school diploma in meeting city, state, and federal civil service requirements. It is also accepted as a high school diploma by business firms and the armed forces. Most colleges admit students whose High School Equivalency Examination scores are in line with their admissions requirements for high school graduates, and accept the scores in place of a full high school transcript. This, of course, usually means that you need to score high on the Examination, and not simply pass.

The purpose of this book is to help you pass the "Interpretation of Literary Materials" section of the High School Equivalency Examination. It contains instruction, drills, and tests covering everything you must know in order to pass the test.

THE TEST YOU WILL TAKE

The Literature section of the High School Equivalency Examination measures your ability to read, understand, and interpret selections from American and English literature. The test can usually be completed in two hours. You may request a reasonable amount of additional time from the examiner, but it is not always practical for him to grant it.

Several different forms of the Literature test are now in use. An average test consists of fourteen or fifteen passages, each fifteen to thirty lines long, with a total of eighty to eighty-five questions. You must read each selection and then answer six to ten questions based on its content. The test contains four complete poems, two dramatic excerpts, and eight passages taken from prose works. Of the prose passages, four are usually selections from fiction (novels and short stories) and four are selected from nonfiction (essays, biographies, and autobiographies). Excerpts from various periods in American and English literary history are presented, with the majority of the selections taken from the works of modern authors. Other forms of the "Interpretation of Literary Materials" test vary slightly. In addition to eight long passages with six to ten questions each, there are several very short passages followed by only one or two questions.

The questions usually require the test taker to: choose the meaning of a word, phrase, or line; select the theme or overall meaning of a selection; infer (determine) the mood, motivation, or point of view of a character; and identify the plot or setting of a passage. Some questions may ask you to identify the author's viewpoint or writing style. You must also be able to identify literary genres (types of literature), poetic forms and structures, and figures of speech. Every question has four possible answer choices, from which you must select the BEST answer. Each answer choice is numbered. On your answer sheet, you must blacken the space under the number of the correct answer. To understand the answering process more clearly, look at the following example.

DIRECTIONS: Read the following passage. Then answer the questions. Choose the BEST answer to each question. Then mark the space under that number in the answer column.

1 Jack and Jill
2 Went up the hill
3 To fetch a pail of water.

1. Jack and Jill went up the hill because they wanted to
   (1) neck.   (3) get some exercise.
   (2) be alone.   (4) get some water.

2. The passage above is an excerpt from which of the following literary genres?
   (1) nursery rhyme   (3) sonnet
   (2) novel   (4) elegy

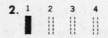

Answer Key

1. **(4)** Although answer choices (1), (2), and (3) may have been true, there is no evidence in the passage for them. We are told (line 3) that their intention was to fetch some water. Choice (4) is the *best* answer.

2. **(1)** We can infer from the short lines, singsong rhythm, and kindergarten content that this excerpt was taken from a nursery rhyme.

HOW THIS BOOK WILL HELP YOU

This book has been designed to help you choose the *correct* answers. It contains instructional materials and exercises to aid you in answering questions based on word or passage meaning, author's tone or style, plot or setting, figurative language, and poetic forms and structures.

Remember that the "Interpretation of Literary Materials" examination tests your reading ability as well as your knowledge of literary terms. If you have trouble with reading comprehension, you are probably weak in one or more of the basic reading skills which everyone must master in order to read with understanding. This book explains what these skills are and shows you how you can develop them. As you study each skill, you will acquire a better understanding of what literature is and how words are used. This knowledge will help you to interpret what you read more accurately and in greater depth.

In the Diagnostic and Simulated Tests, answers have been labeled in the margin. These labels name or identify the principal skill required to answer each question. Department of Education reading specialists responsible for the GED Test specified the particular skills to be tested on each part of the examination. The questions in this book accurately represent these particular skills. It must be understood that the skills-labels name only the principal skill used in answering questions. Several skills are often involved in finding a specific answer because reading and interpretation are very complex processes.

The labels alongside each analyzed answer indicate the most important skill to be used to answer the question. These labels suggest that if you have repeated difficulty with a particular skill, you should reread the text and rework the exercises in that teaching section. The teaching sections should, of course, be used *before* you go on to the practice sections of the book. These teaching sections provide a complete survey of, and practical help in, those skills required to pass the Literature section of the GED Examination.

The *Main Idea* label designates answers to questions that require you to recognize the author's main point or the general theme of the passage. Teaching sections developing skill in recognizing main idea are found on pages 26–51 of this book.

Supporting Detail labels indicate questions that require students to verify details from the passage by checking back with the original text. Techniques for verifying supporting details are given on pages 51–56.

Answers labeled *Inference* require that you recognize what the passage implies as well as what it states. The teaching sections in the chapter on Reading Prose—pages 62–70—trains the student in making inferences.

Style and Tone is used to label answers that require you to infer the author's attitude toward his subject. A short teaching section on this skill is provided on pages 70–73; however, much of the training in earlier sections, especially in the section on inference, lays the groundwork for this skill.

The *Figures of Speech* label indicates questions which require you to interpret or identify words or phrases which, in a particular passage, have meanings different from their dictionary meanings. The teaching section on pages 83–91 explains various types of figures of speech and how to interpret them.

Rhythm and Sound Devices is used to label answers that require an understanding of the particular "musical" effects of words which are achieved in literature—particularly poetry—and of how they are created. Teaching sections on pages 92–107 offer explanations in this area.

Finally, *Literary Forms and Levels of Diction* labels answers which require recognition of different types of literature or of different types of language (formal, informal, etc.). While teaching material which treats these subjects will be found distributed throughout the book, a concise description of each of the literary forms and levels of diction which the student might encounter on the GED Examination will be found in the Glossary, pages 120–124.

To find out how well you can read literature now, take the Diagnostic Test. This test has been designed to point out your present strengths and weaknesses in reading and interpreting literature. Then study the Reading Comprehension section and the chapters on reading prose, poetry, and drama, and review the parts that give you trouble. You should also study the GLOSSARY, which contains additional definitions and examples of terms you may be asked to identify on the High School Equivalency Examination. The Exercises will help you develop particular skills, and the Tests, which duplicate the kinds of questions that appear on the actual High School Equivalency Examination, will provide you with additional practice. Fully explained answers for all Exercises and Tests appear at the end of each chapter.

Following the instructional material is a Simulated High School Equivalency Interpretation of Literary Materials Test. It contains fourteen passages and eighty-four questions. The test reflects the format and kinds of questions asked on the actual High School Equivalency Examination. Take it after you have studied *all* of the material in this book. Allow yourself two hours to take the test, and then check your answers. If you did not do well, review the areas which gave you the most trouble.

Following the Simulated Test is a chapter containing short biographies. In it you will find interesting information about the lives of many of the authors whose works are quoted in this book. You do not have to know specific information about any authors on the High School Equivalency Examination, but the biographies do contain the titles of additional works which you may be interested in reading. The more you read and increase your comprehension skills, the better are your chances of passing the Examination.

TEST-TAKING TIPS

Read the following test-taking tips several times. Remembering and applying these suggestions will result in a higher score.

First, scan the questions to get an idea of the kind of information asked for; *second,* skim (read over quickly) the passage to get a general idea of the topic; *third,* close-read the passage (read the passage thoroughly and carefully, trying to extract all the meaning that the author put in); *fourth,* read each question carefully, then mark the best answer choice, going back to the passage when necessary.

DO answer each question on the basis of information contained in the passage *or* from your knowledge of literary forms and devices. DON'T answer on the basis of what *your* mood or opinion would be if you were the author or one of his characters. If a question inquires about the author's attitude toward religion as expressed in the passage, don't answer in terms of what *you* think his attitude *should* be; answer in terms of what the *passage* implies or states.

DO notice whether a question refers to a specific line, sentence, or quotation from the passage. The answer, or the clue to the answer, to such a question is almost certain to be found in or near the line(s) referred to.

DO work as quickly as you can. This does not mean that you should be in such a hurry that you read the passages only superficially. It means, instead, that you should concentrate on what you are doing and work at a steady pace. Since your time is limited, don't waste precious minutes in worrying or daydreaming.

DO watch out for answers that seem too easy. If the words in a question and an answer choice are almost the same, that answer choice is not *necessarily* correct. Test-writers usually include some tricky questions.

DO choose the *best* answer (the most complete, accurate, or appropriate answer) to each question. Often, more than one choice *seems* correct. You must select the one which is best.

DO answer easier questions first. If a passage or a question seems particularly difficult, jot down the passage or question number on a separate sheet of paper. After you have completed the rest of the test, go back and tackle the hard ones again.

DON'T expect the order of the questions to follow the order of the passage. Often, you must skip from one part of the passage to another in order to find an answer.

DON'T expect to find answers to all of the questions stated directly in the passage. Sometimes, clues to the answer will be stated, and you will need to infer the correct answer on the basis of those clues. At other times, you will be asked to identify the literary genre or device which a particular passage or passage detail illustrates. In such cases, you will not find the answer in the passage, and you will have to rely on your knowledge of various literary genres or devices.

DON'T look in just one sentence or paragraph for information unless you are sure that the correct answer is to be found in that particular part of the passage. Often, the thread of an answer winds through the whole reading selection.

DON'T leave any questions unanswered. On the High School Equivalency Examination, **blank answer spaces are marked wrong. Guess rather than leave an answer blank.**

THE DIAGNOSTIC TEST

The following Diagnostic Test has been carefully designed to measure your present level of ability to understand and interpret literature. The form of the Diagnostic Test closely resembles the form of the "Interpretation of Literary Materials" section of the High School Equivalency Examination, except that: (1) it is only half as long; (2) you should complete it in half the time—one hour, instead of two hours; and (3) you will mark your answers in the spaces provided in the margin of each page instead of on a separate answer sheet.

Before you take this Diagnostic Test, be sure that you have the necessary supplies. You will need a clock or watch and several sharpened pencils. Find a quiet and comfortable place to work where you will not be interrupted.

A word of warning: the Diagnostic Test is *difficult*, as difficult as a real High School Equivalency Examination. On the actual test—and on this test as well—*you only have to answer half of the questions correctly in order to get a passing score.* But don't be satisfied with just a passing score; aim for a high score. If you do poorly on another part of the test, but achieve a high score on the literature test, your overall test average may be high enough for you to receive a diploma or a certificate.

In any case, don't become nervous or upset if you can't understand all of the passages or answer all of the questions. Whatever you do, don't stop working before the hour is up because you feel that the test is too hard and you're not doing well. You may score higher than you expect. Furthermore, this book has been carefully designed to give you the kind of help you need. The less you know now, the more this book has to offer you—if you will study it patiently and thoroughly.

After you have taken the Diagnostic Test you will receive instructions on scoring it and on evaluating your present strengths and weaknesses in interpreting literature.

DIRECTIONS: Read each of the following passages. Choose the BEST answer to each question. Then blacken the space under that number in the answer column.

ANSWERS AND EXPLANATIONS APPEAR AT THE END OF THE TEST

I

1   I met a traveler from an antique land
2   Who said: "Two vast and trunkless legs of stone
3   Stand in the desert. Near them, on the sand,

6

4 Half sunk, a shattered visage lies, whose frown,
5 And wrinkled lip, and sneer of cold command,
6 Tell that its sculptor well those passions read
7 Which yet survive, stamped on these lifeless things,
8 The hand that mocked them and the heart that fed.
9 And on the pedestal these words appear—
10 'My name is Ozymandias, king of kings:
11 Look on my works, ye Mighty, and despair!'
12 Nothing beside remains. Round the decay
13 Of that colossal wreck, boundless and bare
14 The lone and level sands stretch far away."

1. Ozymandias was a
   (1) king.
   (2) traveler.
   (3) sculptor.
   (4) poet.

2. This poem is a
   (1) ballad.
   (2) dirge.
   (3) limerick.
   (4) sonnet.

3. The tone of the poem can be described as
   (1) ironic.
   (2) romantic.
   (3) tragic.
   (4) optimistic.

4. Line 14 of the poem contains examples of
   (1) simile.
   (2) alliteration.
   (3) allusion.
   (4) synecdoche.

5. The sculptor's attitude toward his subject was one of
   (1) respect.
   (2) mockery.
   (3) terror.
   (4) detachment.

6. The style of the poem may be described as
   (1) formal.
   (2) informal.
   (3) humorous.
   (4) romantic.

7. The theme of this poem is
   (1) the futility of vanity.
   (2) the endurance of art.
   (3) the chastisement of wickedness.
   (4) the immortality of greatness.

II

1 A noiseless patient spider,
2 I mark'd where on a little promontory it stood isolated,
3 Mark'd how to explore the vacant vast surrounding,
4 It launch'd forth filament, filament, filament, out of itself.
5 Ever unreeling them, ever tirelessly speeding them.

6 And you O my soul where you stand,
7 Surrounded, detached, in measureless oceans of space,

8 Ceaselessly musing, venturing, throwing, seeking the
   spheres to connect them.
9 Till the bridge you will need be form'd, till the ductile
   anchor hold,
10 Till the gossamer thread you fling catch somewhere, O my soul.

8. 1 2 3 4

8. The poet is
   (1) watching a spider.
   (2) trying to exterminate a spider.
   (3) attempting to catch a spider.
   (4) imitating a spider.

9. 1 2 3 4

9. The spider is attempting to
   (1) escape from the poet.
   (2) spin a web.
   (3) ensnare an insect.
   (4) hide itself from the poet.

10. 1 2 3 4

10. "Musing" (line 8) means
   (1) thinking.
   (2) humming.
   (3) wishing.
   (4) expecting.

11. 1 2 3 4

11. The poet compares his soul to
   (1) a spiderweb.
   (2) the spider.
   (3) the spider's intended victim.
   (4) a promontory.

12. 1 2 3 4

12. The poet is attempting to
   (1) explore his relationship to his soul.
   (2) establish his relationship to the universe.
   (3) learn patience from the spider.
   (4) learn the principles of poetry from the spider.

13. 1 2 3 4

13. The poem is written in
   (1) rhymed iambic pentameter.
   (2) trochaic tetrameter.
   (3) blank verse.
   (4) free verse.

III

1 O, that this too too solid flesh would melt,
2 Thaw and resolve itself into a dew!
3 Or that the Everlasting had not fix'd
4 His canon 'gainst self-slaughter! O God! God!
5 How weary, stale, flat, and unprofitable
6 Seem to me all the uses of this world.
7 Fie on 't! ah fie! 'tis an unweeded garden,
8 That grows to seed; things rank and gross in nature
9 Possess it merely. That it should come to this!
10 But two months dead! nay, not so much, not two:
11 So excellent a king; that was, to this,
12 Hyperion to a satyr; so loving to my mother
13 That he might not beteem the winds of heaven

14 Visit her face too roughly. Heaven and earth!
15 Must I remember? why, she would hang on him,
16 As if increase of appetite had grown
17 By what it fed on; and yet, within a month,
18 Let me not think on 't: Frailty, thy name is woman!
19 A little month; or ere those shoes were old
20 With which she follow'd my poor father's body,
21 Like Niobe, all tears; why she, even she—
22 O God! a beast, that wants discourse of reason,
23 Would have mourn'd longer, —married with my uncle,
24 My father's brother, but no more like my father
25 Than I to Hercules: within a month,
26 Ere yet the salt of most unrighteous tears
27 Had left the flushing in her galled eyes,
28 She married. O! most wicked speed, to post
29 With such dexterity to incestuous sheets!
30 It is not, nor it cannot come to good;
31 But break, my heart, for I must hold my tongue!

14. In this excerpt, the mood of the speaker is
   (1) revengeful.   (3) despairing.
   (2) mocking.   (4) hopeful.

15. "An unweeded garden" (line 7) refers to
   (1) a field.   (3) flesh.
   (2) a bed.   (4) the world.

16. Lines 3 and 4 express the speaker's wish that which of the following was not a sin?
   (1) murder   (3) adultery
   (2) suicide   (4) incest

17. The above excerpt is written in which of the following meters?
   (1) trochaic hexameter   (3) iambic pentameter
   (2) anapestic trimeter   (4) trochaic tetrameter

18. The speaker's feeling toward his mother reflects
   (1) loyalty.   (3) bitterness.
   (2) pity.   (4) apathy.

19. "Incestuous sheets" (line 29) is an example of
   (1) synecdoche.   (3) hyperbole.
   (2) simile.   (4) oxymoron.

20. The above excerpt is a(n)
   (1) eulogy.   (3) dialogue.
   (2) soliloquy.   (4) allusion.

21. The tone of the passage is
   (1) allegorical.   (3) optimistic.
   (2) euphemistic.   (4) tragic.

IV

1 When it was clear that the members of the family were in bed, the
2 Grand Army man hitched his shoulders and, untangling his long
3 legs, caught his heels on the rounds of his chair.
4   "S'pose there'll be a will, Phelps?" he queried in his weak
5 falsetto.
6   The banker laughed disagreeably, and began trimming his
7 nails with a pearl-handled pocket-knife.
8   "There'll scarcely be any need for one, will there?" he queried
9 in his turn.
10   The restless Grand Army man shifted his position again, getting
11 his knees still nearer his chin. "Why, the ole man says Harve's done
12 right well lately," he chirped.
13   The other banker spoke up. "I reckon he means by that Harve
14 ain't asked him to mortgage any more farms lately, so as he could
15 go on with his education."
16   "Seems like my mind don't reach back to a time when Harve
17 wasn't bein' edycated," tittered the Grand Army man.
18   There was a general chuckle.
19   The letters of the book which he had begun to read were
20 swimming before Steavens' eyes. Was it possible that these men did
21 not understand, that the palm on the coffin meant nothing to them?
22 The very name of their town would have remained forever buried
23 in the postal guide had it not been now and again mentioned in the
24 world in connection with Harvey Merrick's. He remembered what
25 his master had said to him on the day of his death, after the
26 congestion in both lungs had shut off any probability of recovery,
27 and the sculptor had asked his pupil to send his body home. "It's
28 not a pleasant place to be lying while the world is moving and doing
29 and bettering," he had said with a feeble smile, "but it rather seems
30 as though we ought to go back to the place we came from, in the
31 end. The townspeople will come in for a look at me; and after they
32 have had their say, I shan't have much to fear from the judgment of
33 God!"

22. From the sentence beginning, "The very name of their town. . ." (lines
   22–24) we infer that
   (1) Merrick was a map-maker.
   (2) Merrick was a famous sculptor.
   (3) the town had a peculiar name.
   (4) the town wasn't listed in the postal guide.

23. The townspeople's attitude toward the deceased is one of
   (1) ridicule.   (3) respect.
   (2) envy.   (4) affection.

24. The tone of the passage can best be described as
    (1)   comic.   (3)   elegaic.
    (2)   sentimental.   (4)   ironic.

25. From the townspeople's conversation we can infer that Merrick's father
    (1)   had enabled his son to get a good education.
    (2)   had wanted Harvey to be a farmer.
    (3)   had wanted Harvey to be a banker.
    (4)   was not proud of his son.

26. The diction of the townspeople is
    (1)   formal.   (3)   colloquial.
    (2)   rhetorical.   (4)   poetic.

27. The palm on the coffin symbolizes
    (1)   the sculptor's artistic achievements.
    (2)   the hand of fate.
    (3)   the dead man's religious faith.
    (4)   Merrick's love of nature.

28. The theme of the passage is the contrast between
    (1)   Merrick the boy and Merrick the man.
    (2)   the differing outlooks of artists and businessmen.
    (3)   country behavior and city behavior.
    (4)   artistic sensibility and the insensitive atmosphere in which it survives.

V

1   ... Nothing showed on the surface of the water but some patches
2   of yellow, sun-bleached Sargasso weed and the purple, formalized,
3   iridescent, gelatinous bladder of a Portuguese man-of-war floating
4   close beside the boat. It turned on its side and then righted itself.
5   It floated cheerfully as a bubble with its long deadly purple filaments
6   trailing a yard behind it in the water.
7   "*Agua mala,*" the man said. "You whore."
8   From where he swung lightly against his oars he looked down
9   into the water and saw the tiny fish that were coloured like the
10 trailing filaments and swam between them and under the small
11 shade the bubble made as it drifted. They were immune to its
12 poison. But men were not and when some of the filaments would
13 catch on a line and rest there slimy and purple while the old man
14 was working a fish, he would have welts and sores on his arms and
15 hands of the sort that poison ivy or poison oak can give. But these
16 poisonings from the *agua mala* came quickly and struck like a
17 whiplash.
18   The iridescent bubbles were beautiful. But they were the
19 falsest thing in the sea and the old man loved to see the big sea
20 turtles eating them. The turtles saw them, approached them from
21 the front, then shut their eyes so they were completely carapaced

22   and ate them filaments and all. The old man loved to see the turtles
23   eat them and he loved to walk on them on the beach after a storm
24   and hear them pop . . . . : . . . .

29. 1 2 3 4

29. The Portuguese man-of-war (line 3) is a
    (1) ship.   (3) sandshark.
    (2) jellyfish.   (4) soldier.

30. 1 2 3 4

30. The old man referred to in the passage is probably a(n)
    (1) scientist.   (3) fisherman.
    (2) sailor.   (4) artist.

31. 1 2 3 4

31. "The iridescent bubbles were beautiful. But they were the falsest thing in
    the sea . . ." (lines 18–19). This means that
    (1) they really weren't beautiful.
    (2) their beauty hid their real danger.
    (3) they burst when touched.
    (4) there was a shell around them.

32. 1 2 3 4

32. The old man's primary feeling towards the *agua mala* was one of
    (1) hostility.   (3) love.
    (2) apprehension.   (4) respect.

33. 1 2 3 4

33. The style of the passage is
    (1) rhetorical.   (3) aphoristic.
    (2) descriptive.   (4) metaphorical.

34. 1 2 3 4

34. "It floated cheerfully as a bubble . . ." (line 5) is a(n)
    (1) apostrophe.   (3) synecdoche.
    (2) metonymy.   (4) simile.

35. 1 2 3 4

35. From a stylistic and logical point of view, the best completion of the final
    sentence is
    (1) with sad, staccato explosions upon the silver sands.
    (2) like firecrackers.
    (3) when he stepped on them with the horny soles of his feet.
    (4) spilling their lavender guts on the dank shore.

VI

1   I encountered in the steep rich woods above the river today the
2   small yellow lady's slipper—my first orchid of the year. I was so late,
3   and so loaded down with natural curiosities for the amusement of
4   my children, that I could not carry it. So I marked the spot and left
5   the little plant where it was.
6   A popular belief has got abroad that orchids are unhealthy. It
7   is true that they live with fungi growing in and around their roots,
8   and cannot exist save when in this "diseased" condition, but men
9   cannot exist either, without a large bacterial flora in the alimentary
10 canal.

11   Such an intimate relation of two different organisms, often with
12   what seem to be mutual adaptations, is a symbiosis. The physical
13   contact is often as close and intense as in a case of parasitism, but
14   in a symbiosis the benefits are mutual, not one-sided. The fungi
15   living in the orchid root purvey to the plant above, which has no
16   rootlets, and hence cannot eat or drink the predigested elements of
17   the soil. Without its particular fungus, each kind of orchid cannot
18   live.

36. "Symbiosis" (line 12) refers to
    (1) an interdependent relationship between two organisms.
    (2) an independent relationship between two organisms.
    (3) a mutually fatal relationship between two organisms.
    (4) a one-sided relationship between two organisms.

36. 1 2 3 4

37. The style of the passage is
    (1) flowery.   (3) idiomatic.
    (2) expository.   (4) trite.

37. 1 2 3 4

38. Fungi associated with orchid plants
    (1) eventually kill the plants.
    (2) cause the plants to turn black.
    (3) assist the plants to obtain food.
    (4) assist the plants in the process of photosynthesis.

38. 1 2 3 4

39. The author of this passage is probably
    (1) a florist.   (3) a naturalist.
    (2) a forest ranger.   (4) a farmer.

39. 1 2 3 4

40. In this passage, the main intent of the author is
    (1) to inform.   (3) to reassure.
    (2) to persuade.   (4) to amuse.

40. 1 2 3 4

41. This passage is an example of the literary genre called the
    (1) novel.   (3) prose-poem.
    (2) short story.   (4) essay.

41. 1 2 3 4

SCORING THE DIAGNOSTIC TEST

Now that you have completed the Diagnostic Test, you are ready to correct your answers. So that the scoring can also be a learning experience, correct your answers for each passage in the following way:

1. Check the list of **Difficult Words Explained** for definitions of words you did not understand.
2. Read the **Summary**.
3. Read the items in the **Answer Key,** marking your own answers either correct or incorrect. Where you marked a wrong answer, try to figure out why you were wrong and why the answer choice given is the correct one. DO NOT CHANGE ANY OF THE ORIGINAL ANSWERS YOU MARKED. To do so will make your Self-Evaluation Profile inaccurate and result in an incorrect estimation of what your learning needs are.

ANSWERS AND EXPLANATIONS

I

"Ozymandias," by PERCY BYSSHE SHELLEY (1792–1822)

```
 1   I met a traveler from an antique land
 2   Who said: "Two vast and trunkless legs of stone
 3   Stand in the desert. Near them, on the sand,
 4   Half sunk, a shattered visage lies, whose frown,
 5   And wrinkled lip, and sneer of cold command,
 6   Tell that its sculptor well those passions read
 7   Which yet survive, stamped on these lifeless things,
 8   The hand that mocked them, and the heart that fed.
 9   And on the pedestal these words appear—
10   'My name is Ozymandias, king of kings:
11   Look on my works, ye Mighty, and despair!'
12   Nothing beside remains. Round the decay
13   Of that colossal wreck, boundless and bare
14   The lone and level sands stretch far away."
```

Difficult Words Explained

LINE
1 **antique:** ancient, very old
2 **vast:** huge
   trunkless: bodiless
4 **shattered:** broken or cracked
   visage: face
5 **sneer:** a scornful, mocking smile

7 **things**: ruins
8 **hand**: the sculptor's hand
9 **pedestal**: base of the statue
11 **ye**: you
    despair: give up hope
12 **beside**: more
    round: around
    decay: the remains
13 **colossal**: huge
    boundless: endless
14 **lone**: empty

Summary

A traveler, returned from an ancient land, tells the narrator of a ruin he observed in the desert. It was once the statue of a mighty king. All that remains, however, are the statue's broken legs and fallen head. The cold and arrogant expression of the ruler, placed there by the sculptor to mock the king, is still evident. On the broken base of the statue is carved the boast: "My name is Ozymandias, king of kings: Look on my works [the things I have built], ye Mighty, and despair!" But Ozymandias is long dead, and his kingdom and power have long since vanished. Only the ruined statue with its boastful inscription remains to mock the foolish pride of tyrants.

Answer Key

1. (1) See line 10, "My name is Ozymandias, king of kings."   **Supporting Detail**

2. (4) A sonnet is a poem of fourteen lines, written in iambic pentameter, with a definite rhyme scheme. You will learn more about the sonnet in the "Reading Poetry" chapter. Iambic pentameter and other rhythms used in poetry are also explained in that chapter. The easiest way to identify "Ozymandias" as a sonnet is to note that it has fourteen lines. See the Glossary for definitions of *ballad*, *dirge*, and *limerick*.   **Rhythm and Sound Devices**

3. (1) Irony is present when our knowledge forces us to conclude the *opposite* of what is stated. The writer *intends* for us to conclude the opposite of what is stated. In this poem, the inscription on the statue of Ozymandias *states* that he is the supreme power; but we *know* that he is long dead, his once mighty empire in ruins (see lines 12–14). In the "Reading Prose" chapter, you will study the *tone* of a literary work, including discussion and examples of *ironic*, *amused*, *pessimistic*, and *optimistic* tone.   **Style and Tone**

4. (2) *Alliteration* is the repetition of the same or very similar consonant sounds. In line 14, "The lone and level sands stretch far away," the *l* sound and the *s* sound are repeated. You will learn about *simile*, *allusion*, and *synecdoche* in the "Reading Poetry" chapter.   **Rhythm and Sound Devices**

5. (2) Lines 4–8 tell us that the sculptor understood the cruel and selfish passions of the king and mocked them when he carved the cold, arrogant expression on the stone face.   **Inference**

Style and Tone

6. (1) Formal style refers to a level of language usage in which certain conventions and rules are carefully observed. Formal language is usually characterized by a large vocabulary and the use of complex sentences, with many subordinate clauses. This sonnet consists of only three sentences, the first 11 lines long. You will study other writing styles in the "Reading Prose" chapter.

Main Idea

7. (1) "Vanity" as used here means conceit or excessive pride. It was vain and futile (useless) of Ozymandias to think that his power (line 10) and kingdom (line 11, "my works") would last forever. Ozymandias' power died with him, and his "works" eventually decayed.

II

"A Noiseless Patient Spider," by WALT WHITMAN (1819–1892)

1   A noiseless patient spider,
2   I mark'd where on a little promontory it stood isolated,
3   Mark'd how to explore the vacant vast surrounding,
4   It launch'd forth filament, filament, filament, out of itself.
5   Ever unreeling them, ever tirelessly speeding them.

6   And you O my soul where you stand,
7   Surrounded, detached, in measureless oceans of space,
8   Ceaselessly musing, venturing, throwing, seeking the spheres to connect them.
9   Till the bridge you will need be form'd, till the ductile anchor hold,
10   Till the gossamer thread you fling catch somewhere, O my soul.

Difficult Words Explained

LINE
2   **mark'd:** noticed
     promontory: projection, something which stands out
3   **vast:** wide empty space
4   **launch'd forth:** sent out
5   **unreeling:** unwinding
8   **musing:** meditating, thinking
     venturing: trying, taking risks
     spheres: heavenly bodies, suns and planets; aspects of reality
9   **ductile:** able to be stretched out
     anchor: the "thread" that connects or relates the poet to the universe
10   **gossamer:** silky and fine

Summary

The poet watches a spider who is standing on a little projection. The spider sends out strand after strand, making the connections necessary for spinning a web. The poet reflects that the spider's efforts are like his own attempts to relate to the universe: the explorations of his soul are like the spider's filaments—both try tirelessly to make connections.

Answer Key

8. **(1)** See lines 1 and 2: "a . . . spider I marked" (noticed or watched).
Supporting Detail

9. **(2)** The spider is "unreeling" filaments (strands of web) "out of itself" (lines 4 and 5).
Supporting Detail

10. **(1)** See DIFFICULT WORDS EXPLAINED.
Inference

11. **(2)** As the spider stands on the promontory, so the poet's soul stands, "surrounded, detached, in . . . space," (lines 6 and 7) attempting to connect itself to other aspects of the universe, as the spider seeks to connect the strands of its web to the surrounding environment.
Inference

12. **(2)** The poet, isolated, in "measureless oceans of space" (line 7), is "ceaselessly musing" on the connections between himself and the rest of the universe. He hopes that the explorations made by his soul will finally "catch somewhere" (line 10), establishing the connection between his soul and the universe.
Main Idea

13. **(4)** Free verse lacks regular rhyme and meter. It does, however, use a variety of internal rhythms and other poetic devices.
Rhythm and Sound Devices

III

from *Hamlet*, by WILLIAM SHAKESPEARE (1564–1616)

1 O, that this too too solid flesh would melt,
2 Thaw and resolve itself into a dew!
3 Or that the Everlasting had not fix'd
4 His canon 'gainst self-slaughter! O God! O God!
5 How weary, stale, flat, and unprofitable
6 Seem to me all the uses of this world.
7 Fie on 't! ah fie! 'tis an unweeded garden,
8 That grows to seed; things rank and gross in nature
9 Possess it merely. That it should come to this!
10 But two months dead! nay, not so much, not two:
11 So excellent a king; that was, to this,
12 Hyperion to a satyr; so loving to my mother
13 That he might not beteem the winds of heaven
14 Visit her face too roughly. Heaven and earth!
15 Must I remember? why, she would hang on him,
16 As if increase of appetite had grown
17 By what it fed on; and yet, within a month,
18 Let me not think on 't: Frailty, thy name is woman!
19 A little month; or ere those shoes were old
20 With which she follow'd my poor father's body,
21 Like Niobe, all tears; why she, even she—
22 O God! a beast, that wants discourse of reason,
23 Would have mourn'd longer,—married with my uncle,
24 My father's brother, but no more like my father

25 Than I to Hercules; within a month,
26 Ere yet the salt of most unrighteous tears
27 Had left the flushing in her galled eyes,
28 She married. O! most wicked speed, to post
29 With such dexterity to incestuous sheets!
30 It is not, nor it cannot come to good;
31 But break, my heart, for I must hold my tongue!

Paraphrase: A modern translation

Oh, if only my body would dissolve and disappear, or if only God had not forbidden suicide. Oh God, how pointless and empty everything in the world seems. Damn this world! It's like a garden overrun with disgusting weeds. That this should happen! My father dead less than two months! Such an excellent, good king. Comparing him with the present king is like comparing the sun god with a beast. He loved my mother so much, that he wouldn't even allow the winds to blow too roughly on her face. Oh why must I remember! Mother used to hold on to Father as though her love grew stronger daily. But within a month after he died . . . I don't want to think about it! God, how weak women are! Just a month, even before the shoes she wore to my father's funeral were old . . . she, who cried like Niobe ("like a fountain," see DIFFICULT WORDS EXPLAINED, below). Oh God, a dumb animal would have grieved longer for its mate . . . married my uncle, my father's brother, a man the very opposite of my father. Within a month, before her eyes had dried from their false tears, she married. How disgusting, to marry her husband's own brother so soon after my father's death. Such a marriage can't possibly come to any good. I'm heartbroken . . . but I must keep silent.

Difficult Words Explained

LINE

2 **resolve itself into:** become
3 **the Everlasting:** God
4 **His canon:** His law, commandment
   'gainst: against
   self-slaughter: suicide
6 **uses:** affairs
7 **Fie on 't!:** Damn it! (the world)
8 **rank:** bad smelling
   gross: low, vulgar
10 **nay:** no
11 **this:** this present king
12 **Hyperion:** in Greek mythology, the sun god.
   a satyr: in Greek mythology, a creature, half man and half goat
13 **beteem:** permit, allow
18 **frailty:** weakness, easily led to sin
19 **ere:** before
21 **Niobe:** in Greek mythology, a mother whose children were slain by the gods. Niobe was turned into a stone from which tears forever flowed.

22 **wants discourse of reason:** lacks reason (a dumb animal)
25 **Hercules:** in Greek mythology, an exceptionally strong hero
26 **unrighteous:** immoral
27 **had left the flushing:** had stopped flowing
    galled: sore from rubbing
28 **post:** hurry
29 **dexterity:** quickness
    incestuous: guilty of incest (sexual relations between close relatives)
30 **come to good:** have happy results
31 **break my heart:** let my heart break

Answer Key

14. **(3)** Lines 1–6, where the speaker expresses his longing to die; and line 31, where he refers to his heartbreak, reveal the speaker's mood of despair (a feeling of great hopelessness and pessimism). — **Style and Tone**

15. **(4)** "It" in the form " 'tis" (it is) refers back to the nearest noun: "world," line 6. — **Figures of Speech**

16. **(2)** In lines 3 and 4 the speaker expresses his wish that the Everlasting (God) had not fixed his canon (commandment) against self-slaughter (suicide). — **Inference**

17. **(3)** An *iamb* is a combination of two syllables, the first unaccented and the second accented. *Pentameter* refers to a poetic meter with *five* syllable groups (in this case, iambs) to one line. *Iambic pentameter*, then, is a meter where each line contains five iambs. See line 31 for an example of iambic pentameter: /"But BREAK,/ my HEART,/ for I/ must HOLD/ my TONGUE!"/ You will study other meters in the "Reading Poetry" chapter. — **Rhythm and Sound Devices**

18. **(3)** Although we understand that the speaker has deep feeling for his mother (otherwise he would not be so shocked by her remarriage), this passage primarily expresses his bitterness over her action. For example, in lines 14–18, recalling his mother's former extremely loving behavior toward his father, Hamlet exclaims how weak women are; in lines 28 and 29 he refers to the "wicked" speed and ease with which she went to his uncle's bed. — **Inference**

19. **(1)** A *synecdoche* is a figure of speech in which a part of something is used to represent the whole, or in which the whole of something is used to represent a part. The "sheets" to which Hamlet's mother hurried represent the marriage bed, or, more broadly, the marriage into which she hurried. "Incest" refers to the act of marrying or having sexual relations with a relative; "incestuous" is the adjectival form of the word. (Legally, the queen's marriage was not incestuous, since she was not a blood relative of her husband's brother. In Hamlet's mind, however, such a marriage constituted incest.) You will learn about *simile, hyperbole,* and *oxymoron* in the "Reading Poetry" chapter. — **Figures of Speech**

**Literary Forms
and Levels
of Diction**

20. (2) A *soliloquy* is a dramatic monologue (only one person speaks) that resembles "thinking aloud." The speaker appears to be talking to himself, expressing whatever thoughts enter his mind (as opposed to conversing with another person). Later in this book you will learn what *eulogy, dialogue,* and *allusion* are.

**Style and
Tone**

21. (4) The suffering of the speaker, the seriousness of his mother's act, the high social position of the characters, and Hamlet's gloomy prophecy that the situation "cannot come to good" all foretell a tragic ending. Later in this book you will learn more about the *tone* of a literary work.

IV

from "The Sculptor's Funeral," a short story by WILLA CATHER (1876–1947)

Difficult Words Explained

LINE

2   **Grand Army man:**   Civil War veteran of the Union Army
4   **S'pose:**   Do you suppose?
    queried: asked
5   **falsetto:**   high-pitched voice
11 **ole:**   old
12 **right well:**   very well
13 **reckon:**   suppose
14 **mortgage:**   use as security to borrow money
17 **edycated:**   educated
    tittered: giggled
18 **chuckle:**   laugh
20 **swimming:**   out of focus, unclear
21 **palm:**   a symbol of greatness
26 **congestion:**   clogging
29 **feeble:**   weak
32 **shan't:**   won't
    the judgment of God: the townspeople would be less merciful than God in judging his faults.

Summary

Harvey Merrick, a great and famous sculptor, has died, and Steavens, his student, has accompanied the body back to Merrick's home town. The coffin lies in the sculptor's home. The family has gone to bed. Steavens and Merrick's neighbors are sitting in the room with the coffin. Two local bankers and an army veteran gossip about Merrick, revealing their low opinion of the sculptor because he had had a greater concern for education than for money. These men are unaware of Merrick's talent and fame. Steavens is shocked by their ignorance and meanness. He now understands what Merrick meant when, asking that his body be returned to his home town, he said that it was not a pleasant place. Merrick revealed his perfect understanding of his neighbor's characters when he predicted that they would criticize him.

Answer Key

22. **(2)** The sentence states that no one would have heard of the town if it hadn't been occasionally mentioned as Harvey Merrick's birthplace. We can infer, then, that Merrick was famous. Later in the paragraph, we learn that Merrick was a sculptor.   **Inference**

23. **(1)** The neighbors' entire conversation reveals their opinion that Merrick was a loafer who was supported by his father. They had great fun discussing Harvey's lack of money and continuous desire for education. See lines 13–17.   **Inference**

24. **(4)** One type of irony is the grim "joke of fate." In this passage, it is a "joke of fate," and an ironic contrast, that a sensitive, great man should have grown up in such an insensitive, crude environment; that he is respected everywhere except in the town where he was born. Furthermore, Harvey Merrick's real worth is the opposite of the statements the townspeople make about him. This is an example of another type of irony.   **Style and Tone**

25. **(1)** In lines 13–15, the banker says that Harvey hasn't asked his father to "mortgage any more farms lately, so as he could go on with his education." The Grand Army man laughingly replies that he couldn't remember a time when Harvey "wasn't bein' edycated." From these remarks, we can infer that Harvey's father made it possible for his son to continue his education at some financial sacrifice.   **Inference**

26. **(3)** Such expressions as "done right well," "ain't," "so as he could go on with his education," "my mind don't reach back," and "bein' edycated" are examples of colloquial (regional) English, rather than standard American English (the speech patterns generally used by newspaper and magazine writers, and by radio announcers).   **Literary Forms and Levels of Diction**

27. **(1)** Since the days of ancient Greece and Rome, the palm branch (often shaped into a wreath) has been an honor awarded to "champions" in sports and in the arts.   **Inference**

28. **(4)** The townspeople reveal themselves to be insensitive and cruel by their mockery of Harvey and by their ignorance of his achievement. Merrick, a sculptor of great sensitivity and genius, is their direct opposite. It is remarkable that so gifted and refined a man developed in such a crude and mindless environment.   **Main Idea**

V

from *The Old Man and the Sea*, a novel by ERNEST HEMINGWAY (1899–1961)

Difficult Words Explained

LINE

2   **Sargasso weed:**   a type of seaweed
     formalized: having a regular shape

3   **iridescent:**   rainbow-tinted
    gelatinous: jelly-like
    bladder: air-filled sac
    Portuguese man-of-war: type of large jellyfish
5   **filaments:**   thread-like, stinging tentacles
7   **Agua mala:**   "evil water," the Cuban name for the jellyfish
11 **immune:**   not affected by
14 **working:**   pulling in
    welts: raised red streaks on the skin
21 **carapaced:**   covered with a protective shell

Summary

The old fisherman, rowing in his boat, sees a beautiful purple jellyfish floating on the sea. He curses the jellyfish, knowing that its floating tentacles are poisonous. When he hauls in his fishing lines, bits of the poison tentacles catch on them and burn his hands and arms. Because he hates the *agua mala,* the old fisherman loves to watch sea turtles eat them, and when they are washed ashore, he loves to step on them and kill them.

Answer Key

Inference

29. **(2)** From the description given in lines 5–6, we learn that the man-of-war resembles a floating bubble with purple filaments. This description could only refer to a jellyfish, *not* to a ship, shark, or soldier.

Inference

30. **(3)** We know the old man is in a boat, because he "swung lightly against his oars" (line 8). Lines 12–15 describe the old man pulling in a fish, and the jellyfish filaments catching on his line. These clues indicate that he is a fisherman, not a biologist, sailor, or artist.

Inference

31. **(2)** We would expect a beautiful bubble to be harmless. This beautiful bubble contains poison and is dangerous. It is "false" because it looks different from what it really is.

Inference

32. **(1)** Although he admires the beauty of the jellyfish, his curse (line 7) and the explanation of the pain the jellyfish can cause, clearly reveal his hostility (extreme unfriendliness).

Style and
Tone

33. **(2)** The author gives us a sharp, detailed picture of the sea, its inhabitants, and the old man's relation to both. His writing style in this passage is realistic and descriptive. Later in this book you will learn about other literary styles.

Figures
of Speech

34. **(4)** A *simile* is a comparison which uses "as" or "like." In line 5, the author compares the floating of the Portuguese man-of-war (the "It") to the cheerful floating of a bubble. Because this comparison is introduced by the word "as," it is a simile. You will learn about *apostrophe, onomatopoeia,* and *metonymy* in the "Reading Poetry" chapter.

Inference

35. **(3)** Choice (1) is too mournful and flowery to be appropriate. Choice (2) is a bad simile. The noise would not be loud enough to sound like

firecrackers. Choice (4) would be too suddenly disgusting and flowery. Only choice (3) is suitably realistic and masculine to fit the realistic, descriptive style.

VI

from *An Almanac for Moderns*, by DONALD CULROSS PEATTIE (1898–1964)

Difficult Words Explained

LINE

1   **encountered:** found

2   **lady's slipper:** a wild orchid, native to North America

3   **curiosities:** unusual plant, animal, or rock specimens

6   **abroad:** around

7   **fungi:** plants, such as mushrooms, which cannot manufacture their own food

8   **save:** except

9   **bacterial flora:** colony of bacteria (single-celled plants)
   alimentary canal: digestive system

12   **mutual:** participated in by both
   adaptations: changes, accommodations
   symbiosis: close relationship between two plants or animals in which each assists the other in some way

13   **parasitism:** a close relationship between two plants or animals in which one lives off the other

15   **purvey:** supply

16   **hence:** therefore
   pre-digested: broken down in advance into substances which can be absorbed by the plant or animal
   elements: substances

Summary

The author, a naturalist (one who studies plants and animals in their natural environments), is walking in the woods, collecting interesting plant, animal, and rock specimens to bring home to his children. He sees a wild yellow orchid. Recalling the popular belief that orchids are unhealthy, he wonders whether this assumption is due to the fact that orchids need fungi growing in their roots to help them obtain food. These fungi, however, are no more unhealthy than the useful bacteria that live in the digestive system of man.

Answer Key

36. **(1)** Symbiosis is defined in lines 11–12 and illustrated in lines 14–17.   **Supporting Detail**

37. **(2)** Expository writing is nonfiction prose designed to communicate information. This passage contains information about symbiotic relationships in plants and animals. The style is factual and informative, or expository.   **Style and Tone**

Supporting
Detail

Inference

Style and
Tone

Literary Forms
and Levels
of Diction

38. **(3)** This information is given in lines 14–17.

39. **(3)** See the first sentence of the SUMMARY for a definition of a naturalist. The author's interest in living things and his scientific knowledge indicate that he is a naturalist.

40. **(1)** While the author clearly hopes to interest the reader, his main interest is to explain symbiosis.

41. **(4)** Essays are works of prose which communicate the author's point of view on a given subject. Novels, short stories, and prose-poems are works of fiction, with literary forms different from that of the essay. You will study literary genres (types) in a later section of this book.

SELF-EVALUATION PROFILE

Although it is impossible to predict precisely how well you will do on the official GED Examination, it is possible to get a good idea of the various areas in which you need further study. The Self-Evaluation Profile (facing page) has been designed for this purpose. After you fill in this chart, you should have an idea of where you stand.

1. Cross out the check for each question you answered incorrectly. Count the number of checks in each column and enter that number in the column *Correct Answers*. Then total your correct answers and enter that number on the bottom line, marked *My Score*.

2. See how well you did on the different types of questions. The pages where you will find special practice in these skills are listed in the last column—"Skills Page."

It is impossible to predict with statistical accuracy how well you would do on an actual High School Equivalency Examination. You will be given any one of several current forms of the test, some of which will seem harder to one individual than to another. Therefore, consider the Self-Evaluation Profile as a guide, not a guarantee. And remember, if you study the material in this book carefully, your score is bound to improve.

READING SKILLS EVALUATION CHART—DIAGNOSTIC TEST

QUESTION NUMBER	MAIN IDEA	SUPPORTING DETAILS	INFERENCE	STYLE AND TONE	FIGURES OF SPEECH	RHYTHM AND SOUND DEVICES	LITERARY FORMS AND LEVELS OF DICTION	CORRECT ANSWERS	SKILLS PAGE
1		✓							51–55
2						✓			92–107
3				✓					69–80
4						✓			92–107
5			✓						62–80, 108–119
6				✓					69–80
7	✓								26–51
8		✓							51–55
9		✓							51–55
10			✓						62–80, 108–119
11			✓						62–80, 108–119
12	✓								26–51
13						✓			92–107
14				✓					69–80
15					✓				81–92
16			✓						62–80, 108–119
17						✓			92–107
18			✓						62–80, 108–119
19					✓				81–92
20							✓		120–129
21				✓					69–80
22			✓						62–80, 108–119
23			✓						62–80, 108–119
24				✓					69–80
25			✓						62–80, 108–119
26							✓		120–129
27			✓						62–80, 108–119
28	✓								26–51
29			✓						62–80, 108–119
30			✓						62–80, 108–119
31			✓						62–80, 108–119
32			✓						62–80, 108–119
33				✓					69–80
34					✓				81–92
35			✓						62–80, 108–119
36		✓							51–55
37				✓					69–80
38		✓							51–55
39			✓						62–80, 108–119
40				✓					69–80
41							✓		120–129

MY SCORE _____

READING COMPREHENSION AND VOCABULARY SKILLS

The literature section of the GED Examination tests your ability to comprehend ideas, relationships, and literary techniques in reading passages. The questions following the selections ask you to think about passages in ways that may be unfamiliar to you. Such thinking often requires learning and practicing new reading skills. This section will help you to grasp the important points in a passage. It will also help you to answer GED questions. Questions are important. Only by answering them correctly can you show that you have understood what you have read.

SECTION 1: Identifying the Main Idea or Theme

When you read social studies or science paragraphs, you will usually find a *main idea sentence* within each paragraph. This main idea sentence is the most important idea in the passage—it is what the passage is all about. When you learn to find the main idea, and understand how the supporting details relate to it, you will understand the paragraph.

In the same way, when you are reading literature, prose, or verse, you must also be able to identify the main idea of the passage. Some selections will contain main idea sentences. In other passages, the main idea will not be stated anywhere in the passage. You must read the passage carefully, digest the information the author gives you, and put the main idea in your own words. This skill is called *inferring the main idea*. For a further discussion on Making Inferences, see page 62.

The Interpretation of Literary Materials test is made up mainly of questions that emphasize knowledge and special skills that you will not often use in ordinary reading. You will be tested on your ability to interpret figures of speech, to handle unusual sentence structure and word meaning, and to recognize mood and purpose, as well as an understanding of literary terms. All these skills are taught in other parts of this book. In this section you will learn what are considered the most important skills in reading of any kind—*the ability to understand what you read*.

The main idea of a literary passage is often referred to as the *theme* of the passage. Questions on the GED Literature Exam often ask what the theme of a particular selection is—or indirectly test your ability to recognize the theme.

26

Locating the Main Idea in an Essay Passage

An *essay* is a statement of a writer's feelings, beliefs, or observations about a particular subject. Finding the main idea of an essay passage is sometimes easier than determining the theme of a poem or of a dramatic or fictional passage. This is true because the essay writer—like the social studies and science writer—usually develops each of his paragraphs around a main idea sentence. When reading the following essay passages, ask yourself these three questions:

What is this passage about? The answer to this question will give you the *topic* of the passage. Then ask yourself:

What is the most important thing the author says about the topic? The answer to this question is the *main idea*. To be sure you really have the main idea, ask yourself:

Do all of the other ideas in the passage support the main idea? If the answer to this question is *yes*, you may be certain that you have found the main idea.

Here is an example. Read the following essay passage and find the main idea.

Passage 1

In the first place, I hate women because they always know where things are. At first blush, you might think that a perverse and merely churlish reason for hating women, but it is not. Naturally, every man enjoys having a woman around the house who knows where his shirt studs and his briefcase are, and things like that, but he detests having a woman around who knows where *everything* is, even things that are of no importance at all, such as, say, the snapshots her husband took three years ago at Elbow Beach.

James Thurber, "The Case Against Women"

1. The most important idea in this paragraph is:

   (1) Every man enjoys having a woman around the house who knows where his shirt studs are.
   (2) Three years ago the author took some snapshots at Elbow Beach.
   (3) The author's reason for hating women is perverse and churlish.
   (4) The author hates women because they always know where everything is.

   (4) **Did you choose answer (4)? It is the correct choice.** Did you ask yourself: *What is this passage about?* It is clear that this paragraph is about the author's dislike of women. This is the *topic* of the paragraph.

   What is the most important thing the author says about the topic? The author says that "I hate women because they always know where things are." This is the main idea of the paragraph. To be absolutely sure this is the main idea, ask yourself:

Do all of the other ideas in the passage support this main idea? There are other ideas in the passage, but they merely add details, explaining that it's all right for a woman to know where important things are, but all wrong for her to always remember where unimportant things are.

Main Ideas in Different Parts of the Paragraph

In the passage which you just read, did you notice that the main idea was contained in the first sentence? In essay passages, main ideas are often found in the beginning sentence, and are illustrated or explained in the sentences which follow. Very often, however, the main idea sentence is located at the end of the paragraph, or even in the middle of the paragraph.

Read the following passages and identify the main idea of each. Keep in mind that the main idea sentence may be at the beginning, in the middle, or at the end of the paragraph.

Passage 2

The human infant, emerging out of fetal unawareness, comes into a world bright with colors and clamorous with sound. So does a fox-cub, or a new-hatched jay. The earthworm's birth is no such transition. Out of the darkness of the egg, the wriggling fragment of flesh and muscle emerges into a world that is hardly more fraught with awareness, hardly more informed by mind, than was the egg mass from which it came. The earthworm is unseeing, for it has no eyes. It is unhearing, for it has no ears. The world into which it has been born is only a darkness and a silence.

Alan Devoe, "Life and Death of a Worm"

2. The theme of this passage is the idea that:

(1) The earthworm is born into a world of darkness and silence.
(2) The human infant comes into a world bright with colors.
(3) The earthworm is unseeing, for it has no eyes.
(4) A new-born earthworm is a wriggling fragment of flesh and muscles.

(1) *What is the passage about?* The topic of Passage 2 is "the earthworm." You may have had more difficulty in locating the topic of this paragraph than you did for the previous passage, since the writer begins by discussing human infants, fox-cubs, and blue-jays. As you read on, however, you discovered that the author mentions warm-blooded newborns with the sole purpose of contrasting their experience with that of the new-born earthworm.

What is the most important thing the author is saying about earthworms? They are born into a world of silence and darkness. This is the main idea of the passage. Notice that it is stated at the *end* of the paragraph.

Do all of the other ideas in the passage support this main idea? The earlier sentences contrast the birth experience of humans, animals, and birds—whose sense organs enable them to experience the world as a place of color, sound, and activity—with the birth experience of the worm. Because of the earthworm's lack of intelligence and sense organs, the world into which he hatches—like the egg from which he came— is a place of darkness and of silence. **Choice (1) is therefore correct.**

Passage 3

I say to you today, my friends, even though we face the difficulties of today and tomorrow, I still have a dream. It is a dream deeply rooted in the American dream. I have a dream that one day this nation will rise up and live out the true meaning of its creed: "We hold these truths to be self-evident, that all men are created equal." I have a dream that one day, on the red hills of Georgia, sons of former slaves and the sons of former slave owners will be able to sit down together at the table of brotherhood.

Martin Luther King, Jr., "I Have a Dream"

3. The main idea of this passage is:

   (1) Today and tomorrow are filled with difficulties.
   (2) The author's dream is deeply rooted in the American dream.
   (3) The author dreams that one day this nation will live according to its creed that "all men are created equal."
   (4) The author dreams often about the red hills of Georgia.

   (3) *What is this passage about?* The topic of Passage 3 is the author's dream.

   What is the most important thing the author is saying about his dream? His dream is "that one day this nation will rise up and live out the true meaning of its creed: 'We hold these truths to be self-evident, that all men are created equal.'" This is the main idea of the passage, stated in the *middle* of the paragraph.

   Do all of the other ideas in the passage support this main idea? Yes, the other sentences simply give details of the writer's dream, as well as one example of what its fulfillment could mean (sons of former slaves and sons of former slaveholders meeting together in brotherhood). **Choice (3) is therefore the correct choice.**

Passage 4

Life will never want for heroes, mostly unhonored and unsung, but always there, and ready to act. Our world has grandeur and life has hope. In spite of the despair of the beats and the wailers, the harp in the air still sings the melody of hope, and hope in action will sing on everlastingly till, maybe, a thousand million years from now time gives its last sigh, and all things go.

Sean O'Casey, "The Harp in the Air Still Sings"

4. The main idea of this passage is:

   (1) Life will never want for heroes.
   (2) Our world has grandeur and life has hope.
   (3) Hope in action will sing on everlastingly.
   (4) The world may end in a thousand million years.

(2) *What is this passage about?* The topic of this passage is the greatness and the hope in human life.

What is the most important thing the author has to say about the topic? "Our world has grandeur and life has hope." This is the main idea of the passage, stated in the second sentence of the paragraph.

Do all of the other ideas in the passage support this main idea? Yes. The first sentence gives an example of the world's grandeur: its heroes and their noble deeds. The sentences which follow the main idea sentence add details concerning hope: the opinion that it will live as long as the world continues. **Choice (2) is therefore the correct choice.**

Let's see if you have learned the technique of finding the main idea sentence in an essay passage. As you read the paragraphs, remember to ask yourself: "What is this passage about?" Determining the topic should help you locate the main idea. Answers and explanations are given on page 31.

EXERCISE 1

Underline the main idea sentence in each of these passages.

Passage A

I may as well let the cat out of the bag right away as far as my opinion goes and say that strictness or permissiveness is not the real issue. Good-hearted parents who aren't afraid to be firm when it is necessary can get good results with either moderate strictness or moderate permissiveness. On the other hand, a strictness that comes from harsh feelings or a permissiveness that is timid or vacillating can each lead to poor results. The real issue is what spirit the parent puts into managing the child and what attitude is engendered in the child as a result.

Benjamin Spock, "Strictness or Permissiveness"

Passage B

It's a beautiful garden. The whole family enjoys its color, its aura of rest and quiet and coolness. Against the house is a foundation planting of mountain laurel and rhododendron rolling down to a low border of Japanese yew along whose edges clumps of star-of-Bethlehem and pasque flower peep out and, in season, autumn crocuses. English ivy climbs the enclosing brick walls against which tall spears of delphinium, foxglove, and monkshood brace, supported in front by lower bushes of daphne, snow-on-the-mountain, larkspur, bleeding heart and Christmas rose. There are patches of delicate wild blue iris, daffodils, and lily of the valley—and a low edging of trimmed box. In one corner is a tall, dramatic castor-bean plant to fill in until the cherry laurel grows taller. It's lovely—and every plant in it is poisonous.

Hubert Creekmore, "Daffodils Are Dangerous"

Passage C

The capacity for getting along with our neighbor depends to a large extent on the capacity for getting along with ourselves. The self-respecting individual will try to be as tolerant of his neighbor's shortcomings as he is of his own. Self-righteousness is a manifestation of self-contempt. When we are conscious of our worthlessness, we naturally expect others to be finer and better than we are. We demand more of them than we do of ourselves, and it is as if we wished to be disappointed in them. Rudeness luxuriates in the absence of self-respect.

Eric Hoffer, "Thoughts on the Brotherhood of Men"

ANSWERS AND EXPLANATIONS

Passage A

"Strictness" versus "permissiveness" is the topic of this passage. The most important thing the author says about the topic is that what matters is neither the strictness nor the permissiveness of parents, but rather the *spirit* in which they are used to manage the child. This idea is stated in the *last* sentence. The earlier sentences build up to the main idea by describing contexts in which both strictness and permissiveness can be either constructive or harmful in their effects on the child.

Passage B

The topic is "garden plants." The most important thing the author says about the topic is that every flower and plant in a beautiful garden may be poisonous. The idea is stated in the *last* sentence. The earlier sentences, describing a variety of plants in a lovely garden, build up to the idea that all of them are poisonous. In this paragraph, the main idea—contained in the last sentence—comes as a "shocker," a surprise ending. The first five sentences communicate a picture of beauty and tranquility. A careless reader—one who did not read the entire passage attentively—might miss the main idea completely. This example illustrates the importance of paying close attention to every element in a passage.

Passage C

The topic is "getting along with our neighbors." The most important thing which the author says about the topic is that our capacity for getting along with others depends on our capacity for getting along with ourselves. This is the main idea. It is stated in the *first* sentence. All of the other sentences describe how self-respect is related to respect for others, and how self-contempt is linked with hostility toward others.

Finding the Theme of a Dramatic Passage

The High School Equivalency Literature Examination will include at least three passages taken from plays and will frequently ask you to identify the *themes* of these passages.

Finding the theme of a dramatic excerpt is a bit trickier than finding the main idea of an essay paragraph. While an essay passage usually includes a main idea sentence, a dramatic passage does not. When reading drama you must *figure out* or *infer* the theme or controlling idea, based on what is happening in the passage.

The reason for this difference is very simple, and is related to the fact that the essay writer and the writer of plays have different purposes. The essayist tells you what he thinks. The dramatist *shows* you what he feels about life or about people by creating characters and situations.

When you read a dramatic passage, imagine that you are witnessing a conversation between real people. Try to imagine the characters actually speaking the lines of the passage. Then ask yourself, *"What does this 'conversation' reveal about events—past, present, or future?"* If necessary, reread the passage so that you are able to answer this question fully. Then ask yourself, *"What does this 'conversation' reveal about the personalities, feelings, and relationships of the leading characters?"* When you have answered this second question, you should be able to combine the information you gathered in answering questions one and two in the form of a single statement which will be the *theme* of the passage.

Read the dramatic passage below. Ask yourself what the "conversation" reveals about *events* and what it reveals about *characters.* Then decide which answer choice best expresses the theme of the passage.

In the following pages, we will show you, through example and practice, how to develop the most important reading skills which will enable you to understand what you read and to score high on the literature part of the GED examination.

You must master these important skills:

Section 1:   Identifying the Main Idea or Theme

    A. In an essay passage
    B. In a drama passage
    C. In a fiction passage
    D. In a poem

Section 2:   Verifying Supporting Details

    A. Supporting Detail Contained in More Than One Sentence
    B. Questions which Paraphrase the Text

Identifying the reading skill to be applied is a first step toward answering the questions correctly. In order to help you master the techniques of identifying reading skills, we have labeled the reading skill that you should have applied to answer the questions correctly.

Passage 1

Scene: David's bedroom, untouched since the day when David went to college. David's mother, Mrs. Phelps, is paying him a late-night visit.

Mrs. Phelps. Why do you look so startled? It's only Mother!

David *(Laconic).* Hello, Mother!

Mrs. Phelps. I came in to ask if you needed anything and . . .

David. Not a thing, thanks.

Mrs. Phelps. And to warn you against opening the window in this weather. Oh, and I brought you that extra cover. I've been picking up after you, too.

David. *(Looking gloomily about).* You needn't have troubled.

Mrs. Phelps. It took me back to the old days when I used to tuck you up in that same little bed . . .

David. *(A strong hint).* Yeah . . . I'm just turning in, Mother.

Mrs. Phelps *(Regardless).* . . . And then sit in this very chair and talk over all my problems with you. I feel that I must talk to my big boy to-night. . . . I must get acquainted with my Dave again.

David. We're not exactly strangers, are we? And besides, it's getting late.

Mrs. Phelps. *(Even more persistent).* It was always in these late hours that we had our talks in the old days when we were still comrades. Oh, are those days gone forever? Don't you remember how we used to play that we had an imaginary kingdom where we were king and queen?

David *(Moribund).* Did we? I wish Chris [David's wife], 'ud come up.

Mrs. Phelps. *(A frown and she speaks quickly).* Have you noticed, Dave boy, that your room is just as you left it? I've made a little shrine of it. . . .

Sidney Howard, "The Silver Cord"

1. Which of the following sentences best expresses the theme of the passage which you have just read?

   (1) Mrs. Phelps, a possessive and over-protective mother, is attempting to "baby" her grown son, an effort which he resists.
   (2) Mrs. Phelps, the loving mother of an only son, is attempting to make David comfortable during his vacation from college.
   (3) David, at home again after a long absence, feels that he and his mother are almost strangers.
   (4) David and his mother are both enjoying a late-night chat such as they have not had since David went away to college.

   (1) *What does the passage reveal about events—past, present and future?* We learn that when David was a little boy, he and his mother were very close (from Mrs. Phelps' fond remembrance of tucking her son into bed "in the old days"; by her reference to their late evening talks, and the game they used to play of being "king and queen"; we learn that David has returned home after a long absence (from Mrs. Phelps' statement that she must get reacquainted with her Dave again, and from her statement that David's room is just as he had left it).

   What does the passage reveal about the personalities, feelings, and relationships of the leading characters? Mrs. Phelps wants to reestablish the intimate, mothering relationship she had with David when he was a small boy. We know this from the little services she has been performing for him; from her fond recollection of their former closeness; from her wanting to "get acquainted with my David again"; and from her statement that she has made a shrine out of his boyhood bedroom. David, on the other hand, feels embarrassed by his mother's possessive, overprotective attitude, and would like her to leave him alone. We know this from his strong hints that he doesn't need anything, that it's getting late, that he is just getting ready to go to bed.

How can the highlights of the above information be combined in a single statement to form the theme of the passage? The most important aspects of this scene are Mrs. Phelps' possessiveness and her attempts to treat David like the small child he once was; and David's polite efforts to resist her babying. **Therefore, answer choice (1) is the correct choice.**

Here is another passage, taken from the same play. Read it, asking yourself what it reveals about events and characters, and how the highlights of the information can be combined to form a statement of the theme.

Passage 2

Christina. Oh, there are normal mothers around; mothers who *want* their children to be men and women and take care of themselves; mothers who are people, too, and don't have to be afraid of loneliness after they've outlived their motherhood; mothers who can look on their children as people and enjoy them as people and not be forever holding on to them and pawing them and fussing about their health and singing them lullabies and tucking them up as though they were everlasting babies. But you're *not* one of the normal ones, Mrs. Phelps! Look at your sons if you don't believe me. You've destroyed Robert. You've swallowed him up until there's nothing left of him but an effete make-believe. And Dave! Poor Dave! How he survived at all is beyond me. . . . If you're choking a bit on David, now, that's my fault because you'd have swallowed him up, too, if I hadn't come along to save him! Talk about cannibals! You and your kind beat any cannibals I've ever heard of. And what makes you doubly deadly and dangerous is that people admire you and your kind. They actually admire you! You professional mothers! . . .

Mrs. Phelps. You are entitled to your opinions, Christina, just as I am to mine and David is to his. I only hope that he sees the kind of woman he's married. I hope he sees the sordidness, the nastiness she offers him for his life.

Christina. *(An involuntary cry of pain).* I'm not nasty! I'm not!

Mrs. Phelps. What have you to offer David?

Christina. A hard time. A chance to work on his own. A chance to *be* on his own. Very little money on which to share with me the burden of raising his child. The pleasure of my society. The solace of my love. The enjoyment of my body. To which I have reason to believe he is not indifferent.

Mrs. Phelps. *(Revolted).* Ugh!

Sidney Howard, "The Silver Cord"

2. The theme of this passage is:

   (1) Christina's lack of gratitude and respect toward Mrs. Phelps, her husband's mother, who has had the kindness to take Christina into her home.

(2) the jealous relationship between David, the more independent and aggressive of the two brothers, and Robert, the younger and weaker son;

(3) the bitter rivalry between Christina and her adult, non-possessive love for David, and Mrs. Phelps, whose love is abnormal and devouring;

(4) the poverty which David and Christina must face, since neither of them has any money.

(3) **Did you choose answer (3)? It is the correct choice.** 1905403

What does this passage reveal about events—past, present, and future? The passage reveals that, in Christina's opinion, Mrs. Phelps has destroyed her son Robert through her abnormal, devouring love, and that she has almost destroyed David in the same manner; that David, in the role of husband and father, can look forward to a future of financial struggle but of independence, emotional and sexual love, and happiness.

What does the passage reveal about the personalities, feelings and relationships of the leading characters? Mrs. Phelps, an over-protective, over-possessive mother, hates her rival and daughter-in-law, Christina; and Christina detests Mrs. Phelps, who in her opinion threatens to destroy David with her abnormal, overpowering love.

How can the highlights of the above information be condensed and combined to form a single statement—the theme of the passage? The scene clearly reveals the hostility between the two women, their rivalry over David's love, and the two contrasting types of love which they have to offer David; **therefore, answer (3) above is the correct answer.**

The next passage is a little tricky. In real life, people do not always mean what they say. Do you think that the characters in the next scene mean everything that they are saying to each other? By determining what the passage reveals concerning both events and personalities, you should arrive at the correct answer.

Passage 3

Tyrone. As I was saying, my throat is parched after the long dusty walk I took just for the pleasure of being your guest.

Hogan. I don't remember inviting you, and the road is hard macadam with divil a speck of dust, and it's less than a quarter mile from the Inn here.

Tyrone. I didn't have a drink at the Inn. I was waiting until I arrived here, knowing that you—

Hogan. Knowing I'd what?

Tyrone. Your reputation as a generous host—

Hogan. The world must be full of liars. So you didn't have a drink at the Inn? Then it must be the air itself smells of whiskey today, although I didn't notice it before you came. You've gone on the water-wagon, I suppose? Well, that's fine, and I ask pardon for misjudging you.

Tyrone. I've wanted to go on the wagon for the past twenty-five years, but the doctors have strictly forbidden it. It would be fatal—with my weak heart.

Hogan. So you've a weak heart? Well, well, and me thinking all along it was your head. I'm glad you told me. I was just going to offer you a drink, but whiskey is the worst thing—

Tyrone. The Docs say it's a matter of life and death. I must have a stimulant —one big drink, at least, whenever I strain my heart walking in the hot sun.

Hogan. Walk back to the Inn, then, and give it a good strain, so you can buy yourself two big drinks.

Josie *(Laughing).* Ain't you the fools, playing that old game between you, and both of you pleased as punch!

Tyrone *(Gives up with a laugh).* Hasn't he ever been known to loosen up, Josie?

Josie. You ought to know. If you need a drink you'll have to buy it from him or die of thirst.

Eugene O'Neill, "A Moon for the Misbegotten"

3. The theme of this passage is:

(1) Tyrone's shame concerning his addiction to whiskey, which makes it impossible for him to come right out and ask for a drink.
(2) Hogan and Josie's disapproval of Tyrone's excessive drinking.
(3) The unspoken, underlying hatred and contempt which Hogan feels for Tyrone on account of his weaknesses.
(4) A playful exchange which Tyrone and Hogan often go through, in which Tyrone hints broadly for whiskey and Hogan, pretending not to understand, insults him.

(4) **The last answer choice is the correct one.**

What does the passage reveal about events? We learn that Tyrone is visiting Hogan, after having stopped at the Inn.

What does the passage reveal about the personalities, feelings and relationships of the leading characters? Tyrone keeps hinting that he would appreciate Hogan's giving him a drink—complaining that his throat is "parched," that his doctors insist that he drink whiskey after walking in the sun, that he knows Hogan's reputation "as a generous host." For his part, Hogan keeps insulting Tyrone—insisting that he hadn't invited him, complaining that the air smells of whiskey, suggesting that Tyrone has a weak head, not a weak heart. We know, however, that their relationship is friendly and their conversation playful, since neither gets angry at the other. Josie's laughing comment about the men "playing that old game between you" confirms the point.

How can we combine the highlights of this information to find the theme of the passage? Highlights of the scene are Tyrone's playful hinting for a drink, Hogan's playful insults—in other words, the "game" they are playing with each other; consequently, **answer choice (4) is correct.**

Now, test your ability to infer the theme of a dramatic selection. Read Passage A below several times. Ask yourself what the "conversation" reveals about events and about characters. Finally, see if you can formulate the theme of the passage in as few words as possible. Answers and explanations are given on page 38.

EXERCISE 2

Write a sentence or two, stating the theme of each passage.

Passage A

Big Daddy. I been quiet here lately, spoke not a word, just sat and stared into space. I had something heavy weighing on my mind but tonight that load was took off me. That's why I'm talking.—The sky looks diff'rent to me. . . . Son, I thought I had it!

Brick. Had what? Had what, Big Daddy?

Big Daddy. Cancer!

Brick. Oh . . .

Big Daddy. I thought the old man made out of bones had laid his cold hand on my shoulder.

Brick. Well, Big Daddy, you kept a tight mouth about it.

Big Daddy. A pig squeals. A man keeps a tight mouth about it. . . . *(grins suddenly, wolfishly).* Jesus, I can't tell you! The sky is open! Christ, it's open again! It's open, boy, it's open!

Brick. You feel better, Big Daddy?

Big Daddy. Better? Well! I can breathe!—All of my life I been like a doubled up fist. . . . Poundin', smashin', drivin'!—now I'm going to loosen these doubled up hands and touch things *easy* with them. . . . *(He spreads his hands as if caressing the air.)* You know what I'm contemplating?

Brick *(vaguely).* No, sir. What are you contemplating?

Big Daddy. Ha ha!—*Pleasure!*—pleasure with *women!*

Tennessee Williams, "Cat on a Hot Tin Roof"

Passage B

Herb. But what's the matter? What's happened? Why isn't my boy a regular fellow? He's had every chance to be since he was knee-high to a grasshopper—boys' camps every summer, boarding schools. What do you think, Laura?

Laura. I'm afraid I'm not the one to ask, Mr. Lee.

Herb. He's always been with men and boys. Why doesn't some of it rub off?

Laura. You see, I feel he's a "regular fellow" . . . whatever that is.

Herb. You do?

Laura. If it's sports that matter, he's an excellent tennis player.

Herb. But Laura, he doesn't even play tennis like a regular fellow. No hard drives and cannon-ball serves. He's a cut artist. He can put more damn twists on that ball.

Laura. He wins. He's the school champion. And isn't he the champion of your club back home?

Herb. I'm glad you mentioned that . . . because that's just what I mean. Do you know, Laura, his winning that championship brought me one of my greatest humiliations? I hadn't been able to watch the match. I was supposed to be in from a round of golf in time, but we got held up on every hole . . . And when I got back to the locker room, I heard a couple of men talking about Tom's match in the next locker section. And what they said cut me to the quick, Laura. One of them said, "It's a damn shame Tom Lee won the match. He's a good player, all right, but John Batty is such a regular guy." John Batty was his opponent. Now what pleasure was there for me in that?

Robert Anderson, "Tea and Sympathy"

Passage C

Johnny. I'm through. . . . I'm quitting.

Polo. Where are you going?

Johnny. I'm a half-hour from hell, Polo. I'm going up to the St. Nicholas and get myself a room. I'm going to kick it . . .

Polo. I was in that room with you once before, Johnny . . .

Johnny. I lock myself up for three days . . . and I won't touch a thing. When I come out, I'll be straight again . . .

Polo. You won't last a day in that room . . .

Johnny. Come with me. You come with me . . . you watch me. You can keep me locked up for three days . . . That's all it takes, Polo. Three lousy days . . .

Polo. Johnny, I can't watch you go through that again . . .

Johnny. I did it once before—and I'll do it again.

Polo. Listen, Johnny. I held you down on that bed for three days! Maybe you can go through that hell again, but I can't watch you again . . . Johnny, sit down, willya . . . ?

Johnny. Polo, my time's running out . . .

Michael V. Gazzo, "A Hatful of Rain"

ANSWERS AND EXPLANATIONS

Passage A

Events. We learn that Big Daddy had believed himself to be dying of cancer, but had recently been told that this was not true. **Characters.** We learn very little about Brick from this conversation. As far as Big Daddy is concerned, now that he is released from the fear of death, he has a new lease on life ("the sky is open again.") All of his life he has been a hard-driving man—but now he decides to live a little, to find pleasure—"with women." **Theme:** *Big Daddy, suddenly relieved of the belief that he was going to die, decides to change his life style and begin "living it up," particularly with women.*

Passage B

Events. Herb Lee's son, Tom, is the tennis champion of his school, and also won the championship of the tennis club in his home town. **Characters.** We learn that Herb is disappointed in his son because he doesn't consider Tom be to a "regular fellow." Instead of being proud of his son's skills in tennis, Herb is ashamed because Tom's style doesn't strike him as being sufficiently masculine. Herb is self-centered and rejecting toward Tom; and when Tom won the club championship, Herb complained that there wasn't any pleasure in it for him. Laura, on the other hand, appreciates and defends Tom. **Theme:** *Expressing disappointment in his son for not being—as he thinks—manly enough, a father reveals his own selfishness and insensitivity.*

Passage C

Events. We learn that Johnny is an addict who wants to kick the habit; and that he had kicked once before, with Polo's help. **Characters.** Johnny is desperate because he knows that very soon he's going to begin to experience withdrawal symptoms ("I'm a half-hour from hell.") He wants to rent a room and lock himself in for three days until the withdrawal period is over; to "quit cold turkey." He begs Polo to stay with him, but Polo refuses, protesting that he can't watch Johnny go through the agony of withdrawal a second time. **Theme:** *A confrontation between Johnny and Polo, in which Johnny begs Polo to help him "kick" his dope habit, and Polo protests he can't watch Johnny go through the agony of withdrawal.*

For additional suggestions and practice in interpreting passages from plays, see the chapter on READING DRAMA which begins on page 86.

Finding the Controlling Idea of a Fiction Passage

When we speak of *fiction,* we are referring to novels and short stories—works in which the plot (story line) and characters are creations of the author's imagination. On the High School Equivalency Literature Examination you will be given at least four passages taken from works of fiction. You will often be asked to identify the *controlling idea of the passage* (the question may not use the term "controlling idea," but may ask you to find the "theme," the "main idea," or "the most important idea"—these terms are often used interchangeably). Or you will be asked related questions, the correct answers to which require an understanding of the controlling idea of the passage.

Short stories and novels are primarily a blend of two types of writing:

1. *Narration,* in which the writer is concerned with telling events, things that have happened or are happening; and

2. *Description,* in which the writer is attempting to give the reader a vivid impression of a person, an animal, a place, an object, an event, etc.

In addition, short story writers and novelists frequently employ *dramatization,* using *dialogue* (conversations between characters) to develop plot and reveal character. When you encounter dramatization in a fictional passage, you may use the techniques described in the last section of this chapter (Finding the Theme of a Dramatic Passage) to analyze and interpret it.

In this section we will be primarily concerned with descriptive, rather than narrative passages, both because they occur more frequently on the GED examination and because you will almost never be asked to identify the controlling idea of a narrative passage. In fact, the main idea of a narrative passage would have to be the briefest possible summary of the events referred to. To illustrate, read the narrative selection below, and tell which of the statements following it best sums up the main events which are mentioned.

Passage 1

Reckless with despair, the girl and the boy planned to elope. Assured of Chang's ability to earn a living, Meilan would take away some of her jewels and they could support themselves in some distant province.

The couple prepared to escape one evening through the back of the garden. As it happened, an old servant saw them at the dark hour of the night and his suspicion was aroused, for the affair was known inside the household. Thinking it his duty to protect the family from a scandal, the servant held the girl and would not let her go. Chang had no choice. He pushed the servant aside. The old man tottered but would not let go and Chang gave him a blow which felled the poor man at the edge of the rockery. His head struck a jagged rock and he lay limp on the ground. Seeing the servant lifeless, they fled.

Lin Yutang, "The Jade Goddess"

1. The statement which best summarizes the main events in this passage is:

   (1) Meilan planned to take some of her jewels with her when she fled to a distant province.
   (2) The affair between Chang and Meilan was well known by the servants of the household.
   (3) The couple prepared to escape in the dark of the night through the back of the garden.
   (4) While eloping with Meilan, Chang accidentally killed one of the household servants.

   (4) **Answer (4) is the correct choice.** Meilan's plan to take her jewels, the servants' knowledge of the affair, and the specifics of the elopement plan are *details*. The two main events in this selection, which, taken together, may be said to constitute the controlling idea, are the planned elopement and the accidental killing, both referred to in answer (4).

When reading a descriptive passage, look for a controlling idea. First, ask yourself, *"What subject is the writer describing?"* Then ask yourself, *"What is the most important thing the writer is saying about the subject?"* The answer to this question should give you the controlling idea of the passage. To check the correctness of your answer, ask yourself,

"Do all of the details in the passage support this controlling idea?" If the answer to this question is *yes,* you may be sure that you have found the controlling idea.

Read the fictional passage below and select the answer choice which best states the controlling idea.

Passage 2

A seat in this boat was not unlike a seat upon a bucking bronco, and by the same token a bronco is not much smaller. The craft pranced and reared and plunged like an animal. As each wave came, and she rose for it, she seemed like a horse making at a fence outrageously high. The manner of her scramble over these walls of water is a mystic thing, and, moreover, at the top of them were ordinarily these problems in white water, the foam racing down from the summit of each wave requiring a new leap and a leap from the air. Then, after scornfully bumping a crest, she would slide and race and splash down a long incline, and arrive bobbing and nodding in front of the next menace.

Stephen Crane, "The Open Boat"

2. The controlling idea in this paragraph is:

   (1) The ocean that day was extremely rough.
   (2) Riding in the small boat was like riding on a plunging horse.
   (3) The foam, racing down from the crest of each wave, nearly capsized the small boat.
   (4) The passengers in the boat were in constant danger of drowning.

(2) Did you choose answer (2)? It is the correct choice.

Did you ask yourself, *"What subject is the writer describing?"* He is obviously describing the movements of a small boat on a rough sea. This is the *subject* of the passage.

What is the most important thing the writer is saying about his subject? The author is saying that a seat in the boat is like a seat on a rearing horse. This is the controlling idea of the passage.

Do all of the details in the passage support this controlling idea? Yes. The author compares riding in the boat to riding either a bucking bronco or a horse jumping an "outrageously high" fence. The boat "leaps" in the air with each wave, and then "races" down the long incline—much as a horse might leap and race.

Now try your hand at interpreting a third practice passage.

Passage 3

We could see the circus performers eating tremendous breakfasts, with all the savage relish of their power and strength: they ate big fried steaks, pork chops, rashers of bacon, a half-dozen eggs, great slabs of fried ham and great stacks of wheat cakes which a cook kept flipping in the air with the skill of a juggler, and which a husky looking waitress kept rushing to their tables on loaded trays held high and balanced marvelously on the fingers of a brawny hand. And above all the maddening odors of the wholesome succulent food, there brooded forever the sultry and delicious fragrance—that somehow seemed to add a zest and sharpness to all the powerful and thrilling life of morning—of strong boiling coffee, which we could see sending off clouds of steam from an enormous polished urn, and which the circus performers gulped down, cup after cup.

Thomas Wolfe, "Circus at Dawn"

3. The controlling idea in this paragraph is:

(1) For breakfast the circus performers ate eggs, meat, pancakes and coffee.
(2) The skill which the circus performers displayed in their acts was not matched by the delicacy of their table manners.
(3) The circus performers drank cup after cup of very strong coffee every morning, the aroma of which permeated the air.
(4) The hugeness of the circus performers' breakfast and appetites reflected the power and strength of the performers themselves.

(4) *What subject is the writer describing?* He is describing the breakfast eaten by the circus performers.

What is the most important thing the writer is saying about his subject? He is emphasizing how strong and powerful these performers are; how huge their breakfasts are and how heartily they eat; and he is making a comparison between the heartiness of the breakfast and the power and animal vigor of the performers.

Do all of the details in the passage support this controlling idea? Yes. We are shown the circus performers "eating tremendous breakfasts, with all the savage relish of their power and strength." The writer then illustrates this "tremendous breakfast," itemizing the foods which were eaten. He emphasizes the power and skill with which the breakfast was cooked and served; the strength of the coffee which the performers gulped down, cup after cup. **Therefore, choice (4) is the correct one.**

Now test your ability to find the controlling or main idea in a descriptive passage. As you read the paragraphs below, remember to ask yourself: *"What subject is the writer describing, and what is the most important thing the writer is saying about this subject?"* Check your answer by verifying whether or not the details in the passage support the controlling idea you have selected. Answers and explanations are given on pages 44–45.

EXERCISE 3

Check the answer which best expresses the controlling idea for each of the passages given below.

Passage A
Big Liam O'Grady was a great raw-boned, sandy-haired man, with the strength of an ox and a heart no bigger than a sour apple. An overbearing man given to berserk rages. Though he was a church-goer by habit, the

true god of that man was Money—red gold, shining silver, dull copper—
the trinity that he worshiped in degree. He and his sister Ellen lived on
the big ranch farm of Moyvalla, and Ellen was his housekeeper and maid
of all work. She was a careful housekeeper, a good cook, a notable baker,
and she demanded no wage. All that suited Big Liam splendidly, and so
she remained single—a wasted woman.

Maurice Walsh, "The Quiet Man"

A. The controlling idea of this passage is:

    (1) Big Liam O'Grady was a bullying and greedy man, prepared to
        sacrifice his sister's happiness for money.
    (2) Although Big Liam went to church every Sunday out of habit, he
        was not a truly religious man.
    (3) Ellen, Big Liam's sister, remained single because she was too busy
        keeping house for her brother to consider marriage.
    (4) Big Liam was a raw-boned, sandy-haired farmer who lived in a big
        ranch house and made a lot of money.

Passage B

About fifteen miles below Monterey, on the wild coast, the Torres family
had their farm, a few sloping acres above a cliff that dropped to the brown
reefs and to the hissing white waters of the ocean. Behind the farm the
stone mountains stood up against the sky. The farm buildings huddled like
the clinging aphids on the mountain skirts, crouched low to the ground as
though the wind might blow them into the sea. The little shack, the rattling,
rotting barn were gray-bitten with sea salt, beaten by the damp wind until
they had taken on the color of the granite hills. Two horses, a red cow
and a red calf, half a dozen pigs and a flock of lean, multicolored chickens
stocked the place. A little corn was raised on the sterile slope, and it grew
short and thick under the wind, and all the cobs formed on the landward
sides of the stalks.

John Steinbeck, "Flight"

B. The controlling idea of this passage is:

    (1) The Torres family owned a few acres of farmland located about
        fifteen miles below Monterey.
    (2) The Torres farm, barely surviving its unfavorable location on a
        slope above the ocean, was a poor one.
    (3) While the farm possessed a few animals, the main business of the
        owners was growing corn.
    (4) Storms, coming in from the ocean, often beat upon the farm and
        were responsible for the decaying condition of its buildings.

Passage C

Once upon a time there was a man who went around selling small rat
traps of wire. He made them himself at odd moments, from material he
got by begging in the stores or at the big farms. But even so, the business
was not especially profitable, so he had to resort to both begging and
petty thievery to keep body and soul together. Even so, his clothes were
in rags, his cheeks were sunken, and hunger gleamed in his eyes.

    No one can imagine how sad and monotonous life can appear to such
a vagabond, who plods along the road, left to his own meditations. But

one day this man had fallen into a line of thought which really seemed to him entertaining. He had naturally been thinking of his rat traps when suddenly he was struck by the idea that the whole world with its lands and seas, its cities and villages,—was nothing but a big rat trap. It had never existed for any other purpose than to set baits for people. It offered riches and joys, shelter and food, heat and clothing, exactly as the rat trap offered cheese and pork, and as soon as anyone let himself be tempted to touch the bait, it closed in on him, and then everything came to an end.

Selma Lagerlof, "The Rat Trap"

C. The controlling idea of this passage is:

(1) The rat-trap seller could not make a decent living from selling his traps, so he was sometimes forced to steal in order to have enough to eat.

(2) Because he was a vagabond, roaming from town to town selling his wares, the man's life was sad, poor and monotonous.

(3) The man, in his poverty and misery, saw life as a giant trap with people as the victims.

(4) The man longed to share in the riches and joys, the luxuries and comforts, that other people possessed.

ANSWERS AND EXPLANATIONS

Passage A

The author is describing Big Liam O'Grady. The aspect of Big Liam's character which the author is emphasizing is his meanness of spirit—particularly his greed for money, to which he has sacrificed his own sister's happiness (by using her as a free housekeeper, rather than encouraging her to marry). This controlling idea is supported by numerous details: the statement that Liam's heart was "no bigger than a sour apple"; that he was overbearing and given to rages; that money was his true god; that his sister worked for him for no wages, which suited him splendidly. **Choice (1) is therefore the correct answer.**

Passage B

The author is describing the Torres farm. In relation to the farm he emphasizes both its poverty and the manner in which it was weatherbeaten and stunted because of its location. This controlling idea is supported by a variety of details: the poverty of the farm is evidenced in such phrases as "a few sloping acres" and "the rattling, rotting barn," the description of a handful of farm animals and a flock of "lean" chickens, and of "a little corn raised on the sterile slope"; the difficult survival of the farm is manifest in the writer's description of how the farm buildings seemed to cling to the mountain side, "as though the wind might blow them away," how the buildings are rotted and weathered by wind and salt, how sterile the land is, and how the corn grew short due to the battering of the ocean wind. **Answer (2) is therefore the correct choice.**

Passage C

The writer is describing a man who sells rat traps. He is emphasizing both the man's poverty and the strange view of life as a giant trap which he deve because of the misery of his existence. His poverty is described in the first paragraph, where we learn that selling rat-traps does not constitute a profitable occupation; that he must beg and steal in order to survive; that he is thin, ragged, and perpetually hungry. His philosophy is described in the second paragraph: that the world is a giant rat trap, that the pleasures and comforts of the world are merely the bait to trap the human victim. **Answer (3) is therefore the correct choice.**

For additional help and practice in interpreting fiction, consult the chapter on **READING PROSE** which begins on page 62.

Identifying the Theme of a Poem

Most GED Literature Examinations ask you to read and interpret four poems; and there are almost always questions concerned with the themes of each of the poems.

In general, poetry is more difficult to understand and interpret than either prose (essays and fiction) or drama. For one thing poets—who love words and like to play with them—frequently use words which are uncommon and which many readers will not understand unless they consult their dictionaries.

For another thing, poets often change around the normal order of words in a sentence ("Now go I," instead of "Now I go") in order to achieve a particular rhyme, rhythm, or emphasis. In addition, the language of poetry is highly condensed, with ideas usually expressed in as few words as possible, and each idea essential to the understanding of the poem as a whole.

Finally, poets habitually use figurative language—symbols and metaphors—in such a way that words in poems do not always have their everyday meanings. For example, a "lamb" in a poem may symbolize innocence; and a "yellow fork" may be a poet's way of referring to a streak of lightning.

In view of these difficulties, you must read a poem slowly and carefully, trying to grasp the meaning of each line. If you do not understand a word in a poem, be sure to look up its meaning in an unabridged dictionary. And finally, if you are having difficulty in understanding the poems in this section, you may want to consult the chapter on READING POETRY which begins on page 81 of this book for help in understanding figurative language.

By and large, the poems given on the GED Examination are short *lyric poems*—poems which communicate a description, a feeling, or an idea.

Poems 1 and 2 are examples of descriptive poetry. In order to find the theme of a descriptive poem, ask yourself: *"What is the writer describing?"* (the subject); and *"What is the most important thing the poet is saying about his subject?"*

Poem 1

Greatly shining,
The Autumn moon floats in the thin sky;
And the fish-ponds shake their backs and flash their dragon scales
As she passes over them.

Amy Lowell, "Wind and Silver"

1. The theme of the poem may be stated as:

   (1) dragons crawling out of the ponds to greet the moon;
   (2) the moon's reflection seeming to turn the ponds into living creatures;
   (3) the effects of the Autumn moon upon the fish in the fish-ponds;
   (4) the brightness of the moon in Autumn.

   (2) **The second answer choice states the theme of the poem.**

   Did you ask yourself, *"What is being described?"* The poet is painting a word picture of the Autumn moon and the fish-ponds below. This is the subject of the poem.

   What is the most important thing the poet is saying about his subject? When he tells us that the fish-ponds "shake their backs" and "flash their dragon scales" he is describing how the moon's reflection in the wavelets of the ponds made them seem alive; **therefore, answer choice (2) is correct.**

Here is a second example of a descriptive poem. Read it and see whether you can identify the theme.

Poem 2

Clean as a lady,
cool as glass,
fresh without fragrance
the tulip was.

The craftsman, who carved her
of metal, prayed:
"Live, oh thou lovely!"
Half metal she stayed.

Humbert Wolfe, "Tulip"

2. Which of the following statements best expresses the theme of the poem?

   (1) The craftsman who carved the tulip fell in love with her.
   (2) A lady is being described, who, in her beauty, resembles a tulip.
   (3) In its crisp perfection, the tulip seems almost metallic.
   (4) The tulip was too stiff and cold to be considered beautiful.

   (3) **The third answer choice is the correct one.** The subject of the poem is, of course, a tulip—a type of flower. The poet is emphasizing the tulip's metallic quality—clean, cool, odorless, perfect. (In fact he imagines a "craftsman" carving her out of metal.)

So far, we have been concerned with descriptive poems. There is another type of poem which communicates a mood or feeling. We can usually find the theme of a poem of this type by asking: *What is the feeling the writer is conveying?* and, *What has given rise to this feeling?*

Poems 3 and 4 communicate different moods. Read them, and see whether you can identify the theme of each.

Poem 3

With rue my heart is laden   By brooks too broad for leaping
  For golden friends I had,   The lightfoot boys are laid;
For many a rose-lipt maiden   The rose-lipt girls are sleeping
  And many a lightfoot lad.   In fields where roses fade.

A. E. Housman, "With Rue My Heart Is Laden"

3. The theme of this poem is

   (1) The poet's joy at remembering the friends of his youth.
   (2) The poet's sadness at remembering the friends of his youth, now dead.
   (3) The poet's amazement at how swiftly the years pass by.
   (4) The poet's bitterness over the fact that his old friends have abandoned him.

> (2) **The second answer is the correct choice.** In this poem the author is sadly recalling the "golden friends" of his young years, now sleeping in the ground.
>
> To find the answer to this question, did you ask yourself: *"What feeling is the author expressing?"* In the first line of the poem, he tells us that his heart is laden with "rue." If you looked up the meaning of "rue" in your dictionary, you discovered that it meant, "sorrow" or "regret." Therefore, we know that the poet's feeling is one of sadness.
>
> *"What has given rise to this feeling?"* The author tells us that his sorrow is for the "golden friends" he had, now laid "by brooks too broad for leaping" or sleeping "in fields where roses fade." In other words, they have died. Thus we know that his sorrow is a lament for the dead friends of his youth.

The following poem describes not one but two emotions. Read it and see whether you can identify the theme.

Poem 4

When I heard the learn'd astronomer,
When the proofs, the figures, were ranged in columns before me,
When I was shown the charts and diagrams to add, divide, and measure them,
When I sitting heard the astronomer where he lectured with much applause in the lecture-room,
How soon unaccountable I became tired and sick,
Till rising and gliding out I wandered off by myself
In the mystical moist night-air, and from time to time,
Look'd up in perfect silence at the stars.

Walt Whitman, "When I Heard the Learn'd Astronomer"

4. The theme of this poem is:

(1) the speaker's boredom with intellectualizations about nature, and his delight in direct experience with nature;

(2) the speaker's anger upon hearing theories with which he disagrees, and his relief upon confirming his own theories;

(3) the speaker's shame at his inability to understand the astronomer, and his relief at escaping outdoors;

(4) the speaker's eagerness to learn about astronomy, and his pride at being able to apply what he has learned.

(1)   **The first answer is the correct choice.**

The speaker became "tired" and "sick"—in other words, bored—listening to the astronomer theorize about the stars; but he recovered when he went outdoors into the night air and gazed up at the stars. Clearly the poet is saying the intellectualizing about nature wearies him, but that direct experience of nature revives him. This, then, is the theme of the poem.

A third type of poem expresses an idea or concept which the poet wishes to share with the reader. When reading a poem of this type, ask yourself: *"What idea about life is the poet expressing?"* This central idea is the theme of the poem. When you believe that you have found the theme, check yourself by asking whether (and how) the details of the poem support the theme.

Read the following poem and identify the theme.

Poem 5

They are not long, the weeping and the laughter,
   Love and desire and hate;
I think they have no portion in us after
   We pass the gate.

They are not long, the days of wine and roses:
   Out of a misty dream
Our path emerges for a while, then closes
   Within a dream.

Ernest Dowson, "Envoy"

5. The theme of the poem is:

(1) Life is a dream.
(2) Our lives, with their joys and sorrows, are brief.
(3) As we mature, we put aside the passions of youth and live more calmly.
(4) Youth swiftly gives way to old age.

(2)   **The second answer choice is the correct one.**

Ask yourself, *"What idea is the writer expressing?* The poet repeats the same theme in various ways: "They are not long—our lives."

"How do the details of the poem support the theme?" The poet first tells us, "They are not long . . ." and then names the various human

passions. He goes on to tell us that he feels that they (our emotions) have no portion (part) in us after we "pass the gate" (die). In the second stanza he repeats that life and its joys ("the days of wine and roses") are not long; and that our brief period of consciousness is bordered at beginning and end by "a misty dream" (sleep, death). Thus we see that individual images of the poem support the theme—that life and its passions are brief.

The next poem presents a very different idea of death. Read it and try to determine the central idea which the poet is expressing.

Poem 6

I never saw a moor,
I never saw the sea;
Yet know I how the heather looks,
And what a wave must be.

I never spoke with God,
Nor visited in Heaven;
Yet certain am I of the spot
As if the chart were given.

Emily Dickinson, "I Never Saw a Moor"

6. The theme of the above poem is:

    (1) the poet's desire to travel and visit the moors and the ocean;
    (2) The poet's doubt that there is a God or a heaven;
    (3) The poet's certainty that God and heaven exist;
    (4) The poet's disbelief in all things that she cannot see.

    (3) **The third answer choice is the correct one.**

What idea is the poet attempting to communicate? She tells us that, although she has never met God nor visited Heaven, she is certain of their existence.

How do the details of the poem support the theme? The poet defends her belief by making a comparison: although she has never seen heather (a type of plant that grows on the moors or flatlands of England and Scotland) or the sea, she is sure of their reality and can imagine very clearly what they must be like; and in the same way she is sure of the reality of God and Heaven.

Now test your ability to identify the themes of the poems which follow. Answers and explanations are given on page 51.

EXERCISE 4

For each of the following poems, decide which answer choice best expresses the theme.

Poem A (Descriptive)

An omnibus across the bridge
  Crawls like a yellow butterfly,
   And, here and there, a passer-by
Shows like a little restless midge.

Big barges full of yellow hay
  Are moved against the shadowy wharf,
  And, like a yellow silken scarf,
The thick fog hangs along the quay.

The yellow leaves begin to fade
  And flutter from the Temple elms,
  And at my feet the pale green Thames
Lies like a rod of rippled jade.

Oscar Wilde, "Symphony in Yellow"

A. The theme of the poem is:

    (1) the ugliness of an urban landscape;
    (2) the many activities taking place by the waterfront;
    (3) the sadness which the writer is feeling as he gazes
       at a river;
    (4) the yellow tones of a city-scene in autumn.

Poem B (Feeling)

My heart is like a singing bird
  Whose nest is in a watered shoot;
My heart is like an apple-tree
  Whose boughs are bent with thick-set fruit;
My heart is like a rainbow shell
  That paddles in a halcyon sea;
My heart is gladder than all these,
  Because my love is come to me.

Christina Rossetti, "A Birthday"

B. The theme of the poem may best be expressed as:

    (1) a dream, in which the poet imagines that she is in a magical forest
       with her love;
    (2) the poet's joy in being reunited with her love;
    (3) the poet's amazement at finding her love after a long absence;
    (4) the poet's joy at receiving gifts from her love—a bird, an apple, and
       a shell.

Poem C (Idea)

Factory windows are always broken.
Somebody's always throwing bricks,
Somebody's always heaving cinders,
Playing ugly Yahoo tricks.

Factory windows are always broken.
Other windows are let alone.
No one throws through the chapel-window
The bitter, snarling derisive stone.

Factory windows are always broken.
Something or other is going wrong.
Something is rotten—I think, in Denmark.
End of the factory-window song.

Vachel Lindsay, "Factory Windows Are Always Broken"

C. The theme of the above poem is:

   (1) people's respect for religion, symbolized by their not throwing rocks at church windows;
   (2) the anti-social behavior of the public, which commits crimes against property;
   (3) the destruction of factories which is presently taking place in Denmark;
   (4) the hostility of workers toward factories and factory-owners, implying that something is wrong with our economic system.

ANSWERS AND EXPLANATIONS

Poem A

What is the poet describing? An urban landscape. *What is the most important thing the poet is saying about the subject?* He is emphasizing the yellow tones of the city scene at his feet—bus, hay in barges, fog, falling leaves. **Therefore (4) is the correct answer choice.**

Poem B

What feeling is the poet describing? She is describing gladness, joy. *What has given rise to this feeling?* Her love has come to her. In the first six lines of the poem, the poet is describing the quality of her joy, comparing her mood with three joyful images from the world of nature. **Answer (2) is the correct choice.**

Poem C

What idea is the poet expressing? He is expressing the hostility of the public toward factories, suggesting that something is rotten, wrong (with the economic system). *How do the details of the poem support this idea?* The poet mentions that, while factory windows are always broken, "other windows are let alone." He concludes that "something is rotten . . . in Denmark," an expression meaning that "something is very wrong here." Clearly he is making a critical comment on our economic system; **hence, answer choice (4) is correct.**

SECTION 2:   Verifying Supporting Details

In previous sections of this chapter, we have been concerned with how to recognize the main idea or theme of a literary excerpt. We have dealt with the *details* of literary passages only insofar as they supported the main idea.

Now we are going to focus on the supporting details themselves. A type of question which is frequently asked on the GED Literature Examination *requires simply that you verify a detail from the passage.*

For example, a passage might state that:

. . . The cactus flowers are all much alike, varying only in color within and among the different species. The prickly pear, for example, produces a flower that may be violet, saffron or red. . . .

You might be asked the following question, based on the information in the passage:

1. Cactus flowers are all:

    (1) very different.
    (2) much alike.
    (3) pear-shaped.
    (4) violet-colored.

In order to answer such a question, all you need to do is to reread the passage carefully in order to determine which of the four possible answer choices is confirmed by details given in the passage. The correct answer is, of course, choice (2): "Cactus flowers are all (2) much alike," a detail which is stated in the first sentence.

This type of question may appear so easy that you suspect that there is a "catch" or a "trick" to the question. But don't worry! The reading specialists who prepared the examination are merely testing your ability to read a passage closely and carefully, and to report accurately on the details of what you have read.

It is true, however, that questions which require you to verify details will not always be as easy as the one given above. For example, the answer to certain questions of this type may not appear in a single sentence, but may require you to check the details of several sentences. Or, the question may use words not contained in the passage, requiring that you have an understanding of certain *synonyms* (words which mean the same thing).

Supporting Detail Contained in More Than One Sentence

Let us use the same passage to illustrate the type of question which requires you to verify a supporting detail which is developed in more than one sentence:

    . . . The cactus flowers are all much alike, varying only in color within and among the different species. The prickly pear, for example, produces a flower that may be violet, saffron or red. . . .

2. A prickly pear is a species of:

    (1) pear tree.
    (2) porcupine.
    (3) cactus.
    (4) thistle.

In order to answer this question, it is necessary to refer to both the first and second sentences of the passage. The first sentence discusses the likenesses and differences among species of cacti. The second sentence begins, "The prickly pear, for example . . ." The words *"for example"* make it plain that the prickly pear is an example of a species of cactus—consequently, we know that (3) is the correct answer.

Warning: a careless reader might be tempted to respond—incorrectly—that a prickly pear is a species of pear tree, due to the similarity between these two terms. Beware of such "sound-alikes." Always verify the correctness of an answer by checking it against the facts contained in the passage.

Questions Which Paraphrase the Text

To *paraphrase* a sentence is to restate the same idea in different words. For example, if I want to paraphrase the sentence, "He likes children," I may say, "He enjoys kids." Both sentences say essentially the same thing, since "enjoys" is a synonym for "likes," and "kids" is a synonym for "children."

Similarly, on the GED Examination, questions often paraphrase the wording of the original passage rather than repeating exactly what was said; and in order to answer the questions correctly, it is necessary to understand what the paraphrase *refers* to.

Reread the sample passage once again, and notice how the question which follows *paraphrases* the content of the passage.

. . . The cactus flowers are all much alike, varying only in color within and among the different species. The prickly pear, for eaxmple, produces a flower that may be violet, saffron or red. . . .

3. The hues of cactus blooms are:

   (1) prickly.
   (2) red.
   (3) alike.
   (4) different.

In order to answer this question correctly, we must know that "hues" is a synonym for "colors," that "blooms" are the same thing as "flowers," that "are different" is another way to express the concept "varying." If we understand the meaning of these synonyms, we know that the question is asking whether the colors of cactus flowers are alike or varying, prickly or red. Referring to the first sentence, we can verify that the correct answer is, of course, (4): "The hues of cactus blooms are (4) different."

Now test your ability to answer questions that require you to verify details contained in a passage. Read each of the paragraphs below carefully. Then read the questions which follow and select the best answer choice, based on supporting details in the passage. Answers and explanations are given on page 55.

EXERCISE 5

Passage A

One prisoner had been brought out of his cell. He was a Hindu, a puny wisp of a man, with a shaven head and vague liquid eyes. He had a thick, sprouting moustache, absurdly too big for his body, rather like the moustache of a comic man in the films. Six tall Indian warders were guarding him and getting him ready for the gallows. Two of them stood by with rifles and fixed bayonets, while the others handcuffed him, passed a chain through his handcuffs and fixed it to their belts, and lashed his arms tight to his sides. They crowded very close about him, with their hands always on him in a careful, caressing grip, as though all the while feeling him to make sure he was there. It was like men handling a fish which is still alive and may jump back into the water. But he stood quite unresisting, yielding his arms limply to the ropes, as though he hardly noticed what was happening.

George Orwell, "A Hanging"

1. The prisoner referred to in the passage was guarded by:

    (1) eight men.
    (2) six men.
    (3) four men.
    (4) two men.

2. The prisoner was about to be:

    (1) released.
    (2) electrocuted.
    (3) hanged.
    (4) shot.

3. The prisoner's manner may be described as:

    (1) passive.
    (2) rebellious.
    (3) hysterical.
    (4) suspicious.

Passage B

After all these years I can picture that old time to myself now, just as it was then: the white town drowsing in the sunshine of a summer's morning; the streets empty, or pretty nearly so; one or two clerks sitting in front of the Water Street stores, with their splint-bottomed chairs tilted back against the walls, chins on breasts, hats slouched over their faces, asleep—with shingle-shavings enough around to show what broke them down; a sow and a litter of pigs loafing along the sidewalk, doing a good business in watermelon rinds and seeds; two or three lonely little freight piles scattered about the "levee"; a pile of "skids" on the slope of the stone-paved wharf, and the fragrant town drunk asleep in the shadow of them; two or three wood flats at the head of the wharf, but nobody to listen to the peaceful lapping of the wavelets against them; the great Mississippi, the majestic, the magnificent Mississippi, rolling its mile-wide tide along, shining in the sun.

Mark Twain, "Old Times on the Mississippi"

1. In this passage, the Mississippi River is described as being:

    (1) polluted.
    (2) congested with small boats.
    (3) dotted with tiny islands.
    (4) about a mile wide.

2. The author jokingly suggests that the clerks had exhausted themselves:

    (1) waiting on customers.
    (2) cleaning out their shops.
    (3) whittling.
    (4) eating watermelon.

3. The town described in the passage is pictured as being:

    (1) somnolent.
    (2) busy.
    (3) noisy.
    (4) flooded.

ANSWERS AND EXPLANATIONS

Passage A

1. In the fourth sentence we are told that "six tall Indian warriors were guarding him." Referring back to the first sentence, we know that "him" refers to the prisoner. Therefore, we know that **choice (2) is the correct answer.**
2. In the fourth sentence we learn that the men guarding the prisoner were "getting him ready for the gallows." A gallows is a platform and scaffold used for hangings; **consequently, answer (3) is the correct choice.**
3. In the last sentence of the passage, we are told that the prisoner "stood quite unresisting . . . as though he hardly noticed what was happening." In paraphrasing this, we may describe his attitude as "passive"; consequently, **answer choice (1) is the correct choice.**

Passage B

1. In the last line of the passage, the Mississippi is described as "rolling its mile-wide tide along"; **hence, answer (4) is correct.**
2. The clerks are described as sleeping, "with shingle-shavings enough around to show what broke them down." "Shingle-shavings" refer to slivers of wood, whittled (carved) with a knife from a shingle (a thin rectangle of wood, used for roofing houses). We can paraphrase this idea by saying that they had exhausted themselves whittling; **consequently, (3) is the correct answer.**
3. Early in the passage the author refers to the white town "drowsing in the sun." Later images—of the clerks sleeping in front of their stores and of the town drunk asleep on the wharf—reinforce this image of drowsing or sleeping. "Somnolent" means "sleepy" or "asleep"; and **therefore (1) is the correct answer choice.** But if you did not understand the meaning of "somnolent" you could have answered correctly by eliminating the three incorrect answer choices: nothing in the passage suggests that the town was busy, noisy, or flooded; in fact it is clear that just the opposite conditions were true, and that the town was idle, quiet, and sunny.

LITERARY LANGUAGE

On the literature section of the GED examination, you will be asked to demonstrate your understanding of *figurative language* as it is used in poems, plays, fiction, and nonfiction. Figurative language (also called *figures of speech*) describes those words and phrases that are used to convey meanings other than literal, or primary, meanings. For instance, when you call a sloppy man a "pig," you are clearly not expressing the literal meaning of the word *pig*. Likewise, you are going beyond the literal meaning of *heart* when you speak of getting down to "the heart of the matter." In these instances, *pig* and *heart* are being used as figures of speech.

Most often, figures of speech are used to suggest a comparison. A writer makes comparisons for a number of reasons. He may want to make his thoughts more dramatic and vivid. Also, he may want to clarify ideas, concepts, and relationships that he feels are too complex. Moreover, he may use a comparison to help you see things and people the way he does. Thus we see that the comparison is a literary instrument used by the writer to bring you, the reader, closer to his mind and world.

On the examination, you will most often come across two types of figures of speech used to make comparisons: *similes* and *metaphors*. A *simile* makes a comparison between two different things by the use of "like" or "as." "Mike is like a tiger," "The ice was as thin as tissue paper," "Sally is as exciting as a wet blanket" are all examples of similes.

A *metaphor*, like a simile, makes a comparison, but a metaphor does its job without using "like" or "as." The following sentences are examples of metaphors:

> Freddy is a fish in the water.
> Sue was an angel to put up with you.
> Mr. Edwards is a dynamo at work.

Writers use metaphors and similes to give familiar ideas a fresh and dramatic appearance. Notice how the poet Langston Hughes uses a metaphor to describe Manhattan in his poem, "Island."

> Black and White,
> Gold and Brown—
> Chocolate custard
> Pie of a town.

He compares the town to a chocolate custard pie. The dark brown chocolate is topped by white whipped cream, in much the same way, Hughes suggests, as black people are dominated by the white people in the city.

In another poem by Hughes, "Dreams," the poet uses a metaphor in which life is compared to an empty field:

> "Life is a barren field
> Frozen with snow."

The idea of life as cold and empty is not a new one. However, the feeling of being in a field that is unmoving, hard and still, lonely and lifeless gives a dramatic meaning to the poet's image of life.

Most literary writing is concerned with feelings, moods, and emotions. The writer is concerned that you see and feel as he does. He selects words that he thinks will make you feel as he wants you to, and then he connects the picture or feeling with his idea, much as Langston Hughes does with Manhattan and chocolate pie. The result in good writing is an immediate understanding of what the writer means.

The result might also be a mood—one of silence, or joy, or fear. Here, too, the writer carefully selects the words he will use to evoke such a mood. For example, look closely at the words that create a depressing tone or ominous feeling in this selection from Edgar Allan Poe's "The Fall of the House of Usher":

> During the whole of a dull, dark and soundless day in the autumn of the year, when the clouds hung oppressively low in the heavens, I had been passing alone, on horseback, through a singularly dreary track of country; and at length found myself, as the shades of the evening drew on, within the view of the melancholy House of Usher. I know not how it was—but, with the first glimpse of the building, a sense of insufferable gloom pervaded my whole spirit.

Words such as *dull*, *dark*, and *soundless*, *oppressively low*, *singularly dreary*, and *melancholy* give a definite sense of foreboding and doom to the paragraph.

In the next example, the short phrases, one following quickly after another, move you through the passage as rapidly as Kino's knife.

> And now a wild fear surged in Kino's breast, and on the fear came rage, as it always did. Kino's hand crept into his breast where his knife hung on a string, and then he sprang like an angry cat, leaped striking and spitting for the dark thing he knew was in the corner of the house. He felt cloth, struck at it with his knife and missed, and struck again and felt his knife go through cloth, and then his head crashed with lightning and exploded with pain. There was a soft scurry in the doorway, and running steps for a moment, and then silence.

In this example of literary writing, the rhythm of the sentences contributes to a mood of fear and anger.

Thus, we see that a writer carefully selects his words and groups them so that they set a pace that is fast or slow, much like a camera jumping or moving slowly from one scene to another.

UNFAMILIAR WORDS

On the literature part of the GED Test, you are often asked to give the meaning of a word that may be unfamiliar to you. For example, you may be asked to choose the correct meaning of *hostile* in the sentence, "At first, the natives were friendly to us, but later they became hostile, attacking and burning the settlements." The word *hostile* means "unfriendly, antagonistic." You can readily determine its meaning by looking for clues or hints in the *context* (the words and phrases surrounding the unfamiliar word). One contextual clue in the example above is the word *but*, which is used to signal a contrast between the unfamiliar word *hostile* and a word you do know—*friendly*. Other contextual clues are the explanatory details—"attacking and burning the settlements"—which follow the word *hostile*. These modifying words, together with signal *but*, tell you that *hostile* is a word used to describe unfriendly persons or acts.

Writers often provide their readers with several kinds of contextual clues to aid them in figuring out the meanings of strange words. One type involves the use of examples. Notice how examples are used to help you understand the meaning of *artifact* ("a man-made object") in the following sentence: "Next to the bones of animals were artifacts, such as arrowheads, spears, pottery, and tools."

Another important contextual clue is restatement—the writer repeats the meaning of the unfamiliar words by using other words. This technique is used to help you understand the meaning of *hyperbole* in the following passage:

> The story was filled with many metaphors and similes. It also contains several hyperboles, or exaggerations, such as "He was centuries old" and "He was as fast as lightning."

Remember, many supposedly unfamiliar words can become clear to you if you keep alert to the many contextual clues used by writers. So, read the passage carefully, and pay special attention to words and phrases surrounding the "demon word." You will often find that the meaning of the word is right in front of you.

EXERCISE 6

DIRECTIONS: What is the meaning of the italicized word in each of the following sentences? Check your answers against the correct answers at the end of the exercise.

1. He didn't *falter* for a minute, but went directly and forcefully to the president.

2. Helen's next attempt to *topple* the chair was unsuccessful. Jane still sat smugly and firmly on it.

3. Simultaneously the light at the left had been rising, slowly, so slowly that it seemed at first they only imagined what it *intimated* in the yard. It vaguely revealed ghost-like figures, silent, waiting.

4. Symbols, comparisons, rhythms, and sounds combine to *evoke* a particular mood in the reader, and if the reader is imaginative, he will respond to the language of imagination.

5. He tried to *simulate* a real garden. He bought trees and plants and bushes. He even let a few canaries fly among the branches. But the setting was artificial, and he knew it.

ANSWERS

1. *Falter* means "hesitate." The words *directly and forcefully* tell how he went to the president. The word *but* is a clue that suggests that *falter* is the opposite of *directly and forcefully*.

2. *Topple* means "make to fall over." What Helen did to the chair was unsuccessful. Jane *still* sat on it. Therefore the chair is still standing and did not fall over.

3. *Intimated* means "vaguely revealed or implied." The words *only imagined* and *vaguely revealed* give a sense of something hinted at or suggested.

4. *Evoke* means "bring forth" or "cause to have a feeling about something." In this sentence, the characteristics of literary writing create or bring forth a mood in the reader. The phrase *respond to* is another clue to the meaning of *evoke*.

5. *Simulate* means to try to duplicate something that is real. The words *but the setting was artificial* help you determine the meaning of *simulate*.

VOCABULARY SKILLS

The vocabulary section of this book has been specially designed to help you do well on the literature part of the GED examination. Here you will study the basic parts of words—prefixes, roots, and suffixes. A knowledge of these commonly used word parts will enable you to figure out the meanings of many unfamiliar words.

English words are constructed of word parts, called *prefixes*, *roots*, and *suffixes*. Different combinations of these word parts produce different words. The *root* is the basic part of any word, the part that gives the word its essential meaning. The essential meaning may be altered or changed completely by adding another word part to the beginning or end of the root. The word part that is attached to the beginning of the root is a *prefix*. The word part that is attached at the end of the root is a *suffix*. By knowing the meanings of these basic word parts that appear over and over again in English words, you will be able to make a good guess as to the meanings of many words that are now totally unfamiliar to you.

To get an idea of how this system of word construction works, look at the following lists.

PREFIXES

Prefix	Meaning	Example	Meaning
1. ante	before	anteroom	a room placed before another room such as a waiting room
2. anti	against or opposite in kind to	antifreeze	a liquid added to the cooling agent in engines to prevent freezing
3. auto	self	autobiography	the story of one's own life
4. circum	around	circumlocution	the use of an unnecessarily great number of words to express an idea; indirect or roundabout expression
5. con	together, with	context	the larger whole in which a word or passage occurs
6. contra	against	contradict	to speak against, to say the opposite of
7. de	down, from, away	decrease	to become less
8. di	two	dialogue	a conversation between two or more people

Prefix	Meaning	Example	Meaning
9. hyper	excessive, above, beyond	hyperbole	an exaggeration
10. re	again	review	to look over again

ROOTS

Root	Meaning	Example	Meaning
1. biblio	book	bibliography	a list of sources of information on a given subject
2. meta	among, akin, along with	metaphor	a comparison made of two things by relating them directly, as in, "He is a pig."
3. meter	measure	hexameter	a line of poetry containing six metrical feet or measures
4. vid, vis	see	video	the picture portion of a television broadcast

SUFFIXES

Suffix	Meaning	Example	Meaning
1. ic	pertaining to, similar, or like	epic	a long narrative poem about the deeds of a traditional hero, poems like the *Iliad* and the *Odyssey*.
2. ion	act or condition of	alliteration	the repetition of sounds in a line of poetry
3. ism	philosophy, act, or practice of	aphorism	a short, pointed sentence expressing a truth or maxim
4. ory	pertaining to	allegory	a story in which people, things, and happenings have another meaning, as in a fable
5. ive	something that accomplishes an action	narrative	a story that tells of events in the order in which they occurred

READING PROSE

Prose is the form of literature that comes closest to ordinary speech. It lacks regular rhyme or rhythm. We will not concern ourselves here with nonliterary prose, such as newspaper and textbook material. We will examine only *literary prose*: imaginative writing that attempts to communicate the author's personal feelings, view of reality, and mental images.

Literary prose can be divided into two main categories: fiction and nonfiction. *Fictional writing*, such as novels and short stories, presents plots and characters that are inventions of the author's imagination. *Nonfictional* writing, such as biographies, autobiographies, essays, and literary articles, describes actual persons and events in an imaginative or creative way, or presents an author's opinions, attitudes, and feelings about real things or events.

Whenever you read a piece of literature, whether prose, poetry, or drama, read it *carefully* and try to *visualize* (picture in your mind) the scenes and characters the author is describing. In good literature, each word or phrase has been included with a purpose, and is intended to communicate information. Therefore, you must pay particularly close attention to details, and relate them to the overall meaning of the passage or work.

FICTION

The passages in this section have been taken from novels and short stories by well-known authors. They are of the same length and quality as the selections on the High School Equivalency Examination. Because these are only excerpts, that is, brief selections from a larger work of literature, you must supply some of the information about the preceding action by making inferences: drawing conclusions from clues in the passage. Do not think, however, that you must make inferences only when reading literary *excerpts*. Inferential skills are necessary for understanding and appreciating literature of *any* length. The kinds of inferences you must make concern the intentions and personalities of the characters, the plot (the story line), the setting (where and when the action takes place), the tone, and the point of view of the author toward the characters and events. In this section you will practice inference-making. Remember to read each passage carefully.

EXERCISE 1: Inferring Plot and Setting

DIRECTIONS: Read the following passage slowly, attempting to visualize (picture in your mind) the action and the characters. Pay attention to each detail, and determine what information it adds to the total meaning of the passage. Then choose the BEST answer to each question, and blacken the space under that number in the answer column.

ANSWERS AND EXPLANATIONS APPEAR AT THE END OF THE CHAPTER

Difficult Words: berry, raven, ghostwise, intent, set you up, thicket, exile, cipher, blind mazes.

1   He told her then that his brother was dead.
2   The woman was silent for a moment. Then she looked at him
3   and said: "He died here, didn't he? In this room?"
4   He told her that it was so. . . .
5   "Oh. . . . How old was he?"
6   "He was twelve."
7   "You must have been pretty young yourself."
8   "I was not quite four."
9   "And—you just wanted to see the room, didn't you? That's why
10 you came back."
11 "Yes."

12   The years dropped off like fallen leaves: the face came back
13 again—the soft dark oval, the dark eyes, the soft brown berry on
14 the neck, the raven hair, all bending down, approaching—the whole
15 appearing to him ghostwise, intent and instant.
16 "Now say it—*Grover!*"
17 "Gova."
18 "No—not Gova.—*Grover!* . . . Say it!"
19 "Gova."
20 "Look, I tell you what I'll do if you say it right. Would you like
21 to go down to King's Highway? Would you like Grover to set you
22 up? All right, then. If you say Grover and say it right, I'll take you
23 to King's Highway and set you up to ice cream. Now say it right—
24 *Grover.*"
25 "Gova."
26 "Ah-h, you-u. Old Tongue-Tie, that's what you are. . . . Well,
27 come on, then, I'll set you up anyway."
28   It all came back, and faded, and was lost again. Eugene turned
29 to go, and thanked the woman and said good-by. . . .
30   And again he was in the street, and found the place where the
31 corners met, and for the last time turned to see where Time had
32 gone.

33 And he knew that he would never come again, and that lost
34 magic would not come again. Lost now was all of it—the street, the
35 heat, King's Highway, all mixed in with the sense of absence in the
36 afternoon, and the house that waited, and the child that dreamed.
37 And out of the enchanted wood, that thicket of man's memory,
38 Eugene knew that the dark eye and the quiet face of his friend and
39 brother—poor child, life's stranger, and life's exile, lost like all of us,
40 a cipher in blind mazes, long ago—the lost boy was gone forever,
41 and would not return.

THOMAS WOLFE, "The Lost Boy"

Difficult Words Explained

LINE

13 **berry:** skin mole, "beauty mark"
14 **raven:** black, like the feathers of a raven
15 **ghostwise:** like a ghost
    intent: concentrated, serious
21 **set you up:** treat you
37 **thicket:** thick growth of bushes
39 **exile:** a person who is forced to live away from his homeland
40 **cipher:** zero, a nobody
41 **blind mazes:** a twisting arrangement of pathways, each of which seems
    to arrive at a dead end; a labyrinth

1. The setting of lines 1–11 is
   (1) King's Highway.
   (2) a front porch.
   (3) a room in a house.
   (4) an enchanted forest.

2. We can infer that the woman with whom Eugene converses
   (1) is his distant relative.
   (2) is Grover's mother.
   (3) resides in a house where Eugene's family once lived.
   (4) was Eugene's neighbor when he was a child.

3. Lines 12–27 represent
   (1) a conversation between Eugene and the woman's son.
   (2) a conversation between the woman's two sons.
   (3) a dream.
   (4) a memory.

4. Grover is the name of
   (1) Eugene's father.
   (2) the woman's husband.
   (3) Eugene's twin.
   (4) Eugene's dead brother.

5. Eugene's brother died
   (1) many years before.
   (2) four years before.
   (3) when Eugene was twelve.
   (4) six months before.

6. Eugene's brother died as a result of
   (1) neglect.
   (2) tuberculosis.
   (3) smallpox.
   (4) It is impossible to tell from the information given.

6. 1 2 3 4

7. "Lost now was all of it" (line 34) means that
   (1) Eugene's parents are dead.
   (2) Eugene's last connection with his brother—and with childhood—has faded forever.
   (3) Eugene's brother is dead.
   (4) the house and the considerable fortune that Eugene's family possessed in his boyhood are gone.

7. 1 2 3 4

8. "The enchanted wood" (line 37) represents
   (1) memory.
   (2) boyhood.
   (3) the forest beyond King's Highway.
   (4) death.

8. 1 2 3 4

EXERCISE 2: Inferring Character

DIRECTIONS: Read the following passage carefully. Infer as much information as you can about the characters from what they say and think. Then choose the BEST answer to each question and blacken the space under that number in the answer column.

ANSWERS AND EXPLANATIONS APPEAR AT THE END OF THE CHAPTER

Difficult Words: alienate, winning, common, dribbling, hinge round, nosing, obnoxious, guffaw, take me in, pretense, placidly, no end

1 As time went on I saw more and more how he managed to alienate
2 Mother and me. What made it worse was that I couldn't grasp his
3 method or see what attraction he had for Mother. In every possible
4 way he was less winning than I. He had a common accent and made
5 noises at his tea. I thought for a while that it might be the news-
6 papers she was interested in, so I made up bits of news of my own
7 to read to her. Then I thought it might be the smoking, which I
8 personally thought attractive, and took his pipes and went round
9 the house dribbling into them till he caught me. I even made noises
10 at my tea, but Mother only told me I was disgusting. It all seemed
11 to hinge round that unhealthy habit of sleeping together, so I made
12 a point of dropping into their bedroom and nosing around, talking
13 to myself, so that they wouldn't know I was watching them, but
14 they were never up to anything that I could see. In the end, it beat
15 me. It seemed to depend on being grown-up and giving people
16 rings, and I realized I'd have to wait.

17   But at the same time I wanted him to see that I was only
18 waiting, not giving up the fight. One evening when he was being
19 particularly obnoxious, chatting away well above my head, I let him
20 have it.

21   "Mummy," I said, "do you know what I'm going to do when I
22 grow up?"

23   "No, Larry," she replied. "What?"

24   "I'm going to marry you," I said quietly.

25   Father gave a great guffaw out of him, but he didn't take me
26 in. I knew it must only be pretense. And Mother, in spite of every-
27 thing, was pleased. I felt she was probably relieved to know that one
28 day Father's hold on her would be broken.

29   "Won't that be nice?" she said with a smile.

30   "It'll be very nice," I said confidently. "Because we're going to
31 have lots and lots of babies."

32   "That's right, dear," she said placidly. "I think we'll have one
33 soon, and then you'll have plenty of company."

34   I was no end pleased about that because . . . .

FRANK O'CONNOR, "My Oedipus Complex"

Difficult Words Explained

LINE

1	**alienate:**	drive apart, come between
4	**winning:**	appealing, charming
	common:	unrefined
9	**dribbling:**	drooling saliva
11	**hinge round:**	depend upon
12	**nosing:**	snooping
19	**obnoxious:**	disagreeable
25	**guffaw:**	belly laugh
	take me in:	fool me
26	**pretense:**	something false
32	**placidly:**	calmly, peacefully
34	**no end:**	very much

1. 1 2 3 4

1. The story is being told from the point of view of
   (1) Mother.   (3) the narrator as a child.
   (2) Father.   (4) the narrator as an adult.

2. 1 2 3 4

2. Larry's attitude toward his father is primarily one of
   (1) love and admiration.   (3) jealousy and disgust.
   (2) respect and awe.   (4) fear and despair.

3. "I knew it must only be pretense" (line 26), is an illustration of

    (1)   Larry's intelligence.

    (2)   Larry's misinterpretation of his parents' attitudes and behavior.

    (3)   Larry's father's attempt to disguise his true feelings.

    (4)   a child's ability to spot phoniness or insincerity in adults.

3. 1 2 3 4

4. The first paragraph describes Larry's attempts to

    (1)   figure out what attracts his mother to his father.

    (2)   alienate his father and mother.

    (3)   hide the fact of his jealousy from his father.

    (4)   reassure his mother that his father's hold on her will one day be broken.

4. 1 2 3 4

5. Larry's announcement that he plans to marry his mother

    (1)   angers his father.   (3)   is not intended seriously.

    (2)   pleases his mother.   (4)   is not intended as a warning.

5. 1 2 3 4

6. Which of his father's habits or characteristics does *not* annoy Larry?

    (1)   his manners   (3)   his conversation

    (2)   his diction   (4)   his smoking

6. 1 2 3 4

7. From what you know about Larry, the best completion of line 34 is:

    (1)   I knew mother had been wanting another child for a long time.

    (2)   I knew how happy the news would make Father.

    (3)   it showed that in spite of the way she gave in to Father she still considered my wishes.

    (4)   it showed that life goes on, that hope is constantly reborn, in spite of the petty frustrations of every day.

7. 1 2 3 4

NONFICTION

Nonfiction differs from fiction in that it describes either real events and characters (as in biography and autobiography), or the author's directly stated opinions and feelings about a particular subject (as in the literary essay). You should be prepared to make inferences and to judge the soundness of the author's reasoning when interpreting essays and other nonfiction works.

Also remember that writers of essays and other nonfictional literature may use figurative language, just as writers of literary fiction do. (You may want to review the discussion of figurative and literal language in the Reading Skills chapter.) In the following passage, most words are used *literally*—in accordance with their dictionary meanings. However, the passage also contains words and phrases that are used *figuratively* to achieve special effects and meanings. In the questions following the next passage, and in *all* your reading of nonfictional prose, watch for words and phrases that are to be interpreted figuratively rather than literally.

EXERCISE 3:   Inferring Word, Line, and Passage Meaning

DIRECTIONS: Read the following passage carefully. Then choose the BEST answer to each question and blacken the space under that number in the answer column.

ANSWERS AND EXPLANATIONS APPEAR AT THE END OF THE CHAPTER

1   Our tragedy today is a general and universal physical fear so long
2   sustained by now that we can even bear it. There are no longer
3   problems of the spirit. There is only the question: When will I be
4   blown up? Because of this, the young man or woman writing today
5   has forgotten the problems of the human heart in conflict with itself
6   which alone can make good writing because only that is worth
7   writing about, worth the agony and the sweat.
8   He must learn them again. He must teach himself that the
9   basest of all things is to be afraid; and teaching himself that, forget
10   it forever, leaving no room in his workshop for anything but the old
11   verities and truths of the heart, the old universal truths lacking
12   which any story is ephemeral and doomed—love and honor and pity
13   and pride and compassion and sacrifice. Until he does so he labors
14   under a curse. He writes not of love but of lust, of defeats in which
15   nobody loses anything of value, of victories without hope and worst
16   of all without pity or compassion. His griefs grieve on no universal
17   bones, leaving no scars. He writes not of the heart but of the glands.
18   Until he relearns these things he will write as though he stood
19   among and watched the end of man. I decline to accept the end of
20   man. It is easy enough to say that man is immortal simply because
21   he will endure; that when the last ding-dong of doom has clanged
22   and faded from the last worthless rock hanging tideless in the last
23   red and dying evening, that even then there will still be one more
24   sound: that of his puny, inexhaustible voice, still talking. I refuse
25   to accept this. I believe that man will not merely endure: He will
26   prevail. He is immortal, not because he alone among creatures has
27   an inexhaustible voice, but because he has a soul, a spirit capable of
28   compassion and sacrifice and endurance. The poet's, the writer's
29   duty is to write about these things.

WILLIAM FAULKNER, "Speech on Receiving the Nobel Prize"

Note: Because this exercise tests your ability to infer the meanings of words and phrases, the **Difficult Words** key has been omitted.

1.
  1 2 3 4

1. "There are no longer problems of the spirit" (lines 2–3), means that
    (1)   mankind has solved its spiritual problems.
    (2)   the author does not believe in the spirit.
    (3)   modern writers do not write about spiritual problems.

(4)   modern scientists have proved that rational solutions can be found to all problems.

2. "Basest" (line 9) means
   (1)   lowest.
   (2)   best.
   (3)   most rigid.
   (4)   most dangerous.

2. 1 2 3 4

3. "Ephemeral" (line 12) means
   (1)   ethereal.
   (2)   eternal.
   (3)   short-lived.
   (4)   self-defeating.

3. 1 2 3 4

4. "He writes not of the heart but of the glands" (line 17) means that he writes only of man's
   (1)   aesthetic concerns.
   (2)   intellectual nature.
   (3)   physical passions.
   (4)   problems.

4. 1 2 3 4

5. The phrase "the last ding-dong of doom" (line 21) suggests
   (1)   an atomic alert.
   (2)   the physical destruction of the earth.
   (3)   the author's death.
   (4)   a funeral.

5. 1 2 3 4

6. In this speech, the author is encouraging young writers (and all men) to
   (1)   rediscover man's spiritual nature.
   (2)   warn everyone of the dangers mankind faces.
   (3)   adopt a materialistic view of the universe.
   (4)   fight for peace and against war.

6. 1 2 3 4

TONE

An author may express his own feelings or attitudes toward his subject or characters. This expression of emotion imparts a *tone* to his writing. To determine the tone of a piece of literature, think of the emotions or attitudes that are expressed throughout the passage. An author's tone may be *serious* or *amused*. He may be *optimistic,* looking forward to better things, or *pessimistic,* expecting the worst. A *tragic* tone reflects the misfortunes and unfulfilled hopes of life. A *satiric* tone mocks and ridicules its subject. An author may use an *ironic* tone to develop a contrast between (1) what is said and what is meant, (2) what actually happens and what appears to be happening, or (3) what happens and what was expected to happen. These are just a few of the emotions or attitudes that influence the tone of a literary work, but they are the ones you will probably be asked to identify on the High School Equivalency Examination.

Think for a moment of the three passages you have read so far in this chapter. How can we describe the tone of each passage?

And out of the enchanted wood, that thicket of man's memory, Eugene knew that the dark eye and the quiet face of his friend and brother—poor child, life's stranger, and life's exile, lost like all of us, a cipher in blind mazes, long ago—the lost boy was gone forever, and would not return.

What feelings are communicated in the above lines (taken from Exercise 1, an excerpt from "The Lost Boy")? "Poor child, life's stranger and life's exile." Clearly, the author is expressing sorrow and pity. "The lost boy was gone forever." The author is expressing nostalgia: a sad yearning for what is gone and will never come again. "Lost like all of us, a cipher in blind mazes." Here Wolfe expresses a pessimistic view of life, in which all of us are lost in a universe which we cannot understand ("blind mazes"). By analyzing the dominant emotions expressed in the passage, we can conclude that its tone is nostalgic and pessimistic.

"I'm going to marry you," I said quietly. Father gave a great guffaw out of him, but he didn't take me in. I knew it must only be pretense. And Mother, in spite of everything, was pleased. I felt she was probably relieved to know that one day Father's hold on her would be broken.

In the above lines (from Exercise 2, "My Oedipus Complex") the author is remembering with amusement his boyhood jealousy. He recalls telling his mother of his plan to marry her. He also remembers his father's laughter (which Larry believed to be hollow laughter, expressing fear), and his mother's pleasure (which he interpreted as relief at the thought of one day being free from his father's "domination"). There is gentle irony in the contrast between Larry's childish misunderstandings and the realities of the situation (which the adult Larry, and of course, the reader, perceive). We can say, then, that the tone of the excerpt in Exercise 2 is humorous and gently ironic.

I believe that man will not merely endure: He will prevail. He is immortal, not because he alone among creatures has an inexhaustible voice, but because he has a soul, a spirit capable of compassion and sacrifice and endurance.

The above lines (taken from the Faulkner speech in Exercise 3) affirm the author's faith in man's spiritual destiny. We can describe the tone of the passage as impassioned (believing with great emotional intensity in an idea or an ideal) and optimistic.

STYLE

Style refers to the manner in which an author has written his work. When you are asked to determine the style of a passage, consider the author's use of language. Is it *formal*, characterized by long, complex sentences and careful attention to the rules of grammar? Is it *informal*, using the standard grammar of spoken English and everyday vocabulary? Is it *colloquial*, containing slang and regional expressions and nonstandard grammar? Is the style *terse*, expressing an idea in as few words as possible? Or is it *flowery*, with each idea ornamented with descriptive words? (For example, "the eye of heaven, the sun; that great orb, the source of all our gladness, all our light, sank in the golden west awash in lilac and amber tints.") Is the style *metaphoric* and *poetic*, using much figurative language? Is it *aphoristic*, full of wise sayings briefly stated.

Referring again to the three passages you have studied in this chapter, let us examine each from the point of view of its style.

The excerpt from Thomas Wolfe's "The Lost Boy" is a blend of *narrative* (storytelling) *style*—in the parts where Eugene describes his conversation with the present owner of his boyhood home, and with Grover, and *poetic style*—in the final lines, where Eugene communicates his sense of loneliness by the use of metaphor.

The excerpt from "My Oedipus Complex" is written in an *informal*, *narrative style*. It tells a story in simple, everyday language. The style of the Faulkner speech is *formal* and *metaphoric*.

EXERCISE 4:   Inferring Tone and Style

DIRECTIONS: Read the following excerpts carefully. From the emotions and attitudes expressed, and from the type of language used, try to determine the author's tone and style. Choose the BEST answer to each question and blacken the space under that number in the answer column.

ANSWERS AND EXPLANATIONS APPEAR AT THE END OF THE CHAPTER

When I go into a bank I get rattled. The clerks rattle me; the wickets rattle me; the sight of the money rattles me; everything rattles me. The moment I cross the threshold of a bank I am a hesitating jay. If I attempt to transact business there, I become an irresponsible idiot.

STEPHEN LEACOCK, "My Financial Career"

1. The tone of this excerpt is
   (1) dramatic.
   (2) humorous.
   (3) informative.
   (4) ironic.

2. The style is
   (1) formal.
   (2) informal.
   (3) terse.
   (4) aphoristic.

Society is commonly too cheap. We meet at very short intervals, not having had time to acquire any new value for each other. We meet at least three times a day, and give each other a new taste of that old musty cheese that we are. We have had to agree on a certain set of rules, called etiquette and politeness, to make this frequent meeting tolerable and that we need not come to open war. We live thick and are in each other's way, and stumble over one another, and I think that we thus lose some respect for one another.

HENRY DAVID THOREAU, *Walden*

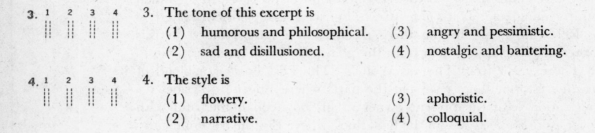

3. The tone of this excerpt is
   (1) humorous and philosophical.
   (2) sad and disillusioned.
   (3) angry and pessimistic.
   (4) nostalgic and bantering.

4. The style is
   (1) flowery.
   (2) narrative.
   (3) aphoristic.
   (4) colloquial.

2:20 A.M. The greatest ship in the world has sunk. From the calm, dark waters, where the floating lifeboats move, there goes up, in the white wake of her passing, "one long continuous moan."

The boats that the *Titanic* had launched pulled safely away from the slight suction of the sinking ship, pulled away from the screams that came from the lips of the freezing men and women in the water.

HANSON W. BALDWIN, *R.M.S. Titanic*

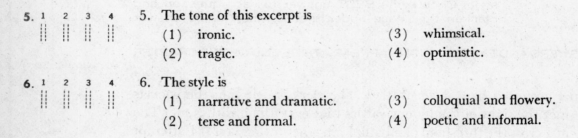

5. The tone of this excerpt is
   (1) ironic.
   (2) tragic.
   (3) whimsical.
   (4) optimistic.

6. The style is
   (1) narrative and dramatic.
   (2) terse and formal.
   (3) colloquial and flowery.
   (4) poetic and informal.

In this chapter you have studied the skills that will help you to read and interpret literary prose. The following two tests are based on those skills and reflect the kinds of reading selections and questions that appear on the High School Equivalency Examination.

DIRECTIONS: Read the following passages and answer each of the questions that come after them. Choose the number of the answer that is BEST. Then blacken the space under that number in the answer column. You may go back to the passages as often as necessary to answer the questions.

ANSWERS AND EXPLANATIONS APPEAR AT THE END OF THE CHAPTER

PROSE TEST 1

Difficult Words: establishment, firing, courses, presses, lavish, quiverings, encroachment, negligence, infinitely, infallible, irreproachable

1 Madame Bovary Senior seemed prejudiced against her daughter-in-
2 law. She thought "her ways too fine for their position"; the wood,
3 the sugar, and the candles disappeared as "at a grand establish-
4 ment," and the amount of firing in the kitchen would have been
5 enough for twenty-five courses. She put her linen in order for her in
6 the presses, and taught her to keep an eye on the butcher when he
7 brought the meat. Emma put up with these lessons. Madame Bovary
8 was lavish of them; and the words "daughter" and "mother" were
9 exchanged all day long, accompanied by little quiverings of the lips,
10 each one uttering gentle words in a voice trembling with anger.
11   In Madame Dubuc's time the old woman felt that she was still
12 the favorite; but now the love of Charles for Emma seemed to her a
13 desertion from her tenderness, an encroachment upon what was
14 hers, and she watched her son's happiness in sad silence, as a ruined
15 man looks through the windows at people dining in his old house.
16 She recalled to him as remembrances her troubles and her sacrifices,
17 and, comparing these with Emma's negligence, came to the con-
18 clusion that it was not reasonable to adore her so exclusively.
19   Charles knew not what to answer: he respected his mother,
20 and he loved his wife infinitely; he considered the judgment of the
21 one infallible, and yet he thought the conduct of the other irre-
22 proachable.

GUSTAVE FLAUBERT, *Madame Bovary*

Difficult Words Explained

LINE

3   **establishment:**   household, estate
4   **firing:**   using firewood to make a fire
5   **courses:**   stages of a meal, served separately
6   **presses:**   upright closet in which linens are kept
8   **lavish:**   generous, plentiful
9   **quiverings:**   tremblings
13   **encroachment:**   "butting in," trespassing
17   **negligence:**   neglect, inattention to duty
20   **infinitely:**   without limitations; very great
21   **infallible:**   not capable of error
      irreproachable: perfect; displaying nothing that could be criticized

1. Madame Bovary Senior disapproved of her daughter-in-law's
   (1) extravagance. (3) rudeness.
   (2) neglect of her husband. (4) miserliness.

2. Emma's response to her mother-in-law's meddling was
   (1) to refuse to let Madame Bovary Senior enter her home.
   (2) obedience to the old woman's wishes and appreciation for her concern.
   (3) angry remarks to the old woman and complaints to her husband about his mother's behavior.
   (4) surface politeness and inner hostility.

3. The real reason for Madame Bovary Senior's resentment of Emma was
   (1) her concern for her son's happiness.
   (2) loyalty to her son's first wife.
   (3) her jealousy at having a rival for her son's affections.
   (4) her intolerance of wastefulness.

4. In the conflict between his wife and mother, Charles sided with
   (1) his mother.
   (2) his wife.
   (3) sometimes one and sometimes the other.
   (4) neither.

5. The phrase, "as a ruined man looks through the windows at people dining in his old house" (lines 14–15) is a(n)
   (1) apostrophe. (3) allusion.
   (2) simile. (4) illusion.

6. We can infer that Emma Bovary
   (1) did not love her husband.
   (2) enjoyed elegant living.
   (3) did not deserve her husband's love.
   (4) was a poor housekeeper.

PROSE TEST 2

Difficult Words: Adam Powell, Ralph Bunche, Leontyne Price, Dr. Martin Luther King, the Nobel Prize, Thurgood Marshall

1 "My boss is white," said Simple.
2 "Most bosses are," I said.
3 "And being white and curious, my boss keeps asking me just
4 what does THE Negro want. Yesterday he tackled me during the
5 coffee break, talking about THE Negro. He always says 'THE
6 Negro,' as if there was not 50–11 different kinds of Negroes in the
7 U.S.A.," complained Simple. "My boss says, 'Now that you-all have
8 got the Civil Rights Bill and the Supreme Court, Adam Powell in
9 Congress, Ralph Bunche in the United Nations, and Leontyne
10 Price singing in the Metropolitan Opera, plus Dr. Martin Luther

11 King getting the Nobel Prize, what more do you want? I am asking
12 you, just what does THE Negro want?' "
13   " 'I am not THE Negro,' I says. 'I am *me*.' "
14   " 'Well,' says my boss, 'you represent THE Negro.' "
15   " 'I do not,' I says. 'I represent my own self.' "
16   " 'Ralph Bunche represents you, then,' says my boss, 'and
17 Thurgood Marshall and Martin Luther King. Do they not?' "
18   " 'I am proud to be represented by such men, if you say they
19 represent me,' I said. 'But all them men you name are *way* up there,
20 and they do not drink beer in my bar.' "
21   " 'Anyhow, you claim you are not THE Negro,' said my boss."
22   " 'I am not,' I said. 'I am *this* Negro.' "
23   " 'Then what do *you* want?' asked my boss."
24   " 'To get out of jail,' I said."
25   " 'What jail?' "
26   " 'The jail you got me in.' "
27   " 'Me?' yells my boss. 'I have not got you in jail. Why, boy,
28 I like you. I am a liberal. I voted for Kennedy. And this time for
29 Johnson. I believe in integration. Now that you got it, though, what
30 more do you want?' "
31   " 'Reintegration,' I said."
32   " 'Meaning by that, what?' "
33   " 'That you be integrated with *me,* not me with you.' "

LANGSTON HUGHES, "Coffee Break"

Difficult Words Explained

LINE

8   **Adam [Clayton] Powell:**   a black Congressman from New York City
9   **Ralph Bunche:**   influential member of the United Nations Secretariat
        Leontyne Price: famous black operatic singer
10   **Dr. Martin Luther King [Jr.]:**   black civil rights leader, winner of the
        Nobel Peace Prize in 1964; assassinated in April, 1968
11   **the Nobel Prize:**   an international award given by the Swedish govern-
        ment to the person considered to have made the most outstanding contri-
        bution to the cause of peace (other Nobel prizes are awarded for out-
        standing contributions in other fields)
17   **Thurgood Marshall:**   black Supreme Court Justice

1. The question, "What does the Negro want?" asked by Simple's boss, indi-
    cates that the speaker does *not*
    (1)   desire to understand the feelings of black people.
    (2)   have any racial prejudice.
    (3)   perceive Negroes as individuals.
    (4)   stereotype black people.

1. 1   2   3   4
    || || || ||

2. 1 2 3 4

2. Simple argues that he represents
    (1) all Negroes.
    (2) only Negroes who live in Harlem.
    (3) only American Negroes.
    (4) only himself.

3. 1 2 3 4

3. By the statement, "They do not drink beer in my bar" (line 20), Simple suggests that
    (1) the gentlemen in question are against drinking alcohol.
    (2) he has not had an opportunity to meet them personally, and therefore does not know their opinions.
    (3) they are not in touch with the feelings of the average black man living in Harlem.
    (4) the bar he frequents would not appeal to celebrities.

4. 1 2 3 4

4. Simple's statement that he wants to get out of jail (line 24) implies that
    (1) he wants white men to stop limiting his opportunities.
    (2) he wants the white establishment to stop putting black men in jail.
    (3) the conversation is taking place in a jail.
    (4) Simple is on parole.

5. 1 2 3 4

5. When Simple states (line 31) that he desires "reintegration," he means
    (1) that the process of racial integration has not been successful, and should be begun again.
    (2) that whites should take the initiative in approaching blacks, moving into black neighborhoods, and adopting black values and attitudes.
    (3) that he dislikes black integration into white society, and wishes to see blacks reintegrate with blacks.
    (4) that efforts to achieve an integrated society must be increased.

6. 1 2 3 4

6. The author's characterization of Simple's boss is
    (1) satirical.   (3) sympathetic.
    (2) bitter.   (4) respectful.

ANSWERS AND EXPLANATIONS

EXERCISE 1: Inferring Plot and Setting

1. (3) The woman's remark in line 3, "He died here, didn't he? In this room?" indicates that the conversation between Eugene and the woman is taking place in a room—the bedroom where Grover died.

2. (3) Line 10 tells us that Eugene has come back, so we know that Eugene does not presently live in the house where the conversation takes place. We are told, however, that his brother died in a room of the house. In line 29, Eugene thanks the woman, presumably for showing him the house. From this evidence we can infer that the woman resides in the house in which Eugene's family once lived.

3. (4) The conversation between Grover and his baby brother, Eugene, is a childhood memory. The sight of the room in which his brother Grover died recalls the scene to Eugene's mind.

4. (4) Eugene is thinking of his dead brother. A conversation flashes to his mind which, judging from Eugene's difficulty in pronouncing words, must have taken place when he was between two and three years old. It is a conversation between Eugene and his brother, in which the brother is trying to teach Eugene to pronounce his name: Grover.

5. (1) Eugene tells the woman that he lost his brother when he himself was only four, and it is clear that Eugene is now an adult. We know then, that Grover died many years before.

6. (4) The passage contains no information and no clues as to the cause of Grover's death.

7. (2) "Lost now was all of it" cannot refer to Grover's death, which happened many years earlier. What is lost is the vivid memory of his dead brother and the other images of his childhood. These memories have been destroyed by seeing his childhood home as it now is.

8. (1) Memory—a mysterious place, filled with unexpected images of scenes half-remembered and half-forgotten—is compared to a thicket, an "enchanted wood."

EXERCISE 2:   Inferring Character

1. (3) The narrator—the "I" of the story—uses the past tense and an adult vocabulary to describe his conflict with his father when he was a child. He tells the story, however, from the point of view which he had *then*, not from his adult point of view.

2. (3) Larry believes that his father is purposely trying to separate him and his mother (lines 1–2). He does everything possible to compete with his "rival" for his mother's attention and affection. He is very jealous of his father, and at the same time disgusted by what he considers to be his father's "common" ways.

3. (2) Larry's father is really amused by Larry's proposal of marriage to his mother, perceiving it as the speech of a little boy who is unaware of the facts of life. Larry, however, wrongly believes that his father is afraid that he *will* steal his mother away, and laughs to hide his fear from Larry. Larry misinterprets his father's laughter because he wants to believe that his father is worried.

4. (1) Larry can't guess what attracts his mother to his father. He adopts one after the other of his father's habits—smoking, reading the newspaper, bad table manners—only to be scolded by his mother. He is no wiser than he was before, except that he finally suspects that his mother's attraction to his father has something to do with being married and sleeping together.

5. **(2)** Larry tells us in lines 26–27 that "Mother . . . was pleased." This is substantiated by his mother's response in line 29: " 'Won't that be nice?' she said with a smile."

6. **(4)** Although his father's bad table manners, "common" accent, and conversation (which Larry can't always understand) annoy the little boy, he considers his father's smoking to be "attractive" (lines 7–8).

7. **(3)** Answer choices (1) and (2) are inconsistent with Larry's character: he is too self-centered to be overjoyed by someone else's good fortune; moreover, he is far too hostile toward his father to be pleased by the fulfillment of his father's wishes. Answer choice (4) is too philosophical to reflect the thinking of a little boy. Only answer choice (3) is consistent with Larry's self-centeredness and dislike for his father.

EXERCISE 3: Inferring Word, Line, and Passage Meaning

1. **(3)** The author suggests that men today are so terrified by the possibility of physical destruction (lines 1–4), that they have forgotten the ever-present problems of man's heart (his deepest feelings) and spirit.

2. **(1)** In the author's opinion, fear is the lowest, the most unworthy emotion; the writer in the grip of fear labors "under a curse" (lines 13–14), and is cut off from true human emotions.

3. **(3)** Art which does not concern itself with universal truths—the truths of the heart and spirit—is doomed to be forgotten quickly.

4. **(3)** The glands of the human body are small organs which manufacture and secrete hormones: chemical substances which influence sexual desire and a number of other physical states. The heart is spoken of symbolically as the source of deep-felt emotions, especially love. Writers who forget that man's true concerns are spiritual ones "write not of the heart but of the glands"; in other words, they speak of lust without love, of material instead of spiritual concerns.

5. **(2)** The following image of "the last worthless rock hanging tideless in the last red and dying evening" signifies that the author is referring to the earth's "doom"—its physical destruction, perhaps by fire.

6. **(1)** The author invites young writers—and all men—to forget their fear of physical death, and to understand that man is more than a physical body. He urges them to concern themselves with man's spiritual nature.

EXERCISE 4: Inferring Tone and Style

1. **(2)** The author is obviously exaggerating his nervousness in banks, as well as making fun of himself, for humorous effect.

2. **(2)** The author uses the language of conversation—informal English. In addition, his subject, making fun of his own unreasonable fear of banks, is humorous and informal.

3. (1) The author philosophizes on the subject of sociability. Although he is speaking seriously, he keeps his sense of humor, as when he refers to our familiar, everyday selves as "musty cheese."

4. (3) The style is aphoristic—full of wise sayings—as in the first and second sentences.

5. (2) The tone of the passage, which describes the sinking of the "greatest ship in the world" amid the moans of the survivors and the screams of the drowning, is tragic.

6. (1) The style is narrative; that is, it faithfully recounts an event. The style is also dramatic; the author describes the incident with emotion and suspense.

PROSE TEST 1

Summary

Madame Bovary Senior, a possessive, interfering woman, is jealous of her son Charles' wife, Emma. She feels that Emma has taken her place in Charles' affections. In the prejudiced opinion of the old woman, Emma lives above her husband's means, wasting money on nonessentials. Madame Bovary Senior constantly tells Emma how she should manage her house; and although the women speak politely to one another, their mutual hostility lies just below the surface. The mother-in-law complains to Charles that Emma does not deserve the great love which he has for her. Charles, who admires and trusts his mother, but adores his wife, cannot agree and does not know what to answer.

Answer Key

1. (1) The old woman thought that Emma used firewood, sugar, and candles too freely (lines 2–5). In other words, she was extravagant (spent too much money unnecessarily).

2. (4) In lines 7–10 we are told that Emma "put up with" her mother-in-law's meddling, called her "mother," and spoke to her with "gentle words" —but in a voice trembling with anger. We can therefore describe Emma's response as a combination of polite overt (external) behavior and inner hostility (anger).

3. (3) In the second paragraph we are told that, to Madame Bovary Senior, Charles' love for Emma seemed like a "desertion." She observed their happiness as a "ruined man" watches people dining in the house that was formerly his. Clearly, the old woman felt that Emma now possessed the love that had been hers. She is intensely jealous of Emma, the "rival" who has replaced her in Charles' affections.

4. (4) Loving both his mother and his wife, and believing each to be perfect, Charles could not take sides in the conflict between them.

5. (2) The phrase is a simile because it is a comparison expressed with "as."

6. (2) Emma made plentiful use of firewood (for cooking), sugar, and candles. Her mother-in-law described Emma's ways as "too fine for their posi-

tion." We can infer, therefore, that Emma was fond of elegant living. Although Madame Bovary Senior feels that Emma is a poor house-keeper and does not deserve her husband's love, there is no evidence in the passage to suggest that the old woman's opinion is correct; nor does the passage suggest that Emma does not love her husband.

PROSE TEST 2

Summary

Simple, a character who represents Harlem's "man in the street," describes a conversation with his white boss, who kept prodding Simple for an answer to his question, "What does THE Negro want?" It is obvious from his constant reference to "THE Negro" that the boss stereotypes black men. He imagines that they all think alike. Simple keeps insisting that he is not "THE Negro," but himself. Simple finally answers his boss's question by saying that he wants to get out of jail, meaning that he wants to live free of the restrictions that white society has imposed on black people. He adds that he wants white society to integrate with *him*. He resents the whole concept of integration—blacks moving into white neighborhoods and adopting "white" culture—because it is a form of discrimination.

Answer Key

1. **(3)** His reference to "THE Negro" indicates that he assumes there is only one type of Negro; that all black men think alike and are alike. He does *not* think of black people as individuals.

2. **(4)** "I am not THE Negro," says Simple in line 13. "I am *me*." And in line 15, "I represent my own self."

3. **(3)** A bar is a place where men meet as equals and speak freely. "They do not drink in my bar" suggests that men like Ralph Bunche, Thurgood Marshall, and Dr. King do not associate with Simple (or his neighbors) as equals and, therefore, cannot be familiar with their feelings and attitudes.

4. **(1)** We know that Simple is a working man (the conversation with his boss takes place during a coffee break), so he cannot really be in jail. Therefore, his statement that he wants to get out of "the jail you got me in" must be understood symbolically. Simple means that he wants to escape from the restrictions that white society has imposed on him: restrictions in the areas of jobs, housing, education, etc.

5. **(2)** Simple defines "reintegration" to mean "that you be integrated with *me,* not me with you." Since "integration" typically refers to black people entering previously all-white neighborhoods, schools, jobs, etc., "reintegration" means the reverse, with whites doing the moving in.

6. **(1)** The author satirizes (ridicules) Simple's boss and all whites who think of themselves as "liberal" and pro-black, but whose attitudes and behavior toward black people reveal their underlying prejudices.

READING POETRY

When most people think of poetry, they imagine stanzas that have a regular rhythm and words that rhyme at the end of lines. For example:

Once upon a midnight dreary, while I pondered, weak and weary,
Over many a quaint and curious volume of forgotten lore,—
While I nodded, nearly napping, suddenly there came a tapping,
As of someone gently rapping, rapping at my chamber door.

EDGAR ALLAN POE,
"The Raven"

Although many poems *do* have both regular rhythm and rhyme, other poems have regular rhythm, but do *not* rhyme:

Before I built a wall I'd ask to know
What I was walling in or walling out,
And to whom I was like to give offense.
Something there is that doesn't love a wall . . .

ROBERT FROST,
"Mending Wall"

Many modern poems have neither rhyme nor regular rhythm. They may, however, use punctuation, capitalization, and spacing in unusual ways in order to achieve special effects:

in Just-
spring   when the world is mud-
luscious the little
lame balloonman

whistles   far   and wee
E. E. CUMMINGS,
"in Just-"

If poetry does not always have rhyme or regular rhythm, what distinguishes it from prose? One of the major characteristics of poetry is its highly *condensed language*. One or two words can communicate many feelings, ideas, and images. For example, if a poet writes of a "popsicle sky" (a figure of speech, of course, since the sky is not really made of ice cream), with only two words he communicates that the sky is the color of popsicles (orange and red), the time of day is either dawn or sunset, and he is feeling playful. Perhaps he is remembering his childhood, when he ate popsicles.

Another characteristic of poetry is the "music" of its language, achieved by *rhythm, repetition,* and *sound devices.* The devices poets use to achieve the sound effects they desire have special names, such as onomatopoeia, alliteration, and refrain. Do not worry about these strange-sounding words. They are carefully explained in this chapter. If you study their meanings, pronunciations and the examples given, you will soon become familiar with them.

Good poets choose every word with great care, often to increase the emotional effect of the poem. For example, if the poet wishes to express powerful and blunt emotion, he may use "strong" words—short words with harsh consonants:

> And all is seared with trade; bleared, smeared with toil;
> And wears man's smudge and shares man's smell: the soil
> Is bare now, nor can foot feel, being shod.
>
> GERARD MANLEY HOPKINS,
> "God's Grandeur"

The poet is expressing his despair over the loss of beauty in the world. Everything in nature has been dirtied and corrupted by man, and man has ruined his own spirit. To communicate these feelings in as few words as possible, Hopkins uses strong, hard sounds. Notice the hissing effect created by the "s" sound which begins the words "seared," "smeared," "smudge," "smell," and "soil." The poet reveals his distaste for what man has done by the meanings and sounds of the words he chooses.

Poems also tend to have *multiple meanings.* Not only do the figures of speech used in poetry communicate several ideas, but many whole poems have both a surface meaning (the obvious meaning expressed by the poet's images) and a deeper meaning—often a truth about people or about life:

> The sword sung on the barren heath,
> The sickle in the fruitful field:
> The sword he sung a song of death,
> But could not make the sickle yield.
>
> WILLIAM BLAKE,
> "The Sword and the Sickle"

Although the surface meaning of the poem appears to be a contest between two blades, one cutting down lives, the other reaping grain, the deeper meaning of the poem is the poet's conviction that the life force is more powerful than the death force, and will triumph.

Some of the questions on the High School Equivalency Examination ask you to choose the correct interpretation of a particular word, line, or poem. In addition, you must also be able to identify meters, rhythms, figures of speech, and other poetic devices. Therefore, in addition to providing you with practice in understanding and interpreting poetry, this chapter also teaches you about the specific kinds of figures of speech, devices of repetition and sound, and rhythms used by poets.

FIGURES OF SPEECH

In the Reading Comprehension chapter, you were introduced to figurative and literal language. *Literal language* uses words to mean what they commonly stand for. *Figurative language* refers to words and phrases that are used in ways which differ from their dictionary meanings. Read the examples below and note the way a word can be used literally and figuratively.

Literal Use of a Word

She hung the *wet blanket* on the clothesline to dry.

I could feel the beating of my *heart*.

Figurative Use of a Word

She's a *wet blanket*. (She "dampens" other people's pleasure.)

Let's get to the *heart* of the matter. (Let's examine the central, most important part of the matter.)

Figurative language can be used in many different ways. The different types of figurative language are called *figures of speech*. When you take the High School Equivalency Examination, you will be asked to identify at least some of the figures of speech which are explained below.

Simile /SIM-ih-lee/ A simile is a comparison introduced by "like" or "as."

. . . I lost my boyhood and
    found my wife.
A girl *like* a Salem* clipper;†
A woman straight *as* a hunting-
    knife
With eyes as bright *as* the
    Dipper.*

* a New England seaport;
† a fast sailing ship

* a group of seven stars which suggests the outline of a dipper (long-handled drinking cup)

STEPHEN VINCENT BENÉT,
"The Ballad of
William Sycamore"

Notice how the three similes in the stanza communicate both a mental picture and a "feeling" of what the wife was like: proud, graceful, and when in motion, like a ship in full sail; straight and strong and practical as a hunting knife; bright-eyed and as much a part of nature as the Big Dipper. Notice that all of the similes are related to nature or to active outdoor life. We can infer that the woman would cope very well with a rugged environment.

Metaphor /MET-uh-for/ Metaphor refers to the figurative use of a word (or words) to suggest a comparison, but *without* the use of "like" or "as." Instead of saying that one thing is *like* another, a metaphor simply calls one thing by another's name, or says that one thing *is* another, or gives one thing the qualities or actions of another. Below are several metaphors. Each one is followed by a literal explanation.

> The road was a ribbon of moonlight . . . .

This metaphor suggests that the road was a long, narrow, winding strip (like a ribbon), lighted by the moon.

> The Lord is my Shepherd . . .
> PSALM 23

God takes care of me, as a shepherd looks after his sheep.

An **extended metaphor** is a single image that is developed and expanded throughout a number of lines:

> "Hope" is the thing with feathers—
> That perches in the soul—
> And sings the tune without the words—
> And never stops—at all—
>
> And sweetest—in the Gale—is heard—
> And sore must be the storm—
> That could abash the little Bird
> That kept so many warm—
>
> I've heard it in the chillest land—
> And on the strangest Sea—
> Yet, never, in Extremity,
> It asked a crumb—of Me.
>
> EMILY DICKINSON,
> " 'Hope' is the thing with feathers"

In the above poem, "hope" is metaphorically represented as a small bird which nests in the human soul. The bird's warm and gallant song cheers us on in times of trouble and discouragement.

Personification /per-sahn-ih-fih-KAY-shun/ Personification is the attribution of human qualities, actions, or feelings to things or concepts.

Night is a curious child, wandering
Between earth and sky, creeping
In windows and doors, daubing
The entire neighborhood
With purple paint.

FRANK MARSHALL DAVIS,
"Four Glimpses of Night"

Apostrophe /uh-PAHS-truh-fee/   Apostrophe is the poetic convention of addressing (talking to, in the poem) someone or something that is not present. Study the examples and explanations below:

Ah, Sun-flower! weary of time,
Who countest the steps of the Sun,
Seeking after that sweet golden clime*   * climate, realm
Where the traveler's journey is done.

WILLIAM BLAKE,
"Ah Sun-flower"

The poet is addressing the sunflower.

Roll on, thou deep and dark blue Ocean—roll!

GEORGE GORDON, LORD BYRON,
"Childe Harold's Pilgrimage"

The poet is addressing the ocean.

Milton! thou shouldst be living at this hour:
England hath need of thee . . .

WILLIAM WORDSWORTH,
"London, 1802"

Wordsworth is addressing the dead poet, John Milton.

Allusion /uh-LOO-zhun/   A reference to a person, place, or event from history, literature, religion, mythology, or any other field of knowledge.

. . . Great God! I'd rather be
A Pagan* suckled in a creed outworn,   *an unbeliever, raised in a
                                                heathen religion
So might I, standing on this pleasant lea,*   *pasture, grassland
Have glimpses that would make me less forlorn;* *sad, lonely
Have sight of *Proteus* rising from the sea;
Or hear old *Triton* blow his wreathèd horn.

WILLIAM WORDSWORTH,
"The World Is Too Much With Us"

The allusions here are to "Proteus" and "Triton," gods of the sea in Greek mythology.

> On desperate seas long wont to roam,
>   Thy hyacinth hair, thy classic face,
> Thy *Naiad* airs, have brought me home . . .
>
> > EDGAR ALLAN POE,
> > "To Helen"

Poe alludes to "Naiad," the mythical goddess of nature who lived in streams.

Hyperbole /hi-PER-buh-lee/ A deliberate exaggeration used for emphasis.

> By the rude bridge that arched the flood,
>   Their flag to April's breeze unfurled,
> Here once the embattled farmers stood
> And fired *the shot heard round the world*.
>
> > RALPH WALDO EMERSON,
> > "Concord Hymn"

The allusion is to the episode that triggered the American Revolution, when a band of Massachusetts farmers shot at a group of British soldiers. The suggestion that the shot was "heard round the world" is an example of *hyperbole*. The poet means that the incident had world-wide social and political implications.

> Will all great Neptune's* ocean wash this blood   *an allusion to the sea god of Roman mythology
> Clean from my hand? No; *this my hand will rather*
> *The multitudinous seas incarnadine,**   *turn red
> *Making the green one red*.
>
> > WILLIAM SHAKESPEARE,
> > *Macbeth*

The speaker suggests that if he were to try to wash the blood from his hand in the ocean, he would succeed only in turning the whole ocean red—a *hyperbolic* statement. The statement reflects Macbeth's guilt about his involvement in the murder of Duncan.

Oxymoron /ox-ih-MOHR-ahn/ The bringing together of two opposite or contradictory ideas.

> And you, my father, there on the sad height,
> *Curse, bless,* me now with your fierce tears, I pray.
>
> > DYLAN THOMAS,
> > "Do Not Go Gentle into That Good Night"

> Why then, O *brawling love! O loving hate!*
> O *anything! Of nothing* first create.
> O *heavy lightness! Serious vanity!*
>> WILLIAM SHAKESPEARE,
>> *Romeo and Juliet*

Synecdoche /sin-EK-duh-kee/   A *part* of something is used to represent the whole, or the *whole* is used to represent a part.

> So, we'll go no more a-roving
>   So late into the night,
> Though the *heart* be still as loving,
>   And the moon be still as bright.
>> GEORGE GORDON, LORD BYRON,
>> "We'll Go No More A-Roving"

In the third line Byron uses the word "heart" as a synecdoche to represent the emotional life, or human desire.

> And when we meet at any time again,
> Be it not seen in either of our *brows*
> That we one jot of former love retain.
>> MICHAEL DRAYTON,
>> "Since There's No Help"

The word "brows" in the above lines is used to mean faces.

Metonymy /me-TAHN-uh-mee/   The name of one thing is used for that of another thing with which it is closely associated.

> The paths of glory lead but to *the grave.*
>> THOMAS GRAY,
>> "Elegy Written in a Country Churchyard"

The grave is used to represent death.

Symbol /SIM-bl/   A symbol is an idea or an object used to represent something else. For example, a white dove is a common symbol for peace; a lily is a common symbol for purity.

> Out of the *night* that covers me,
>   Black as the Pit from pole to pole,
> I thank whatever gods may be
>   For my unconquerable soul.
>> WILLIAM ERNEST HENLEY,
>> "Invictus"

"Night" is frequently used to symbolize spiritual darkness, doubt, despair, and confusion.

EXERCISE 1:   Figures of Speech

DIRECTIONS: Each of the following questions consists of a passage of poetry followed by an incomplete statement about that passage. Choose the BEST completion to the statement and blacken the space under that number in the answer column.

ANSWERS AND EXPLANATIONS APPEAR AT THE END OF THE CHAPTER

The Lightning is a *yellow Fork*
From Tables in the sky
By inadvertent fingers dropped

EMILY DICKINSON,
"The Lightning is a yellow Fork"

1. The phrase "yellow Fork" is a(n)
   (1)   oxymoron.
   (2)   synecdoche.
   (3)   metaphor.
   (4)   symbol.

Lay a garland on my hearse
   Of the dismal *yew;*
Maidens, *willow-branches* bear,
   Say I died true.

JOHN FLETCHER,
"Lay a Garland on my Hearse"

2. In this excerpt, "yew" and "willow-branches" are each examples of
   (1)   symbol.
   (2)   metonymy.
   (3)   hyperbole.
   (4)   simile.

Till *Phoebus*, dipping in the west,
Shall lead the world the way to rest.

JOHN DRYDEN,
"Evening Quatrains"

3. The reference to Phoebus is a(n)
   (1)   simile.
   (2)   metaphor.
   (3)   hyperbole.
   (4)   allusion.

The green field *sleeps* in the sun . . .

WILLIAM WORDSWORTH,
"Written in March"

4. The image of the green field sleeping is an example of
   (1)   metonymy.
   (2)   hyperbole.
   (3)   oxymoron.
   (4)   personification.

"*O Swallow*, flying from the golden woods,
Fly to her, and pipe and woo her, and make her mine,

ALFRED, LORD TENNYSON,
"O Swallow, Swallow"

5. "O Swallow" is an example of
   (1) simile.
   (2) metaphor.
   (3) apostrophe.
   (4) allusion.

5. 1 2 3 4

And even yet, I dare not . . .
Dare not indulge in memory's *rapturous pain* . . .

EMILY BRONTË,
"Cold in the Earth"

6. "Rapturous pain" is an
   (1) allusion.
   (2) oxymoron.
   (3) simile.
   (4) metonymy.

6. 1 2 3 4

. . . the world which seems
So various, so beautiful, so new,
Hath really neither joy, nor love, nor light . . .

MATTHEW ARNOLD,
"Dover Beach"

7. The final line of this excerpt illustrates
   (1) hyperbole.
   (2) personification.
   (3) allusion.
   (4) oxymoron.

7. 1 2 3 4

The long day wanes; the slow moon climbs; *the deep*
Moans round with many voices.

ALFRED, LORD TENNYSON,
"Ulysses"

8. "The deep" is an example of
   (1) metonymy.
   (2) apostrophe.
   (3) personification.
   (4) simile.

8. 1 2 3 4

EXERCISE 2: Figures of Speech

DIRECTIONS: Each of the following questions consists of a passage of poetry followed by an incomplete statement about that passage. Choose the BEST completion to the statement and blacken the space under the number in the answer column.

ANSWERS AND EXPLANATIONS APPEAR AT THE END OF THE CHAPTER

Oh, I wish to the lord that I'd never seen your face,
Or heard your *lyin' tongue,* my lord . . .

AMERICAN FOLK SONG,
"Lonesome Road"

1. 1 2 3 4   1. "Lyin' tongue," is a(n)
    ‖ ‖ ‖ ‖   (1)   synecdoche.   (3)   metonymy.
                      (2)   symbol.   (4)   oxymoron.

> The *Grape* that can with Logic absolute . . .
> Life's leaden metal into Gold transmute . . .
>
> EDWARD FITZGERALD,
> *The Rubáiyát of Omar Khayyám*

2. 1 2 3 4   2. "Grape" is used as a(n)
    ‖ ‖ ‖ ‖   (1)   hyperbole.   (3)   metonymy.
                      (2)   apostrophe.   (4)   simile.

> The brightness of her cheek would shame
>   those stars,
> As daylight doth a lamp . . .
>
> WILLIAM SHAKESPEARE,
> *Romeo and Juliet*

3. 1 2 3 4   3. This statement is a(n)
    ‖ ‖ ‖ ‖   (1)   oxymoron.   (3)   personification.
                      (2)   allusion.   (4)   hyperbole.

> Tomatoes, redder than *Krakatoa's** fire,   *volcano in Indonesia
> Oranges like old sunsets over *Tyre** . . .   *ancient capital of Phoenicia
>
> WILFRID WILSON GIBSON,
> "Sight"

4. 1 2 3 4   4. The references to "Krakatoa" and "Tyre" are examples of
    ‖ ‖ ‖ ‖   (1)   synecdoche.   (3)   apostrophe.
                      (2)   allusion.   (4)   metonymy.

> . . . I saw a bright green snake . . .
> *Green as the herbs* on which it couched.
>
> SAMUEL TAYLOR COLERIDGE,
> "Christabel"

5. 1 2 3 4   5. "Green as the herbs" is a(n)
    ‖ ‖ ‖ ‖   (1)   metaphor.   (3)   personification.
                      (2)   simile.   (4)   apostrophe.

> A careless shoe-string, in whose tie
> I see a *wild civility,*
> Do more bewitch me, than when art
> Is too precise in every part.
>
> ROBERT HERRICK,
> "Delight in Disorder"

6. "Wild civility" is a(n)
   (1) oxymoron.
   (2) apostrophe.
   (3) hyperbole.
   (4) simile.

6. 1 2 3 4

> Sweet day, so cool, so calm, so bright,
> The *bridal* of the earth and sky:
> The dew shall weep thy fall tonight;
> For thou must die.
>
> GEORGE HERBERT,
> "Virtue"

7. "Bridal" is a(n)
   (1) synecdoche.
   (2) simile.
   (3) metaphor.
   (4) hyperbole.

7. 1 2 3 4

> *Tyger! Tyger!* burning bright
> In the forests of the night,
> What immortal hand or eye
> Could frame thy fearful symmetry?
>
> WILLIAM BLAKE,
> "The Tyger"

8. "Tyger! Tyger!" is a(n)
   (1) apostrophe.
   (2) synecdoche.
   (3) allusion.
   (4) oxymoron.

8. 1 2 3 4

> The *Sea* said "Come" to the *Brook,*
> The Brook said "Let me grow!"
> The Sea said "Then you will be a Sea—
> I want a brook, Come now!"
>
> EMILY DICKINSON,
> "The Sea said 'Come' to the Brook"

9. "Sea" and "Brook" are
   (1) similes.
   (2) oxymorons.
   (3) personifications.
   (4) hyperboles.

9. 1 2 3 4

> Bright star! would I were steadfast as thou art—
> Not in lone splendor hung aloft the night,
> And watching, with eternal lids apart . . .
>
> JOHN KEATS,
> "Bright Star"

10. The word "star" is used as a(n)
   (1) symbol.
   (2) hyperbole.
   (3) allusion.
   (4) simile.

10. 1 2 3 4

DEVICES OF REPETITION AND SOUND

Poets use many techniques (poetic devices) to achieve special rhythmic and sound effects in their poetry. The devices of *rhyme, assonance, alliteration, onomatopoeia, refrain,* and *parallelism* are described below.

Rhyme   Rhyme is the repetition, in two or more words, of the stressed vowel sound and the sounds of the consonants or syllables following that vowel. The lists below contain words that rhyme:

owl	weather
towel	feather
foul	together

We determine the *rhyme scheme* (pattern of rhymes) of a poem by giving a letter to the last word in each line. Words that rhyme get the same letter. Label the last word in the first line *a*. If the last word in the second line rhymes with the last word in the first line, label it *a* also. If it does not rhyme, label it *b*. All lines whose last words rhyme should be labeled with the same letter. Observe the rhyme scheme of the following excerpt:

	Rhyme Scheme
Love is not all: it is not meat nor drink	*a*
Nor slumber nor a roof against the rain;	*b*
Nor yet a floating spar to men that sink	*a*
And rise and sink and rise and sink again;	*b*
Love can not fill the thickened lung with breath,	*c*
Nor clean the blood, nor set the fractured bone;	*d*
Yet many a man is making friends with death	*c*
Even as I speak, for lack of love alone.	*d*

EDNA ST. VINCENT MILLAY,
"Love Is Not All"

Assonance   Assonance is the repetition of vowel sounds, but *not* the consonants that follow. In the lines below, note that the *y* in "sky" repeats the long *i* sound in "lilacs" and "night." Also notice the repetition of the *oo* sound.

When lilacs last in the dooryard bloom'd,
And the great star early droop'd in the western sky in the night, . . .

WALT WHITMAN,
"When Lilacs Last in the Dooryard Bloom'd"

Alliteration Alliteration is the repetition of *consonant sounds,* usually at the beginning of words, to achieve a desired effect. Note the alliteration of *d* and *s* in the following lines:

> When I am *d*ead, my *d*earest,
> *S*ing no *s*ad *s*ongs for me;
> CHRISTINA ROSETTI,
> "When I Am Dead, My Dearest"

Onomatopoeia /ahn-uh-mah-tuh-PEE-uh/   When a poet wants to imitate a sound, he selects a word whose pronunciation is similar to that sound. This device is called "onomatopoeia." Words such as hiss, buzz, crash, bang, jingle, whisper, murmur, and stutter are onomatopoeic (sound-imitating) words.

> And thumping and plumping and bumping and jumping,
> And dashing and flashing and splashing and clashing . . .
> All this way the water comes down at Lodore!
> ROBERT SOUTHEY,
> "How the Water Comes Down at Lodore"

The poet has used words that imitate the sounds of falling water.

Refrain A refrain is one or more lines of a poem (or a major portion of a line) repeated at regular intervals. The refrain usually appears at the end of a stanza.

> I have had playmates, I have had companions,
> In my days of childhood, in my joyful school-days;
> All, all are gone, the old familiar faces.   *(refrain)*
>
> I have been laughing, I have been carousing,
> Drinking late, sitting late, with my bosom cronies;
> All, all are gone, the old familiar faces.   *(refrain)*
> CHARLES LAMB,
> "The Old Familiar Faces"

Parallelism Parallelism refers to the purposeful repetition of a word or group of words. The repeated words occur in lines that have parallel (matching) grammatical structures. In the following excerpt, note the parallelism in the first two lines and in the last four lines:

> Heart-leaves of lilac all over New England,
> Roots of lilac under all the soil of New England,
> Lilac in me because I am New England,
> Because my roots are in it,

> Because my leaves are of it,
> Because my flowers are for it,
> Because it is my country. . . .

AMY LOWELL,
"Lilacs"

EXERCISE 3:   Devices of Repetition and Sound

DIRECTIONS: Each of the following questions consists of a passage of poetry followed by an incomplete statement about that passage. Choose the BEST completion to the statement from the four answer choices and blacken the appropriate space in the answer column.

ANSWERS AND EXPLANATIONS APPEAR AT THE END OF THE CHAPTER

1   Oh, the bells, bells, bells!
2   What a tale their terror tells
3   Of Despair!
4   How they clang, and clash, and roar!
5   What a horror they outpour
6   On the bosom of the palpitating air!

EDGAR ALLAN POE,
"The Bells"

1. 1 2 3 4

1. The rhyme scheme is
    (1) abcabc.
    (2) aabbcc.
    (3) aabccb.
    (4) aabccd.

2. 1 2 3 4

2. Line 2 contains examples of
    (1) alliteration and onomatopoeia.
    (2) alliteration and assonance.
    (3) assonance and onomatopoeia.
    (4) parallelism and alliteration.

3. 1 2 3 4

3. Lines 2 and 5 both contain
    (1) alliteration.
    (2) onomatopoeia.
    (3) refrain.
    (4) parallelism.

4. 1 2 3 4

4. The line which best illustrates onomatopoeia is
    (1) line 2.
    (2) line 4.
    (3) line 5.
    (4) line 6.

5. 1 2 3 4

5. Lines 1 and 4 contain examples of
    (1) rhyme.
    (2) alliteration.
    (3) refrain.
    (4) rhyme scheme.

1   Little Lamb, who made thee?
2   Dost thou know who made thee?
3   Gave thee life and bid thee feed

4 By the stream and o'er the mead;*   * meadow
5 Gave thee clothing of delight,
6 Softest clothing, woolly, bright;
7 Gave thee such a tender voice,
8 Making all the vales* rejoice?   * valleys
9   Little Lamb, who made thee?
10   Dost thou know who made thee?

WILLIAM BLAKE,
"The Lamb"

6. The lines, "Little Lamb, who made thee?/Dost thou know who made thee?"   6. 1 2 3 4
   illustrate
   (1) refrain.   (3) assonance.
   (2) onomatopoeia.   (4) parallelism.

7. The best example of assonance is found in   7. 1 2 3 4
   (1) lines 3 and 4.   (3) lines 6 and 7.
   (2) lines 5 and 6.   (4) lines 8 and 9.

8. Lines 3, 5, and 7 best illustrate   8. 1 2 3 4
   (1) alliteration.   (3) assonance.
   (2) onomatopoeia.   (4) parallelism.

9. This selection contains no examples of   9. 1 2 3 4
   (1) parallelism.   (3) alliteration.
   (2) onomatopoeia.   (4) assonance.

10. The rhyme scheme is   10. 1 2 3 4
    (1) aaaabbccaa.   (3) aabbccddaa.
    (2) aabbccddee.   (4) aaaabbccdd.

RHYTHM AND METER

Like figures of speech, rhythm and meter are used in poetry to achieve special effects. Rhythm in poetry, or in any writing, is similar to rhythm in music. Both depend on the patterning of accented and unaccented units. In music, the units are notes; in poetry, they are syllables. *Rhythm in poetry then, is the alternation of stressed (accented) and unstressed syllables.*

The rhythm of a poem, as in a musical composition, is related to its meaning. Joyful poetry and music both have lively rhythms. Serious or mournful subjects require slow rhythms.

On the High School Equivalency Examination you will be asked to identify the most common poetic rhythms. These are explained below. You should also study the examples of other poetic rhythms listed in the GLOSSARY under **Poetic Foot** and **Poetic Meter.**

All poetry has rhythm, but many poems have an *ordered rhythm*, which is called *meter*. The flow of stressed and unstressed syllables is given a specific order or pattern by the poet. This pattern is determined by two things: (1) the number of stressed and unstressed syllables in each unit or beat (each unit is called a *poetic foot*), and (2) the number of feet in a line. *Meter*, then, is determined by the *kind and number of feet in a line*. Although meter may vary slightly from line to line, a whole poem is said to be written in one meter.

To identify meter, then, you must first identify the kind of feet that the poem contains. The most common types of poetic feet are:

iambic /eye-AM-bik/ *da DUM*   Two syllables, the first unstressed and the second stressed.

/When I/ con-SID-/ er HOW/ my LIGHT/ is SPENT/

anapestic /an-uh-PES-tik/ *da da DUM*   Three syllables, the first two unstressed, and the third stressed.

/The As-SYR-/ ian came DOWN/ like a WOLF/ on the FOLD/

trochaic /troh-KAY-ik/ *DUM da*   Two syllables, the first stressed and the second unstressed.

/SAY that/ HEALTH and/ WEALTH have/ MISS'D me/

dactylic/ dak-TILL-ik/ *DUM da da*   Three syllables, the first stressed and the next two unstressed.

/WHAT if a/ MUCH of a/ WHICH of a/ WIND/

spondaic/ spahn-DAY-ik/ *DUM DUM*   Two stressed syllables.

/HOLD HANDS!/ KNEEL DOWN!/ PRAISE GOD!/

The second thing you must determine in identifying meter is the number of feet in a line:

dimeter /DYE-mee-ter/   A line containing *two* poetic feet.

/TOUCH her not/ SCORN-ful-ly/

trimeter /TRY-mee-ter/   A line containing *three* poetic feet.

/A BIRD/ came DOWN/ the WALK/

tetrameter /teh-TRAHM-ih-ter/   A line containing *four* poetic feet.

/Be-CAUSE/ I COULD/ not STOP/ for DEATH/

pentameter /pehn-TAM-ih-ter/   A line containing *five* poetic feet.

/KNOW then/ thy-SELF,/ pre-SUME/ not GOD/ to SCAN/

hexameter /hek-ZAHM-ih-ter/   A line containing *six* poetic feet.

/YE who be-/ LIEVE in af-/ FEC-tion that/ HOPES and en-/
DURES and is/ PA-tient/

When you are asked to identify the meter of a poem, indicate (1) the type of foot used, and (2) the number of feet in a line, as follows:

/To ME,/ fair FRIEND,/ you NE-/ ver CAN/ be OLD;/
iambic pentameter

/My LIFE/ closed TWICE/ be-FORE/ its CLOSE/
iambic tetrameter

/CAN-non to/ RIGHT of them/
dactylic dimeter

/HAIL to/ THEE, blithe/ SPIR-it/
trochaic trimeter

/TELL me/ NOT in/ MOURN-ful/ NUM-bers/
trochaic tetrameter

/You LEFT/ us in TAT-/ ters, with-OUT / shoes or SOCKS,/
anapestic tetrameter (Notice that the first foot is iambic.)

Before you test your knowledge of foot and meter, one word of caution: poets frequently vary the rhythm within a particular line so that the poem will not sound too regular or mechanical, like the ticking of a clock. For example:

1 In Reading gaol* by Reading town   *is pronounced and means the same as "jail"
2   There is a pit of shame,
3 And in it lies a wretched man
4   Eaten by teeth of flame.
5 In a burning winding-sheet he lies,
6   And his grave has got no name.

OSCAR WILDE,
"The Ballad of Reading Gaol"

Lines 1, 3, and 5 are written in *iambic tetrameter*; however, in order to vary the rhythm, the poet has begun line 5 with an *anapestic* foot, rather than an *iambic* foot. Lines 2, 4, and 6 are written in *iambic trimeter*, varied by the use of a *trochaic* foot to begin line 4, with an *anapestic* foot beginning line 6. When identifying the meter of a poem, though, be concerned only with the basic meter, not with the occasional variations.

There are several standard forms of poetry that use particular patterns of rhyme and meter. On the High School Equivalency Examination, however, it is unlikely that you will be asked to identify specific poetic forms, with one important exception: the **sonnet.**

A **sonnet** is a poem consisting of 14 lines. (If a poem has 13 lines, or 15, or 16, it is *not* a sonnet.) Most English language sonnets are written in iambic pentameter. A sonnet generally begins with a statement of a theme or problem. The poet develops his ideas in the body of the poem, and ends the sonnet with a conclusion or summary statement of the main theme.

The following sonnet, "How Do I Love Thee?" is by Elizabeth Barrett Browning.

> How do I love thee? Let me count the ways.
> I love thee to the depth and breadth and height
> My soul can reach, when feeling out of sight
> For the ends of Being and ideal Grace.
> I love thee to the level of everyday's
> Most quiet need, by sun and candlelight.
> I love thee freely, as men strive for Right;
> I love thee purely, as they turn from Praise.
> I love thee with the passion put to use
> In my old griefs, and with my childhood's faith.
> I love thee with a love I seemed to lose
> With my lost saints—I love thee with the breath,
> Smiles, tears, of all my life!—and, if God choose,
> I shall but love thee better after death.

EXERCISE 4:   Identifying Meter

DIRECTIONS: Read each of the following excerpts from poems and identify their basic meter. You may wish to read each excerpt aloud several times in order to get a better sense of its rhythm. Select the BEST answer and blacken the space under that number in the answer column.

ANSWERS AND EXPLANATIONS APPEAR AT THE END OF THE CHAPTER

> A Robin Red breast in a Cage
> Puts all Heaven in a Rage.
>
> WILLIAM BLAKE,
> "Auguries of Innocence"

1. ¹ 2 3 4
   ‖ ‖ ‖ ‖

1. The meter of these lines is
   (1)   iambic tetrameter.
   (2)   anapestic trimeter.
   (3)   dactylic hexameter.
   (4)   trochaic dimeter.

The Sun does arise,
And make happy the skies . . .

WILLIAM BLAKE,
"The Echoing Green"

2. The meter of these lines is
   (1) trochaic trimeter.
   (2) spondaic hexameter.
   (3) anapestic dimeter.
   (4) iambic tetrameter.

2. 1 2 3 4

Little Lamb, who made thee?
Dost thou know who made thee?

WILLIAM BLAKE,
"The Lamb"

3. These lines are written in
   (1) anapestic tetrameter.
   (2) anapestic trimeter.
   (3) dactylic pentameter.
   (4) trochaic trimeter.

3. 1 2 3 4

Honor the charge they made!
Honor the Light Brigade,

ALFRED, LORD TENNYSON,
"The Charge of the Light Brigade"

4. The meter of these lines is
   (1) trochaic pentameter.
   (2) iambic dimeter.
   (3) dactylic tetrameter.
   (4) dactylic dimeter.

4. 1 2 3 4

I sent my Soul through the Invisible,
Some letter of that After-life to spell,
And by and by my Soul returned to me,
And answered "I Myself am Heav'n and Hell"

EDWARD FITZGERALD,
The Rubáiyát of Omar Khayyám

5. The meter of these lines is
   (1) iambic pentameter.
   (2) iambic trimeter.
   (3) iambic hexameter.
   (4) iambic tetrameter.

5. 1 2 3 4

Now courting is pleasure, and parting is grief.
But a false-hearted lover is worse than a thief.

AMERICAN FOLK SONG,
"On Top of Old Smokey"

6. The meter of these lines is
   (1) trochaic tetrameter.
   (2) dactylic tetrameter.
   (3) anapestic tetrameter.
   (4) spondaic tetrameter.

6. 1 2 3 4

For sweetest things turn sourest by their deeds;
Lilies that fester smell far worse than weeds.

WILLIAM SHAKESPEARE,
"Sonnet 94"

7. 1 2 3 4
∥ ∥ ∥ ∥

7. The meter of these lines is
   (1)   iambic pentameter.   (3)   spondaic trimeter.
   (2)   anapestic tetrameter.   (4)   trochaic dimeter.

All your strength is in your union.
All your danger is in discord;
Therefore be at peace henceforward,
And as brothers live together.

HENRY WADSWORTH LONGFELLOW,
The Song of Hiawatha

8. 1 2 3 4
∥ ∥ ∥ ∥

8. The meter of these lines is
   (1)   iambic pentameter.   (3)   trochaic trimeter.
   (2)   dactylic hexameter.   (4)   trochaic tetrameter.

In this chapter you have studied the skills that will help you to read and interpret poetry. The following two tests are based on those skills, and reflect the kinds of reading selections and questions that appear on the High School Equivalency Examination.

DIRECTIONS: Read the following passages and answer each of the questions that come after them. Choose the number of the answer that is BEST. Then blacken the space under that number in the answer column. You may go back to the passages as often as necessary to answer the questions.

ANSWERS AND EXPLANATIONS APPEAR AT THE END OF THE CHAPTER

POETRY TEST 1

Difficult Words: frigate, coursers, prancing, traverse, oppress, toll, frugal

1   There is no frigate like a book
2   To take us lands away,
3   Nor any courser like a page
4   Of prancing poetry.

5   This traverse may the poorest take
6   Without oppress of toll;
7   How frugal is the chariot

8   That bears a human soul!

EMILY DICKINSON,
"There Is No Frigate Like a Book"

Difficult Words Explained

LINE
1 **frigate:** ship
3 **coursers:** horses
4 **prancing:** high-stepping playfully
5 **traverse:** journey
6 **oppress:** a burden
  toll: a fee
7 **frugal:** economical, inexpensive

1. "This traverse" (line 5) refers to
   (1) a trip to foreign lands.   (3) an ocean crossing.
   (2) a flight of the imagination.   (4) dying.

2. The "chariot" referred to in line 7 is a metaphor representing
   (1) a stagecoach.   (3) death.
   (2) a two-wheeled cart, drawn by horses.   (4) a book.

3. Lines 3 and 4 contain
   (1) alliteration.   (3) allusion.
   (2) onomatopoeia.   (4) iambic pentameter.

4. "There is no frigate like a book" (line 1) means that
   (1) frigates do not look like books.
   (2) frigates and books are completely dissimilar.
   (3) frigates can take us where books cannot.
   (4) books can take us where frigates cannot.

5. The poet suggests that
   (1) freedom is a condition of the mind.
   (2) the poor should be frugal.
   (3) ships and horses are unnecessary.
   (4) traveling is wasteful.

	1	2	3	4
1.	‖	‖	‖	‖
2.	‖	‖	‖	‖
3.	‖	‖	‖	‖
4.	‖	‖	‖	‖
5.	‖	‖	‖	‖

POETRY TEST 2

Difficult Words: grieving, Goldengrove, unleaving, fresh, wanwood, springs, ghost, blight

1 Márgarét are you gríeving
2 Over Goldengrove unleaving?
3 Leáves, líke things of man, you
4 With your fresh thoughts care for, can you?
5 Ah! ás the heart grows older

6 It will come to such sights colder
7 By and by, nor spare a sigh
8 Though worlds of wanwood leafmeal lie;
9 And yet you will weep and know why.
10 Now no matter, child, the name:
11 Sórrow's springs are the same.
12 Nor mouth had, no nor mind, expressed
13 What heart heard of, ghost guessed:
14 It is the blight man was born for,
15 It is Margaret you mourn for.

Difficult Words Explained

LINE

1 **grieving:** sorrowing
2 **Goldengrove:** a group of golden-leaved trees
    unleaving: losing their leaves
4 **fresh:** young
8 **wanwood:** a "made-up" word suggesting the paleness and lifelessness of the fallen leaves ("wan" means pale, faint)
11 **springs:** origins, sources
13 **ghost:** soul, spirit
14 **blight:** sorrow, curse

1. The phrase "Goldengrove unleaving" (line 2) describes
   (1) the departure of Mr. Goldengrove.
   (2) the theft of a treasure.
   (3) the loss of a valuable prize.
   (4) the falling of autumn leaves.

2. "The blight man was born for" (line 14) is man's
   (1) mortality.   (3) sickness.
   (2) sorrow.   (4) wickedness.

3. We can infer that Margaret is
   (1) a young child.   (3) the poet's sweetheart.
   (2) the poet's wife.   (4) an old lady.

4. A title appropriate to the tone and theme of the poem is
   (1) "Gold and Silver."   (3) "Sorrow and Happiness."
   (2) "Spring and Fall."   (4) "Male and Female."

5. An idea *not* suggested in the poem is that Margaret
   (1) does not understand the real reason for her sorrow.
   (2) will one day be indifferent to the falling of autumn leaves.
   (3) will one day grieve for the passing of youth.
   (4) is grieving over the death of her mother.

6. The word "ghost" in line 13 refers to
   (1) the dead leaves.   (3) the spirit of a living person.
   (2) the ghost of a dead man.   (4) the spirit of approaching winter.

ANSWERS AND EXPLANATIONS

EXERCISE 1:   Figures of Speech

1. (3) The poet compares the branching streak of lightning to a "yellow Fork" which has been dropped from the sky. This is a metaphor because it is a comparison made without "like" or "as."

2. (1) The branches of yew (a type of evergreen) and willow trees were formerly placed on graves. They have become symbols of death and mourning.

3. (4) The allusion is to Phoebus Apollo, the sun god of Greek mythology, who drove the chariot of the sun across the sky each day.

4. (4) Sleeping is a human function. Therefore, the image of the field "sleeping" is an example of personification.

5. (3) The poet is addressing the swallow which is not present. Therefore, this is an apostrophe.

6. (2) "Rapturous pain" is an oxymoron—the bringing together of words with opposite meanings.

7. (1) By stating that the world contains no joy, no love, and no light, the poet is creating an hyperbole—exaggeration for the purpose of achieving a powerful poetic effect.

8. (1) "The deep" is an expression commonly used to refer to the ocean. This is an example of metonymy, in which a thing is referred to by the name of something that resembles or suggests it.

EXERCISE 2:   Figures of Speech

1. (1) The use of the words "lyin' tongue" to mean "the lying words you spoke" is an example of synecdoche. A part of something is used to represent the whole. Here the "tongue" represents the whole act of speaking, which, in reality, involves the brain, lips, tongue, and the words themselves.

2. (3) "The Grape," meaning "wine," is an example of metonymy. The name of something is used to represent something else with which it is closely associated. Because wine is made from grapes, the poet has used "The Grape" to represent wine.

3. (4) Her cheek (Juliet's) could not really outshine the stars. Romeo feels great love for Juliet, and therefore, exaggerates her beauty.

4. (2) "Krakatoa" and "Tyre" are used as allusions. The poet compares the golden red color of fresh tomatoes to the flame of a volcano. The color of oranges reminds him of the orange-gold of the sunsets of ancient Tyre.

5. **(2)** "Green as the herbs" is a simile. Coleridge compares the snake's green color to the green plants on which the snake lay.

6. **(1)** "Wild civility" is an oxymoron because it brings two opposite meanings or ideas (wildness and order) together.

7. **(3)** The comparison of the harmony of earth and sky to a "bridal" (wedding), without the use of "like" or "as," is a metaphor.

8. **(1)** The poet is addressing the "Tyger," which is not present. Therefore, this is an apostrophe.

9. **(3)** Both the sea and the brook are represented as having the human abilities of thought and speech. They are, therefore, personifications.

10. **(1)** Keats uses the "star" to symbolize constancy. He considers the star something that never changes, and wishes that he could be as "steadfast."

EXERCISE 3:   Devices of Repetition and Sound

1. **(3)** The lines end in the following words:
"bells" (*a*); "tells" (*a*); "despair" (*b*); "roar" (*c*); "outpour" (*c*); "air" (*b*).

2. **(2)** The repetition of the *t* sound in "tale," "terror," and "tells" is an example of alliteration. Assonance is illustrated by the repeated *e* sound in "terror," and "tells."

3. **(4)** The similar beginning of lines 2 and 5 ("What a tale . . . ," "What a horror . . .") constitutes parallelism.

4. **(2)** Line 4 contains three examples of onomatopoeia: "clang," "clash," and "roar."

5. **(2)** Alliteration is found in line 1 in the triple repetition of the *b*, and in line 4, in the double repetition of *cl*.

6. **(1)** These two lines constitute a refrain because they are repeated. See lines 1–2 and 9–10.

7. **(1)** In lines 3 and 4 the *ee* sound is repeated five times: "th*ee*," "th*ee*," "f*ee*d," "str*ea*m," "m*ea*d."

8. **(4)** The phrase "Gave thee . . ." introduces lines 3, 5, and 7—an illustration of parallelism.

9. **(2)** None of the words in the selection are onomatopoeic. We have already examined illustrations of parallelism, alliteration, and assonance.

10. **(3)** The lines of the selection end in the following words:
thee (*a*); thee (*a*); feed (*b*); mead (*b*); delight (*c*); bright (*c*); voice (*d*); rejoice (*d*); thee (*a*); thee (*a*).

EXERCISE 4: Identifying Meter

1. **(1)** /a ROB-/ in RED/ breast IN/ a CAGE/
   /PUTS/ all HEA-/ ven IN/ a RAGE/
   4 iambs to the line: *iambic tetrameter*

2. **(3)** /The SUN/ does a-RISE,/
   /And make HAP-/ py the SKIES;/
   2 anapests to the line: *anapestic dimeter* (Notice that the first foot is iambic.)

3. **(4)** /LIT-tle/ LAMB, who/ MADE thee?/
   /DOST thou/ KNOW who/ MADE thee?/
   3 trochees to the line: *trochaic trimeter*

4. **(4)** /HON-or the/ CHARGE they made!/
   /HON-or the/ LIGHT Bri-gade,/
   2 dactyls to the line: *dactylic dimeter*

5. **(1)** /I SENT/ my SOUL/ THROUGH the/ in-VIS-/ i-ble,/
   /Some LET-/ ter OF/ that AF-/ ter LIFE/ to SPELL:/
   /And BY/ and BY/ my SOUL/ re-TURNED/ to ME/
   /And ANS-/ wered "I/ my-SELF/ am HEAV'N/ and HELL:"/
   5 iambs to a line: *iambic pentameter* (Notice that the first line has only three iambs.)

6. **(3)** /Now COURT-/ ing is PLEA-/ sure, and PART-/ ing is GRIEF;/
   /But a FALSE-/ heart-ed LOV-/ er is WORSE/ than a THIEF./
   4 anapests to the line: *anapestic tetrameter* (Notice that the first foot is iambic.)

7. **(1)** /For SWEET-/ est THINGS/ turn SOUR-/ est BY/ their DEEDS;/
   /LIL-ies/ that FES-/ ter SMELL/ far WORSE/ than WEEDS./
   5 iambs to the line: *iambic pentameter* (Notice that the first foot in the second line is trochaic.)

8. **(4)** /ALL your/ STRENGTH is/ IN your/ UN-ion./
   /ALL your/ DAN-ger/ IS in/ DIS-cord;/
   /THERE-fore/ BE at/ PEACE hence-/ FOR-ward,/
   /AND as/ BRO-thers/ LIVE to-/ GE-ther./
   4 trochees to the line: *trochaic tetrameter*

POETRY TEST 1

Summary

Literature enables our minds to travel. Ships and horses can only carry our bodies on physical journeys. Books, which are so inexpensive, can transport our souls.

Answer Key

1. **(2)** "This traverse" is the adventuring of our imaginations when we read books.

2. **(4)** Books are the "chariots" which transport our minds wherever the author has chosen to take us.

3. **(1)** Alliteration appears in the repetition of the *p* sound in the words "page," "prancing," and "poetry."

4. **(4)** Ships can only sail on actual oceans. Books can take us to every area of the mind and the imagination.

5. **(1)** The mind can have an adventure even if the body does not. We can travel by reading books even though we are poor. Freedom, then, is of the mind.

POETRY TEST 2

Summary

The poet, Gerard Manley Hopkins, addresses a child who is saddened by the falling of autumn leaves. He reflects that as she grows older she will no longer care about the death of leaves, but will mourn that the autumn of her own life is near. The poet suggests that, although she doesn't know or understand it, in mourning the dying of leaves she is mourning her own mortality, her own eventual death. "It is Margaret you mourn for."

Answer Key

1. **(4)** A grove is a group of trees. A "goldengrove" is a group of golden (yellow) trees. One meaning of "leave" is to produce leaves; a meaning of the prefix "un-" is "remove from." The poet has made up a word, putting "un-" and "leave" together to form "unleaving"—meaning "shedding leaves."

2. **(1)** The poet suggests throughout the poem, and particularly in the last line, that Margaret, in grieving over the leaves (their death), is unknowingly grieving over her gradual aging and eventual death. ("It is Margaret you mourn for.")

3. **(1)** In line 4 the poet refers to Margaret's "fresh thoughts" ("fresh" here means young). He calls her "child" (line 10) and suggests that as her "heart grows older" (line 5) she will not mourn for dying leaves. All of these clues tell us that Margaret is a little girl.

4. **(2)** The idea of "fall" is clearly stressed in the imagery of falling yellow leaves. "Fall" is later equated with old age. Childhood, then—and the child Margaret—must represent spring. In her "spring" (childhood), Margaret grieves for the death of leaves in the fall. In her own "fall" (old age), she will grieve for her own approaching death.

5. **(4)** In line 9 the poet suggests that when Margaret is older, she will "know why" she weeps, implying that as a child, she does *not* know; therefore choice (1) is incorrect. It *is* suggested that Margaret will one day be indifferent to falling leaves (lines 6–7), hence choice (2) is wrong. The

poet implies that Margaret will one day grieve for the loss of her youth, eliminating choice (3). Nowhere, however, does the poet mention Margaret's mother.

6. (3) Although Margaret has not yet thought about her own death, her heart has "heard of" and her "ghost guessed" the mortality of all living things. The only meaning of "ghost" that makes sense here is "spirit" or "soul" (an archaic meaning of the word "ghost," as in Holy Ghost, meaning Holy Spirit).

READING DRAMA

A play is a literary composition, written in poetry or prose, that tells a story through dialogue (conversation) and action, and is performed by actors and actresses. Drama originated in ancient religious rituals. A surviving example of drama as religious ritual is the Nativity Play, in which the events surrounding the birth of Christ are portrayed by costumed actors.

Understanding drama requires basically the same skills as understanding novels, short stories, essays, and poems. The main difference in drama is that a play is meant to be seen and heard rather than to be read on a printed page.

It is important to remember that a play, performed before an audience, is the creation not only of its author but also of its director, stage designer (who creates the settings and costumes) and actors. All of them play a part in *interpreting* the author's characters, mood, and message. Each interpretation of a play will vary in accordance with the understanding, personalities, and skill of the people who stage and perform it.

But when you *read* a play, your own imagination must supply the interpretations. You must visualize the characters and settings and imagine the actors speaking to one another. You must also infer the emotions and motives that underlie their words and actions.

When you are asked on the High School Equivalency Examination to interpret a brief excerpt taken from a play, you must gather as much meaning as possible from the "clues" in the excerpt.

Although most modern plays are written in prose, many great plays of the past (for example, the dramas of Shakespeare) were written in poetry. When you take the High School Equivalency Examination you will probably be asked to interpret excerpts from both types of dramas. For this reason, this chapter provides you with instruction and practice in interpreting excerpts from plays written in both prose and poetry.

PROSE DRAMA

The excerpt presented in Exercise 1 has been selected to give you practice in inferring *plot*, the plan of the action, and *setting*, the place where, and the time when, the action occurs.

EXERCISE 1: Inferring Plot and Setting

DIRECTIONS: Read the following passage slowly, attempting to visualize (picture in your mind) the action and the characters. Pay attention to each detail, and determine what information it adds to the total meaning of the passage. Then choose the BEST answer to each question, and blacken the space under that number in the answer column.

ANSWERS AND EXPLANATIONS APPEAR AT THE END OF THE CHAPTER

Difficult Words: Greenwich, ghastly, critic, the St. Regis, paneling, Third Avenue, stunning, run-of-the-bowl

(**Bob and Mary, a husband and wife, are examining their old check-books. Oscar, their tax lawyer, is helping them.**)

1 **Oscar:** *And* we have Mrs. Robert Connors—three hundred dollars.
2 **Bob:** Mrs. Connors?
3 **Mary:** I thought so long as you walked this earth you'd remember
4 Mrs. Connors. Bootsie Connors and her fish?
5 **Bob:** Oh, God. That ghastly weekend in Greenwich.
6 **Oscar:** Okay, tell Daddy.
7 **Bob:** Do you remember that young English critic, Irving Mannix?
8 **Oscar:** The angry young man?
9 **Bob:** This was two years ago, when he was just a cross young man.
10 At that time he was writing long scholarly articles proving that
11 Shakespeare was a homosexual. Anyway, he was staying here.
12 And we'd been invited to a party at the Connors'.
13 **Mary:** So we brought along dear old Irving.
14 **Bob:** Do you know the Connors' place in Greenwich?
15 **Oscar:** No.
16 **Bob:** Well, the living room is about the size of the ballroom at the
17 St. Regis. You feel it would be just the place to sign a treaty.
18 Anyway, it was all too rich for Irving, and he started to lap up
19 martinis. In fifteen minutes he was asking our hostess if it was
20 true that the Venetian paneling had been brought over piece
21 by piece from Third Avenue.
22 **Oscar:** Why didn't you take this charmer home?
23 **Bob:** Because he passed out. In the library.
24 **Mary:** On that damn velvet sofa.
25 **Bob:** But he came to just long enough to light a cigarette. Presently
26 the sofa was on fire—really on fire. Our hero jumped up and,
27 with stunning presence of mind, put out the blaze with a tank
28 of tropical fish.
29 **Mary:** And these were no run-of-the-bowl goldfish. They came from
30 Haiti and were friends of the family. I mean, they had *names.*

JEAN KERR, *Mary, Mary*

Difficult Words Explained

LINE

5   **Greenwich:**   a wealthy community in Connecticut.

      ghastly: awful.

7   **critic:**   person who writes reviews of literature, plays, films, or other works of art

17   **the St. Regis:**   an expensive Manhattan hotel.

20   **paneling:**   wall-covering, usually made of wood

21   **Third Avenue:**   an avenue in New York City where many antique shops are located

27   **stunning:**   amazing

29   **run-of-the-bowl:**   Mary's variation of "run-of-the-mill," an expression which means "ordinary"

1. 1   2   3   4

1. The episode Bob and Mary are recalling occurred how many years before?
    (1)   one year   (3)   three years
    (2)   two years   (4)   more than three years

2. 1   2   3   4

2. Irving Mannix was
    (1)   the Connors' friend.   (3)   Bob and Mary's friend.
    (2)   Oscar's friend.   (4)   unacquainted with any of them.

3. 1   2   3   4

3. Bob and Mary went to the Connor home in Greenwich
    (1)   to sign a treaty.   (3)   to attend a party.
    (2)   to attend a ball.   (4)   to meet Irving Mannix.

4. 1   2   3   4

4. Irving set fire to the Connors' velvet sofa
    (1)   on purpose, because he disliked the Connors.
    (2)   on purpose, because he didn't want to be taken home.
    (3)   accidentally, because he was too drunk to know what he was doing.
    (4)   accidentally, when examining some tropical fish.

5. 1   2   3   4

5. The result of the evening was that
    (1)   Mrs. Connors never spoke to Bob and Mary again.
    (2)   Bob and Mary never spoke to Irving again.
    (3)   Bob and Mary paid Mrs. Connors for the damage Irving had caused.
    (4)   Irving paid Mrs. Connors for the damage he had caused.

POETIC DRAMA

Most plays written in poetry are composed in *blank verse*: unrhymed iambic pentameter. (Review the definition and examples of iambic pentameter.)

Just as poems are characterized by the use of figurative language, plays in verse tend to contain more figures of speech and other literary devices than do plays in prose. Furthermore, most plays in verse were written several centuries ago. They therefore contain many archaic or obsolete words (words no longer in common use), and tend to be more difficult to read and understand than prose plays.

Below is an excerpt from *Volpone*, a play written in blank verse by Ben Jonson. As you read it, try to apply your knowledge of the literary devices often used by poets (metaphor, simile, etc.). Also, remember that this excerpt requires you to infer plot, character, and setting, just as a play written in prose does.

EXERCISE 2: Interpreting Poetic Drama

DIRECTIONS: This exercise consists of a dramatic passage followed by questions about that passage. Read the passage carefully. Then choose the BEST answer to each question and blacken the space under that number in the answer column.

ANSWERS AND EXPLANATIONS APPEAR AT THE END OF THE CHAPTER

Difficult Words: without, Cupid, bolting, except, thou, 'las, would, nay, effect, aught, compass, plate

1   **Volpone:** Oh, I am wounded!
2   **Mosca:** Where, sir?
3   **Volpone:** Not without;
4   Those blows were nothing: I could bear them ever.
5   But angry Cupid, bolting from her eyes,
6   Hath shot himself into me, like a flame;
7   I cannot live, except thou help me, Mosca.
8   **Mosca:** 'Las, good sir!
9   Would you had never seen her.
10   **Volpone:** Nay, would thou
11   Had'st never told me of her.
12   **Mosca:** Sir, 'tis true;
13   I do confess, I was unfortunate,
14   And you unhappy: but I'm bound in conscience,
15   No less than duty, to effect my best
16   To your release of torment, and I will, sir.
17   **Volpone:** Dear Mosca, shall I hope?
18   **Mosca:** Sir, more than dear,
19   I will not bid you to despair of aught
20   Within a human compass.
21   **Volpone:** Oh, there spoke
22   My better angel. Mosca, take my keys,
23   Gold, plate, and jewels, all's at thy devotion;
24   Employ them how thou wilt; nay, coin me too:
25   So thou, in this, but crown my longings, Mosca.

BEN JONSON, *Volpone*

Difficult Words Explained

LINE

3	**without:**	externally
5	**Cupid:**	the god of love
	bolting:	darting, coming from
6	**hath:**	has
7	**except:**	unless
	thou:	you
8	**'las:**	alas
9	**would:**	I wish
10	**nay:**	no
15	**effect:**	do
19	**aught:**	anything
20	**compass:**	range of ability or possibility
23	**plate:**	dishes made from precious metal

1. "Oh, I am wounded!" (line 1) refers to the fact that Volpone
   - (1) has been shot.
   - (2) has been stabbed.
   - (3) has fallen in love.
   - (4) has been betrayed.

2. Volpone begs Mosca to help him
   - (1) live.
   - (2) get revenge.
   - (3) guard his possessions.
   - (4) win the love of a lady.

3. "Crown my longings" (line 25) means that Volpone
   - (1) wishes to satisfy his desires.
   - (2) wishes to become a king.
   - (3) is comparing himself to a king.
   - (4) is comparing his longings to a crown.

4. The "keys" referred to in line 22 are probably
   - (1) the keys to a dungeon.
   - (2) the keys to a strongbox.
   - (3) the keys to the speaker's heart.
   - (4) the keys to a lady's bedroom.

5. The reference to "angry Cupid" (line 5) suggests
   - (1) love's power to hurt.
   - (2) Volpone's bad temper.
   - (3) the anger of his beloved.
   - (4) Volpone's anger over the wound that Cupid has inflicted.

6. Lines 5 and 6 contain examples of
   - (1) apostrophe, allusion, metaphor, and simile.
   - (2) allusion, metaphor, and simile.
   - (3) metaphor and simile.
   - (4) simile only.

In this chapter you have studied the skills that will help you to read and interpret drama. The following two tests are based on those skills and reflect the kinds of reading selections and questions that appear on the High School Equivalency Examination.

DIRECTIONS: Read the following passages and answer each of the questions that come after them. Choose the number of the answer that is BEST. Then blacken the space under that number in the answer column. You may go back to the passages as often as necessary to answer the questions.

ANSWERS AND EXPLANATIONS APPEAR AT THE END OF THE CHAPTER

DRAMA TEST 1

1 **Virginia:** Years and years ago, not long after Mother died, I wrote
2 you a letter that you still quote as a great joke. I was in love
3 with you then.
4 **Barney:** You should have loved your mother more.
5 **Virginia:** You loved her so much, how could I? She was always out
6 with you or away with you. You were both away on one of
7 those trips when she died. When you returned, you told me
8 she was still away. It was only long after, after I had accepted
9 her absence, that I learned the truth from a schoolteacher.
10 Then—I hopefully stole Mother's old wedding ring. But even
11 though she was gone, you were still trying to find her.
12 **Barney:** She loved me completely: you were a child, you didn't
13 understand: what letter do I quote as a joke?
14 **Virginia:** "Dearest Daddy. You never want me around because I
15 am not pretty. Therefore, I am a stepchild and so I am running
16 away. Your loving daughter, Virginia."
17 **Barney:** Don't you think that's funny coming from a kid of seven or
18 eight?
19 **Virginia:** I put it on your desk and sat in my room with the door
20 open, waiting for you. Company came. You read them the letter.
21 Everyone laughed. You called to the maid, "Pack a bag for Miss
22 Virginia." She put me out on the veranda, with my little red
23 suitcase. A clear, bright, autumn day. I pull the shades on days
24 like that now.
25 **Barney:** I was watching from behind the curtains. I wouldn't have
26 let you get very far.
27 **Virginia:** Why didn't you say something when I came in? Why
28 didn't you even look at me? Why did you laugh? That night, I
29 cut your new trousers.

ARTHUR LAURENTS, *A Clearing in the Woods*

1. Lines 5–7 imply that Virginia's parents
    (1) did not love her.
    (2) did not give her enough attention.
    (3) did not really love each other.
    (4) were engaged in an illegal occupation.

1. 1   2   3   4

2. 1 2 3 4

2. "I hopefully stole mother's old wedding ring" (line 10) implies that
  (1) the little girl had a habit of stealing.
  (2) Virginia had always wanted to own a ring.
  (3) Virginia wanted to take her mother's place in her father's affections.
  (4) Virginia wanted a keepsake to remind her of her dead mother.

3. 1 2 3 4

3. After his wife's death, Barney
  (1) found consolation in loving his little daughter.
  (2) became a sad, solitary person.
  (3) went away, leaving his daughter with the maid.
  (4) was absorbed in the memory of the love he and his wife had shared.

4. 1 2 3 4

4. Virginia wrote a letter to her father because
  (1) she was planning to run away.
  (2) she wanted his attention.
  (3) she believed that she had been adopted.
  (4) she wanted to make her father laugh.

5. 1 2 3 4

5. Barney told the maid to pack Virginia's suitcase because
  (1) he believed that she really intended to run away.
  (2) he wanted to punish his daughter by making her believe that he was sending her away.
  (3) he wanted to get rid of Virginia.
  (4) he was amused by the letter, and was making a game of it.

6. 1 2 3 4

6. Barney's reaction to the letter demonstrates that he
  (1) was insensitive.
  (2) had a good sense of humor.
  (3) didn't believe in spoiling children.
  (4) took pleasure in hurting other people.

7. 1 2 3 4

7. "I pull the shades on days like that now" (lines 23–24) suggests that Virginia
  (1) has weak eyes.
  (2) is indifferent to the past.
  (3) has never gotten over her hurt.
  (4) rejects her father.

8. 1 2 3 4

8. Virginia's reaction to the episode of the letter was
  (1) sadness and withdrawal.
  (2) despair and rage.
  (3) laughter at her own silliness.
  (4) to really run away from home.

DRAMA TEST 2

Difficult Words: wilt thou, yon, herald, morn, severing, jocund, exhales, torch-bearer, reflex, Cynthia, hie hence, woes

1   **Juliet:** Wilt thou be gone? It is not yet near day:
2   It was the nightingale, and not the lark,
3   That pierc'd the fearful hollow of thine ear;

4   Nightly she sings on yon pomegranate tree:
5   Believe me, love, it was the nightingale.
6 **Romeo:** It was the lark, the herald of the morn,
7   No nightingale: look, love, what envious streaks
8   Do lace the severing clouds in yonder east:
9   Night's candles are burnt out, and jocund day
10   Stands tiptoe on the misty mountain tops:
11   I must be gone and live, or stay and die.
12 **Juliet:** Yon light is not daylight, I know it, I:
13   It is some meteor that the sun exhales,
14   To be to thee this night a torch-bearer,
15   And light thee on thy way to Mantua:
16   Therefore stay yet; thou need'st not to be gone.
17 **Romeo:** Let me be ta'en, let me be put to death;
18   I am content, so thou wilt have it so.
19   I'll say yon grey is not the morning's eye,
20   'T is but the pale reflex of Cynthia's brow;
21   How is 't, my soul? let's talk; it is not day.
22 **Juliet:** It is, it is; hie hence, be gone, away!
23   It is the lark that sings so out of tune.
24   O! now be gone; more light and light it grows.
25 **Romeo:** More light and light; more dark and dark our woes!

WILLIAM SHAKESPEARE, *Romeo and Juliet*

Difficult Words Explained

LINE

1   **wilt thou:** will you
4   **yon:** yonder, that one over there
6   **herald:** one who announces
     morn: morning
8   **severing:** parting
9   **jocund:** cheerful, merry
13   **exhales:** gives out
14   **torch-bearer:** one who carries a burning torch to light the way
20   **reflex:** reflection
     Cynthia: goddess of the moon in Roman mythology
22   **hie hence:** hurry away
26   **woes:** sorrows, troubles

1. When Juliet says that "It was the nightingale, and not the lark" (line 2), she is

    (1) implying that Romeo does not know much about bird-songs.
    (2) attempting to persuade Romeo to stay with her.
    (3) trying to start an argument.
    (4) suggesting that Romeo is hard of hearing.

1. 1   2   3   4
    || || || ||

2. ¹ ² ³ ⁴   2. "Envious streaks" (line 7) implies that
                    (1)   day is jealous of the lovers' happiness and seeks to end it.
                    (2)   the moon is jealous of the lovers' happiness and seeks to end it.
                    (3)   a jealous rival is approaching.
                    (4)   Juliet's brow is wrinkled with lines of envy.

3. ¹ ² ³ ⁴   3. Juliet's reference to a meteor (line 13) is motivated by
                    (1)   her belief in astrology.
                    (2)   her ignorance of astronomy.
                    (3)   wishful thinking.
                    (4)   her tendency to lie.

4. ¹ ² ³ ⁴   4. "The morning's eye" (line 19) is a(n)
                    (1)   allusion.
                    (2)   personification.
                    (3)   simile.
                    (4)   oxymoron.

5. ¹ ² ³ ⁴   5. Romeo's statement "it is not day" (line 21), indicates that
                    (1)   he is agreeing with Juliet because he is reluctant to leave her.
                    (2)   what he thought was the light of dawn was merely a meteor.
                    (3)   he is agreeing with Juliet to be polite.
                    (4)   he had mistaken moonlight for the sunrise.

6. ¹ ² ³ ⁴   6. Juliet reacts to Romeo's statement in line 21 with
                    (1)   pleasure.
                    (2)   fear.
                    (3)   irritation.
                    (4)   argumentativeness.

7. ¹ ² ³ ⁴   7. Juliet tells Romeo to "be gone" (line 24) because
                    (1)   she is tired of arguing with him.
                    (2)   she wishes to sleep.
                    (3)   his life is in danger if he stays.
                    (4)   her reputation will be ruined if he is discovered.

8. ¹ ² ³ ⁴   8. Juliet's description of the lark's song as being "out of tune" (line 23) suggests that
                    (1)   she does not really hear a lark.
                    (2)   the song exists only in her mind.
                    (3)   the lark's song is harsh and unmelodious.
                    (4)   the lark's song is unwelcome.

ANSWERS AND EXPLANATIONS

EXERCISE 1:   Inferring Plot and Setting

1. **(2)** See line 9, where Bob mentions that the event had occurred two years before.

2. **(3)** We can infer that Irving was Bob and Mary's friend because he was staying with them (line 11).

3. **(3)** In line 12, Bob explains that they had been invited to a party at the Connors'.

4. **(3)** In lines 18–19 we learn that Irving had drunk several martinis. Irving accidentally set fire to the sofa—on which he had passed out—when he "came to" (line 25) just long enough to light a cigarette, and then passed out again.

5. **(3)** In line 1, Oscar refers to a check for three hundred dollars made out to Mrs. Connors. We later learn that Bob and Mary's friend ruined Mrs. Connors' sofa and killed her valuable tropical fish. From this information we can infer that Bob and Mary paid for the damage.

EXERCISE 2:   Interpreting Poetic Drama

1. **(3)** Volpone tells Mosca that his wound is not "without," meaning, not a wound to the body, but rather an emotional wound inflicted by Cupid. (In Greek mythology, when Cupid shot someone with his magic arrows, that person would fall passionately in love.)

2. **(4)** In line 7, Volpone moans that he "cannot live" (recover from the pains of love) unless Mosca helps him (to win the lady he longs for).

3. **(1)** "Crown my longings" (line 25) means "satisfy my desires." In this case, it refers to Volpone's longing to possess the lady with whom he has fallen in love.

4. **(2)** Volpone tells Mosca to take his keys (line 22). All of Volpone's treasures ("gold, plate, and jewels") are at Mosca's disposal—presumably to either impress or bribe the lady. The keys in question, therefore, are to the strongbox where Volpone keeps his treasure.

5. **(1)** Cupid is referred to as "angry" (line 5) because of his power to wound his victims with the painful arrows of love.

6. **(2)** The reference to Cupid in line 5 is an allusion which refers to a character from Greek mythology. The descriptions of Cupid "bolting from the lady's eyes," and shooting himself into Volpone are metaphors because they make comparisons without using "like" or "as." "Like a flame" is a simile because it *does* use "like" to make a comparison. The lines do not contain an apostrophe (a figure of speech in which the poet or a character addresses himself to an absent person or to a thing).

DRAMA TEST 1

Summary

Virginia, now an adult, confronts her father with an incident from the past that had hurt her deeply. She recalls that when her mother was alive, her parents had not given her much attention. When Virginia's mother died, the lonely little girl hoped that her father's love would be hers. Instead, her father treated her as he always had, searching elsewhere to recapture the love he had lost. Virginia hoped to call attention to her loneliness. She wrote her father a letter, telling him that because he didn't want her, she was running away. Insensitive to his daughter's needs, Barney treated the letter as a joke. Virginia realized that she would never have her father's love. Her yearning then turned to despair and rage.

Answer Key

1. **(2)** Virginia felt rejected by her parents because of the frequency with which they went out socially or went on trips together, leaving her alone in the care of the maid.

2. **(3)** By stealing her mother's wedding ring, Virginia was symbolically attempting to "steal" her mother's status as Barney's wife.

3. **(4)** After his wife died, Barney did not turn to his daughter for affection, as Virginia had hoped. Instead, he was "still trying to find her [his wife]" (line 11); in other words, his emotions still centered around the love he had shared with his dead wife.

4. **(2)** Virginia tells her father that she put the letter on his desk and "waited for him" (lines 19–20). She believed that her father, on reading the letter, would be filled with pity, love, and understanding and would come to her.

5. **(4)** Barney thought the letter, coming from a little girl, was a huge joke. He played along with the joke, telling the maid to pack Virginia's suitcase. We know that he didn't really intend to let her run away, because he was "watching from behind the curtains" (line 25), and wouldn't have let her go far.

6. **(1)** In refusing to understand and respond with compassion to the pain which had motivated his daughter's letter, Barney showed great insensitivity.

7. **(3)** We can infer that bright, sunny days remind Virginia so painfully of this childhood incident that she cannot bear them, and pulls down the shades to blot out both the sunlight and the memory. In other words, Virginia has never gotten over her hurt.

8. **(2)** Virginia responded to her father's rejection by cutting his new pair of trousers—an act prompted by the despair and rage which replaced her frustrated love.

DRAMA TEST 2

Summary

Romeo and Juliet have spent the night together in Juliet's bedroom. Romeo notices the light of dawn in the sky, and knows that he must go or risk being killed.

Juliet cannot bear the thought of parting from Romeo, and insists that the bird they hear is the nightingale (a bird that sings at night), not the lark (a bird that sings at daybreak). She also insists that the light in the sky is a meteor, not dawn. Romeo, equally unhappy about leaving, pretends that it is not yet daybreak. Juliet knows very well that it is morning. She becomes terrified that her beloved will be discovered and killed, and urges him to go.

Answer Key

1. **(2)** Knowing that Romeo must leave at daybreak and desiring to have him stay a little longer, Juliet denies that the birdsong they hear is the lark's (a bird that sings at daybreak), and insists that it is the call of the nightingale (a bird that sings at night).

2. **(1)** The "streaks" referred to are rays of sunlight. Romeo's reference to them as "envious" implies that the day desires to part the lovers because it is jealous of their happiness.

3. **(3)** Juliet, who cannot bear to admit that the light in the sky is really daylight and that Romeo must leave, suggests that the light may come from a meteor. She is engaging in wishful thinking.

4. **(2)** The figure of speech, "the morning's eye" (line 19), illustrates personification: attributing human qualities or characteristics (in this case, an eye) to a thing or concept.

5. **(1)** Romeo is well aware that day is breaking, but he is so tempted to stay that he agrees with Juliet's pretense that it is not yet morning, declaring that the light in the sky is the moon shining.

6. **(2)** In spite of her protests to the contrary, Juliet knows that it is really morning, and that if Romeo stays, he will be discovered and killed (see line 11). Consequently, when Romeo agrees that "it is not day," Juliet realizes that he has decided to stay with her, and is terrified for his life.

7. **(3)** Juliet knows that Romeo will be killed if he stays (see line 11).

8. **(4)** The song of the lark, heralding the morning, is "out of tune" with Juliet's desires, therefore, unwelcome.

GLOSSARY: TERMS YOU SHOULD KNOW

In the preceding three chapters you have practiced reading, analyzing, and answering questions about prose, poetry, and drama. In those chapters you studied many literary terms. The following pages contain an alphabetical list of those terms with references to where they are defined. In addition, you will find explanations of a few terms that were not included in the previous chapters.

Use this glossary as a handy study-reference. Knowing these definitions will help you on the Simulated Test at the end of this book, and more important, you will be able to answer many of the questions on the actual High School Equivalency Examination.

allegory: the use of fictional characters and actions to symbolize (represent) truths or generalizations about human conduct or experience.

alliteration: *See* page 93.

allusion: *See* page 85.

anapest, anapestic: *See* page 96.

aphorism, aphoristic: An aphorism is a short, concise statement of a truth or principle. EXAMPLE: "The paths of glory lead but to the grave." Aphoristic writing contains many aphorisms.

apostrophe: *See* page 85.

assonance: *See* page 92.

autobiography: The life story of a person, told by himself; one of the literary genres (types).

ballad: An old narrative song, whose author often is unknown. The refrain is a main feature. EXAMPLE: "In Scarlet town, where I was born,/ There was a fair maid dwellin',/ Made every youth cry *Well-a-day*!/ Her name was Barbara Allen./"

biography: The life story of a person, written by someone else; one of the literary genres (types).

cliché: an overused phrase which has lost most of its original meaning. EXAMPLES: "few and far between"; "as pretty as a picture"; "quick as a flash."

colloquialism: A word or expression used in informal conversation or in a particular geographic area. EXAMPLE: "C'mon, kids, wash up, it's chow time." (As opposed to the more formal, "Come, children, wash your hands. It's suppertime.")

connote: To suggest. For example, the words "slender" and "thin" can both be used to refer to a person who is underweight; but, whereas "slender" connotes grace and attractiveness, "thin" connotes an unattractive degree of undernourishment. *See* **denote** below.

dactylic: *See* page 96.

denote: To mean, according to the dictionary definition of a word. For example, the word "home" *denotes* a dwelling. But the word "home" often *connotes* a place of warmth, love, and security. *See* **connote** above.

dialogue: A conversation between two or more speakers.

diction: The word choice and pronunciation of a speaker, which tell us a great deal about his background. For example, if a character says, "Man, that's cool!" we may infer that the character is "hip."

dimeter: *See* page 96.

dirge: *See* **elegy.**

drama: *See* page 108.

elegy: A poem of sorrow, usually over someone who is dead; also called a **dirge.**

epic: A long dramatic poem that tells the story of a notable or heroic action or series of actions.

essay: A literary composition in prose that discusses a particular subject from the personal point of view of the author; one of the literary genres (types).

eulogy: A poem (or statement) praising someone in the highest terms.

exposition, expository: Exposition is nonliterary writing such as that which appears in news items, textbooks, and scientific articles. It attempts to set forth facts, undistorted by the writer's personal opinion.

extended metaphor: *See* **metaphor.**

fiction: *See* page 62.

figurative language: *See* page 83.

figures of speech: *See* page 83.

flowery: *See* page 71.

foot: *See* **poetic foot.**

formal: *See* page 71.

free verse: Poetry that has no regular meter or rhyme.

genre: A type of literary composition. EXAMPLES: novel, short story, essay, poem, play.

hexameter: *See* page 97.

hyperbole: *See* page 86.

iamb, iambic: *See* page 96.

idiom, idiomatic: An expression whose meaning is understood from continual use, but which loses meaning when looked at word for word. EXAMPLE: "His remark *made my blood boil*, and I *let fly at* him"; meaning, "His remark made me furious, and I hit him."

image, imagery: An *image* is a picture (or a perception of a sound, smell, taste, or touch) in the mind of a writer. The *imagery* in a literary work refers to the literal or figurative descriptions by means of which the writer communicates his mental images. For example, in describing a young country girl, William Wordsworth used the images of a sheltered wildflower and a solitary star: "A violet by a mossy stone / Half hidden from the eye! / Fair as a star, when only one / Is shining in the sky."

informal: *See* page 71.

inversion: A change in normal word order, either to emphasize a particular idea or to adjust the words of a poem to the poem's meter. EXAMPLE: "Something there is that doesn't love a wall . . ." (instead of, "There is something that doesn't love a wall).

irony: *See* page 69.

limerick: A five-line humorous poem with a special rhyme scheme.

lyric: A short poem which expresses a personal emotion (as opposed to *narrative* poetry, which relates a story, or *dramatic* poetry, which reveals character or action through monologue or dialogue).

metaphor: *See* page 84.

meter: *See* page 95.

metonymy: *See* page 87.

monologue: A long, uninterrupted speech by one person.

mood: *See* **tone.**

narrative: *See* page 71.

narrator: The person (in a work of literature) who is telling the story.

nonfiction: *See* page 67.

ode: A long lyric poem with a serious subject and many stanzas.

onomatopoeia: *See* page 93.

optimism, optimistic: Optimism is a faith that everything will turn out all right and that the future will be better. Arthur Hugh Clough's "Say Not the Struggle Naught Availeth" is an optimistic poem.

oxymoron: *See* page 86.

paradox: A statement that seems foolish or contradictory, but may actually be true. EXAMPLE: "The more things change, the more they remain the same."

parallelism: *See* page 93.

pentameter: *See* page 96.

personification: A figure of speech which gives human qualities, characteristics, and behavior to things or ideas. EXAMPLE: "Ten thousand [daffodils] saw I at a glance / *Tossing their heads* in sprightly *dance*." Daffodils do not really have heads, nor can they dance.

pessimism, pessimistic: Pessimism is the tendency to expect the worst. The tone of certain works of literature is pessimistic. EXAMPLE: "Beyond this place of wrath and tears / Looms but the horror of the shade [death] . . ."

plot: *See* page 62.

poetic foot: *See* page 96.

poetic meter: *See* page 95.

poetry: *See* page 81.

prose: *See* page 62.

quatrain: A four-line stanza of poetry, usually rhymed.

refrain: A regularly recurring phrase or line, usually at the end of each stanza of a poem.

rhetoric, rhetorical: The presenting of ideas in clear and elegant language. A rhetorical literary style tends to be formal and elaborate. EXAMPLE: "Four-score and seven years ago our fathers brought forth on this continent a new nation, conceived in liberty and dedicated to the proposition that all men are created equal."

rhyme: The similarity of sound between two or more words due to the repetition of the stressed vowel sound and the consonants or syllables which follow. EXAMPLE: pink, think, ink; pillow, billow, willow.

rhyme scheme: *See* page 92.

rhythm: *See* page 95.

satire: A literary work that ridicules human vices, faults, and weaknesses.

simile: *See* page 83.

soliloquy: In a play, a monologue in which the character thinks aloud. EXAMPLE: One of Hamlet's soliloquies, which begins, "To be, or not to be? That is the question."

sonnet: *See* page 98.

spondee, spondaic: *See* page 96.

stanza: A division of a poem consisting of a group of lines. The stanzas of a poem usually have the same number of lines and the same rhyme scheme.

style: *See* page 70.

symbol: *See* page 87.

synecdoche: *See* page 87.

tetrameter: *See* page 96.

tone: *See* page 69.

tragedy: A serious drama having a sorrowful or disastrous ending.

trimeter: *See* page 96.

trite: Describes an expression that is unoriginal or overused; the same as a cliché.
EXAMPLES: "and they lived happily ever after"; "her teeth were as white as ivory."

trochee, trochaic: *See* page 96.

THE SIMULATED TEST

It is a well-known fact that astronauts prepare themselves for space travel by training under conditions that *simulate*, or imitate, the environment of outer space. Astronauts do this in order to ensure success on a real mission. In a similar manner, you increase your chances of passing the official High School Equivalency Examination by taking a test that simulates the form and content of the real thing. The test that follows is just such a device. It is a simulated version of the "Interpretation of Literary Materials" section of the High School Equivalency Examination.

The Simulated Test reflects the format of the Examination that is most frequently used. Other test forms vary slightly in the number and length of the reading passages. This test has approximately the same number of questions as the official test. The kinds of questions, the forms of literature tested, and the proportions allotted to each form, are similar to the real test. And finally, the level of difficulty of the questions on the actual test has been maintained here.

Read the directions to the simulated test carefully before you start. Give yourself two hours to finish. (Experience has shown that approximately two hours is adequate to complete the official examination, although additional time may be permitted.)

An important note: don't leave any questions unanswered. On the High School Equivalency Examination, **blank answer spaces are marked wrong. Guess rather than leave an answer blank.**

DIRECTIONS: Read each of the following passages. Choose the BEST answer to each question. Then blacken the space under that number in the answer column.

ANSWERS AND EXPLANATIONS APPEAR AT THE END OF THE TEST

I

1   That time of year thou mayst in me behold
2   When yellow leaves, or none, or few, do hang
3   Upon those boughs which shake against the cold,
4   Bare ruin'd choirs, where late the sweet birds sang.
5   In me thou see'st the twilight of such day
6   As after sunset fadeth in the west;
7   Which by and by black night doth take away,
8   Death's second self, that seals up all in rest.

9   In me thou see'st the glowing of such fire,
10   That on the ashes of his youth doth lie,
11   As the deathbed whereon it must expire,
12   Consumed with that which it was nourish'd by.
13   This thou perceivest, which makes thy love more strong,
14   To love that well which thou must leave ere long.

1. The "time of year" to which the poet refers in the first four lines of the above poem is
   (1) summer.   (3) spring.
   (2) winter.   (4) autumn.

2. The word "late" (line 4) means
   (1) after dark.   (3) long ago.
   (2) after midnight.   (4) recently.

3. "Death's second self" (line 8) is a metaphor for
   (1) twilight.   (3) sunset.
   (2) night.   (4) winter.

4. The "glowing . . . fire" (line 9) represents
   (1) the poet's waning life.
   (2) the poet's passion for the person addressed.
   (3) the poet's fireplace.
   (4) the poet's literary inspiration.

5. We can infer that the poet is
   (1) in his teens.   (3) approaching middle age.
   (2) in his twenties.   (4) past middle age.

6. What strengthens the friend's love for the poet?
   (1) The awareness that love often dies.
   (2) The knowledge that the friend's life will soon be over.
   (3) The friend understands that the poet does not have many more years to live.
   (4) none of the above

7. The above poem is a(n)
   (1) ode.   (3) sonnet.
   (2) limerick.   (4) dirge.

8. In line 8, the poet uses
   (1) simile.   (3) onomatopoeia.
   (2) alliteration.   (4) hyperbole.

II

1 The host, he says that all is well
2 And the fire-wood glow is bright;
3 . . . .
4 But on the window licks the night.

5 Pile on the logs . . . Give me your hands,
6 Friends! No,—it is not fright . . .
7 But hold me . . . somewhere I heard demands. . . .
8 And on the window licks the night.

9. Line 3 above is omitted. Which of the following did the poet write?
   (1)   Methinks I can hear a funeral knell,—
   (2)   The food has a warm and tempting smell,—
   (3)   Alas, I can hear the beast of hell,—
   (4)   The food, the friends, and the wine are swell,—

9. 1 2 3 4

10. The mood of the poem is one of
    (1)   apprehension.   (3)   nostalgia.
    (2)   conviviality.   (4)   excitement.

10. 1 2 3 4

11. Lines 4 and 8 serve as a(n)
    (1)   cliché.   (3)   epigram.
    (2)   aphorism.   (4)   refrain.

11. 1 2 3 4

12. The poem consists of two
    (1)   couplets.   (3)   strophes.
    (2)   quatrains.   (4)   spondees.

12. 1 2 3 4

13. "On the window licks the night" is an example of
    (1)   inversion and onomatopoeia.
    (2)   inversion and personification.
    (3)   metonymy and oxymoron.
    (4)   metonymy and hyperbole.

13. 1 2 3 4

14. The rhyme scheme of the poem is
    (1)   *abab baba*   (3)   *abab cdcd*
    (2)   *abab cbcb*   (4)   *abba cddc*

14. 1 2 3 4

III

1   Do not weep, maiden, for war is kind.
2   Because your lover threw wild hands toward the sky
3   And the affrighted steed ran on alone,
4   Do not weep.
5   War is kind.

6   Hoarse, booming drums of the regiment,
7   Little souls who thirst for fight,
8   These men were born to drill and die.
9   The unexplained glory flies above them,
10   Great is the battle-god, great, and his kingdom—
11   A field where a thousand corpses lie.

12   Do not weep, babe, for war is kind.
13   Because your father tumbled in the yellow trenches,
14   Raged at his breast, gulped and died,
15   Do not weep.
16   War is kind.

17   Swift blazing flag of the regiment,
18   Eagle with crest of red and gold,
19   These men were born to drill and die.
20   Point for them the virtue of slaughter,
21   Make plain to them the excellence of killing
22   And a field where a thousand corpses lie.

23   Mother whose heart hung humble as a button
24   On the bright splendid shroud of your son,
25   Do not weep.
26   War is kind.

15. 1 2 3 4   15. "Do not weep. / War is kind" is intended as
  (1)   irony.   (3)   poetic license.
  (2)   rhetoric.   (4)   persuasion.

16. 1 2 3 4   16. The poet contrasts the pomp and glory of war with
  (1)   the splendor of drums and   (3)   the kindness of war.
        flags.   (4)   the courage of individual sol-
  (2)   the reality of suffering.   diers.

17. 1 2 3 4   17. How does the poet feel about war?
  (1)   Mourning is wrong.   (3)   War is kind.
  (2)   War is glorious.   (4)   War is cruel.

18. 1 2 3 4   18. Lines 2–3 describe
  (1)   a soldier's death.   (3)   a soldier riding a horse.
  (2)   a lover's passion.   (4)   a stampede.

19. Which of the following is *not* contained in the above poem?
    (1)   simile   (3)   rhythm
    (2)   a regular rhyme scheme   (4)   stanzas

19. 1 2 3 4

20. "Do not weep. / War is kind" is a(n)
    (1)   stanza.   (3)   refrain.
    (2)   allusion.   (4)   simile.

20. 1 2 3 4

IV

Excerpt 1

1   The gallows in my garden, people say,
2   Is new and neat and adequately tall.
3   I tie the noose on in a knowing way
4   As one that knots his necktie for a ball;
5   But just as all the neighbors—on the wall—
6   Are drawing a long breath to shout "Hurray!"
7   The strangest whim has seized me. . . . After all
8   I think I will not hang myself today.

21. The tone of the above excerpt is
    (1) pessimistic.   (3) ironic.
    (2) tragic.   (4) bitter.

22. The excerpt illustrates all of the following *except*
    (1) extended metaphor.   (3) blank verse.
    (2) multiple meaning.   (4) iambic pentameter.

Excerpt 2

1   It sifts from leaden sieves,
2   It powders all the wood,
3   It fills with alabaster wool
4   The wrinkles of the road.

23. In these lines, the poet is describing
    (1) atomic fallout.   (3) a snowfall.
    (2) a sandstorm.   (4) the rain.

24. "Leaden sieves," (line 1) describes
    (1) the gray sky.   (3) window screens.
    (2) a slate roof.   (4) skyscrapers and machinery.

Excerpt 3

1   my specialty is living said
2   a man(who could not earn his bread
3   because he would not sell his head)

25. "He would not sell his head" (line 3) means that the speaker
    (1) did not want to go to the guillotine.
    (2) refused to commercialize his thoughts.
    (3) had a price on his head.
    (4) owned a piece of sculpture which he refused to sell.

26. This excerpt suggests that the speaker treasured
    (1) independence.   (3) bread.
    (2) money.   (4) success.

V

1 **Miss M:** I had no idea that you felt like this.
2 **Morgan:** Because you are not interested in me.
3 **Miss M:** (*incredulously*) Not interested in you?
4 **Morgan:** (*losing control*) How can you be interested in a machine
5   that you put a penny in and if nothing comes out you give it a
6   good shake? "Evans, write me an essay, Evans, get up and bow,
7   Evans, what is a subjunctive!" My name is Morgan Evans! and
8   all my friends call me Morgan, and if there is anything gets on
9   the wrong side of me it is callin' me Evans! . . . And do you
10   know what they call me in the village? *Ci bach yr ysgol!* The
11   schoolmistress's little dog. What has it got to do with you if my
12   nails are dirty? Mind your own business! (*He bursts into sobs
13   and buries his head in his hands. A pause. She is extremely
14   upset, but tries hard not to show it. She waits for him to
15   recover.*)
16 **Miss M:** I never meant you to know this. I have spent money on
17   you—I don't mind that, money ought to be spent. But time is
18   different. Your life has not yet begun, mine is halfway over.
19   And when you're a middle aged spinster, some folk say it's
20   pretty near finished. Two years is valuable currency. I've spent
21   two years on you. Ever since that first day, the mainspring of
22   this school has been your career. Sometimes, in the middle of
23   the night, when I have been desperately tired, I have lain
24   awake, making plans. Large and small. Sensible and silly. Plans
25   for you. And you tell me I have no interest in you. If I say any
26   more I shall start to cry; and I haven't cried since I was younger
27   than you are, and I'd never forgive you for that. (*Walking
28   brusquely to the front door.*) I am going for a walk. I don't like
29   this sort of conversation, please never mention it again. If you
30   want to go on, be at school tomorrow. (*Going.*) If not, don't.
31 **Morgan:** (*Muttering, fiercely*) I don't want your money, and I
32   don't want your time! . . . I don't want to be thankful to no
33   strange woman—for anything!

27. The above passage is a(n)
    (1) prologue.   (3) monologue.
    (2) epilogue.   (4) dialogue.

28. We can infer that the speakers in the above excerpt are
    (1) a youth and his mother.   (3) a man and his mistress.
    (2) a husband and wife.   (4) a teacher and pupil.

29. Which of the following replies to Morgan's final retort (lines 31–33) would
    be most consistent with Miss M.'s character?
    (1) "I don't understand you. I don't understand you at all."

(2)   "After all I've done for you, you should be ashamed of yourself for acting this way."

(3)   "Very well. Then I shan't waste any more of my time on you."

(4)   "Damn you! You owe it to me to win that scholarship so that you can repay me for all the money I've spent on you."

30. 1 2 3 4   30.   We can infer that Miss M. devoted particular attention to Morgan because of his

(1)   youth and good looks.

(2)   poverty and deprivation.

(3)   slowness.

(4)   intellectual ability.

31. 1 2 3 4   31.   It is evidently *not* difficult for

(1)   Miss M. to express deep emotion.

(2)   Morgan to take direction from a woman.

(3)   Morgan to do well in his studies.

(4)   Morgan and Miss M. to understand each other.

32. 1 2 3 4   32.   When Miss M. says that "two years is valuable currency" (line 20), she implies that

(1)   time is more precious than money.

(2)   Morgan should repay her for her time.

(3)   the present moment can never be recaptured.

(4)   Morgan should spend more time on his studies.

VI

1 **Scene: Garden at the Manor House.**
2 **Miss Prism:** (*Calling.*) Cecily, Cecily! Surely such a utilitarian
3 occupation as the watering of flowers is rather Moulton's duty
4 than yours? Especially at a moment when intellectual pleasures
5 await you. Your German grammar is on the table. Pray open it
6 at page fifteen. We will repeat yesterday's lesson.
7 **Cecily:** (*Coming over very slowly.*) But I don't like German. It isn't
8 at all a becoming language. I know perfectly well that I look
9 quite plain after my German lesson.
10 **Miss Prism:** Child, you know how anxious your guardian is that you
11 should improve yourself in every way. He laid particular stress
12 on your German, as he was leaving for town yesterday. Indeed,
13 he always lays stress on your German when he is leaving for
14 town.
15 **Cecily:** Dear Uncle Jack is so very serious! Sometimes he is so
16 serious that I think he cannot be quite well.
17 **Miss Prism:** (*Drawing herself up.*) Your guardian enjoys the best
18 of health, and his gravity of demeanour is especially to be
19 commended in one so comparatively young as he is. I know no
20 one who has a higher sense of duty and responsibility.

33. The author's intent is to
    (1) instruct.
    (2) moralize.
    (3) entertain.
    (4) describe.

34. We can infer that Cecily and Miss Prism
    (1) share a fondness for German.
    (2) share a dislike for German.
    (3) have different ideas about German.
    (4) are German nationals.

35. From the information given, which of the following can be characterized as frivolous?
    (1) Moulton.
    (2) Cecily.
    (3) Uncle Jack.
    (4) Miss Prism.

36. The phrase "gravity of demeanour" (line 18) means
    (1) seriousness of purpose.
    (2) seriousness of manner.
    (3) weightiness of cares.
    (4) acceptance of responsibility.

37. We can assume that Cecily is Jack's
    (1) daughter.
    (2) mistress.
    (3) fiancée
    (4) ward.

38. The word "utilitarian" means
    (1) useful.
    (2) foolish.
    (3) wasteful.
    (4) intellectual.

VII

1 **Portia:** Brutus, my lord!
2 **Brutus:** Portia, what mean you? Wherefore rise you now?
3   It is not for your health thus to commit
4   Your weak condition to the raw cold morning.
5 **Portia:** Nor for yours neither. You've ungently, Brutus,
6   Stole from my bed. And yesternight, at supper,
7   You suddenly arose, and walked about,
8   Musing and sighing, with your arms across,
9   And when I asked you what the matter was,
10   You stared upon me with ungentle looks.
11   I urged you further; then you scratched your head,
12   And too impatiently stamped with your foot;
13   Yet I insisted; yet you answered not,
14   But, with an angry wafture of your hand,
15   Gave sign for me to leave you. . . . .
16   Make me acquainted with your cause of grief.
17 **Brutus:** I am not well in health, and that is all.
18 **Portia:** Brutus is wise, and, were he not in health,
19   He would embrace the means to come by it.

39. "Wherefore" (line 2) means
(1) where. (2) why. (3) when. (4) how.

40. "Nor for yours neither" (line 5) is an example of what kind of diction?
(1) archaic (2) incorrect (3) idiomatic (4) modern

41. How many poetic feet does each line of verse contain?
(1) four (2) five (3) ten (4) eleven

42. Portia's mood can best be described as
(1) angry. (2) injured. (3) anxious. (4) teasing.

43. We can infer that Brutus' restlessness is probably due to
(1) his poor health.   (3) his wife's nagging.
(2) some matter which trou-   (4) his insanity.
bles him.

44. A completion of line 15 consistent with the form, style, and tone of the passage is
(1) For the sake of your family,   (3) Dear my lord,
(2) For Pete's sake,   (4) Evil man,

VIII

1 The widow she cried over me, and called me a poor lost lamb, and
2 she called me a lot of other names, too, but she never meant no
3 harm by it. She put me in them new clothes again, and I couldn't
4 do nothing but sweat and sweat, and feel all cramped up. Well,
5 then, the old thing commenced again. The widow rung a bell for
6 supper, and you had to come on time. When you got to the table
7 you couldn't go right on eating, but you had to wait for the widow
8 to tuck down her head and grumble a little over the victuals, though
9 there warn't really anything the matter with them—that is, nothing
10 only everything was cooked by itself. In a barrel of odds and ends
11 it is different; things get mixed up, and the juice kind of swaps
12 around, and things go better.

13 After supper she got out her book and learned me about Moses
14 and the Bulrushers, and I was in a sweat to find out all about him;
15 but by and by she let it out that Moses had been dead a considerable
16 long time; so then I didn't care no more about him, because I don't
17 take no stock in dead people.

18 Pretty soon I wanted to smoke, and asked the widow to let me.
19 But she wouldn't. She said it was a mean practice and wasn't clean,
20 and I must try not to do it any more. That is just the way with some
21 people. They get down on a thing when they don't know nothing
22 about it. Here she was a-bothering about Moses, which was no kin
23 to her, and no use to anybody, being gone, you see, yet finding a
24 power of fault with me for doing a thing that had some good in it.
25 And she took snuff, too; of course, that was all right, because she
26 done it herself.

45. The style of the narrative is
    (1) colloquial.   (3) terse.
    (2) romantic.   (4) poetic.

46. "Victuals" (line 8) means
    (1) prayers.   (3) food.
    (2) dishes.   (4) barrels.

47. The narrator attributes the widow's disapproval of his smoking to her
    (1) religion.   (3) ignorance.
    (2) stern sense of morality. (4) cleanliness.

48. The "poor lost lamb" of this passage is apparently a child who
    (1) had learned to mistrust and fear all adults.
    (2) has an inferiority complex.
    (3) craves elegant meals.
    (4) is not used to middle class manners.

49. The narrator's attitude toward the widow can best be described as
    (1) impudent and mischievous.   (3) grateful and worshipful.
    (2) respectful and somewhat   (4) bitter and resentful.
        uncomfortable.

45. 1 2 3 4

46. 1 2 3 4

47. 1 2 3 4

48. 1 2 3 4

49. 1 2 3 4

50. 1 2 3 4

50. The author's tone is
   (1) straightforward.
   (2) moralizing.
   (3) satirical.
   (4) outraged.

51. 1 2 3 4

51. The narrator may symbolize
   (1) ingratitude.
   (2) natural man.
   (3) the transition from boyhood to manhood.
   (4) irreligion.

IX

1   It ran in his knowledge before he ever saw it. It looked and towered
2   in his dreams before he even saw the unaxed woods where it left
3   its crooked print, shaggy, huge, red-eyed, not malevolent but just
4   big, too big for the dogs which tried to bay it, for the horses which
5   tried to ride it down, for the men and the bullets they fired into
6   it; too big for the very country which was its constricting scope.
7   It was as if the boy had already divined what his senses and intellect
8   had not encompassed yet:—that doomed wilderness whose edges
9   were being constantly and punily gnawed at by men with plows
10   and axes who feared it because it was wilderness, men myriad and
11   nameless even to one another in the land where the old bear had
12   earned a name, and through which ran not even a mortal beast
13   but an anachronism indomitable and invincible out of an old dead
14   time, a phantom, epitome and apotheosis of the old wild life which
15   the little puny humans swarmed and hacked at in a fury of abhor-
16   rence and fear, like pygmies about the ankles of a drowsing elephant;
17   —the old bear solitary, indomitable, and alone; widowered childless·
18   and absolved of mortality. . . .

52. What towered in the boy's dreams before he ever saw it?
    (1)   the wilderness   (3)   a man on a horse
    (2)   a drowsing elephant   (4)   the great bear

53. How did the men with axes and plows feel toward the wilderness?
    (1)   They feared it.
    (2)   They respected it.
    (3)   They wished to preserve it.
    (4)   They were impressed by its wild beauty.

54. The writer's attitude toward the bear is one of
    (1)   abhorrence.   (3)   fear.
    (2)   impatience.   (4)   respect.

55. An "anachronism" (line 13) is
    (1)   something which belongs to another time.
    (2)   something which one wishes to get rid of.
    (3)   a destructive force.
    (4)   doom.

56. The great bear probably symbolizes
    (1)   the dangers which pioneers must confront.
    (2)   the fact that the wilderness is doomed.
    (3)   the struggle between man and animals.
    (4)   wild nature which can never be conquered.

57. The phrase "The puny humans swarmed . . . like pygmies about the ankles
    of a drowsing elephant" (lines 15–16) is a
    (1)   simile.   (3)   rhyme.
    (2)   metaphor.   (4)   apostrophe.

X

1 True! Nervous, very very dreadfully nervous I had been and am;
2 but why *will* you say that I am mad? The disease had sharpened
3 my senses, not destroyed, not dulled them. Above all was the sense
4 of hearing acute. I heard all things in the heaven and in the earth.
5 I heard many things in hell. How, then, am I mad? Hearken! And
6 observe how healthily—how calmly I can tell you the whole story.

7   It is impossible to say how first the idea entered my brain; but
8 once conceived, it haunted me day and night. Object there was
9 none. Passion there was none. I loved the old man. He had never
10 wronged me. He had never given me insult. For his gold I had no
11 desire. I think it was his eye! Yes, it was this! One of his eyes
12 resembled that of a vulture—a pale blue eye, with a film over it.
13 Whenever it fell upon me, my blood ran cold; and so by degrees,
14 very gradually, I made up my mind to take the life of the old man
15 and thus rid myself of the eye forever.

58. The narrator says that he is
(1) nervous.   (3) mad.
(2) delirious.   (4) feverish.

59. He believes that which of his senses has become abnormally acute?
(1) hearing   (3) smell
(2) sight   (4) touch

60. The narrator decided to kill the old man
(1) because he hated the old man.
(2) because the old man had offended him.
(3) in order to steal the old man's gold.
(4) none of the above

61. From the narrator's statement that he "heard many things in hell" (line 5)
we can infer that
(1) he was in league with the Devil.
(2) his senses were abnormally acute.
(3) he was mentally unbalanced.
(4) he had supernatural powers.

62. The word "conceived" (line 8) means
(1) sharpened sight.   (3) convinced.
(2) received.   (4) thought of.

63. The mood of the passage is one of
(1) horror and suspense.
(2) pessimism and gloom.
(3) reminiscence and nostalgia.
(4) regret and self-recrimination.

XI

1   He [Little Chandler] looked coldly into the eyes of the photograph
2   and they answered coldly. Certainly they were pretty and the face
3   itself was pretty. But he found something mean in it. Why was it
4   so unconscious and ladylike? The composure of the eyes irritated
5   him. They repelled him and defied him: there was no passion in
6   them, no rapture. He thought of what Gallaher had said about rich
7   Jewesses. Those dark oriental eyes, he thought, how full they are
8   of passion, of voluptuous longing! . . . Why had he married the
9   eyes in the photograph?
10   He caught himself up at the question and glanced nervously
11 round the room. He found something mean in the pretty furniture
12 which he had bought for his house on the hire system. Annie had
13 chosen it herself and it reminded him of her. It too was prim and
14 pretty. A dull resentment against his life awoke within him. Could
15 he not escape from his little house? Was it too late for him to try
16 to live bravely like Gallaher? Could he go to London? There was
17 the furniture still to be paid for. If he could only write a book and
18 get it published, that might open the way for him.
19   A volume of Byron's poems lay before him on the table. He
20 opened it cautiously with his left hand lest he should waken the
21 child and began to read the first poem in the book.

. . .

22   The child awoke and began to cry. He turned from the page
23 and tried to hush it: but it would not be hushed. He began to rock
24 it to and fro in his arms but its wailing cry grew keener. He rocked
25 it faster while his eyes began to read the second stanza.

. . .

26   It was useless. He couldn't read. He couldn't do anything. The
27 wailing of the child pierced the drum of his ear. It was useless,
28 useless! He was a prisoner for life. . . .

64. The word "keener" means
    (1)   quieter.
    (2)   happier.
    (3)   more intense.
    (4)   sadder.

64. 1 2 3 4

65. To Little Chandler, the face of his composed, pretty wife symbolizes
    (1)   the pleasures of marriage.
    (2)   the beauty of Byron's poetry.
    (3)   the lack of excitement and rapture in his life.
    (4)   the economic hardships which they suffered.

65. 1 2 3 4

66. The short, choppy sentences in lines 26–28
    (1)   reflect the mood of frustration and impatience.
    (2)   imitate a baby's wailing.
    (3)   balance the lengthier sentences at the beginning of the passage.
    (4)   imitate the style of Byron's poems.

66. 1 2 3 4

67. | 1 2 3 4

67. The meaning of the word "composure" in line 4 is
   - (1) passion.
   - (2) intelligence.
   - (3) calmness.
   - (4) anger.

68. | 1 2 3 4

68. The main feeling of the passage is Little Chandler's sense of being
   - (1) a gifted poet.
   - (2) inferior to Gallaher.
   - (3) trapped.
   - (4) interrupted.

69. | 1 2 3 4

69. Which of the following sentences, placed immediately after line 28, matches the mood, tone, and style of the passage?
   - (1) He placed the book on the table, deciding to relinquish his dream.
   - (2) "There now, love! There now!... *Lambabaun*!" he crooned sadly to the wailing babe.
   - (3) But, he thought, he was blessed with a pretty wife, a pretty home, and an infant son.
   - (4) His arms trembled with anger and suddenly bending to the child's face he shouted: "Stop!"

XII

1 I am more of a host than a guest. I like people to stay with me but
2 do not much care about staying with them, and usually say that
3 I am too busy. The only people we ask to stay with us are people
4 we like—I do not believe in business hospitality, which has the seed
5 of corruption in it—and all Fridays I work in a pleasant glow just
6 because I know some nice people are coming down by the last
7 train. I am genuinely glad to see them. But I suspect that I am
8 still more delighted when they go, and the house is ours again.
9 They leave more room in which to live properly. Meals are quicker
10 and easier. There is no more hanging about, no more sight-seeing,
11 no further necessity for bright talk. My mind, like my body, puts
12 on its old clothes again. I enjoy hard work (my own kind) and
13 foolish play, and both are difficult when you are cluttered up with
14 guests. I like to think about life in this world, and it is not easy
15 to do this when animated and talkative pieces of it are all over
16 the place. With guests about I am conscious of myself as a solid,
17 but as soon as they have gone I expand into a gas again. And a
18 gas can have more delight than a solid. So——Good-by! . . .
19 Good-by! . . . Good—

70. The literary genre represented by this passage is the
    (1) biography.   (3) short story.
    (2) novel.   (4) essay.

70. 1 2 3 4

71. The author is delighted when his guests leave because he
    (1) dislikes people.
    (2) dislikes entertaining business clients.
    (3) is more relaxed when there are no guests.
    (4) would rather be a guest than a host.

71. 1 2 3 4

72. "My mind . . . puts on its old clothes again" (lines 11–12) is a(n)
    (1) hyperbole.   (3) oxymoron.
    (2) metaphor.   (4) antithesis.

72. 1 2 3 4

73. The author suggests that most of his actions are determined by
    (1) his own needs.   (3) social convention.
    (2) a sense of duty.   (4) his friends' desires.

73. 1 2 3 4

74. The last sentence (So—Good-by! . . . Good-by! . . . Good—) playfully sug-
    gests that the author has
    (1) fallen asleep.   (3) no more to say.
    (2) run out of ink.   (4) risen into the air.

74. 1 2 3 4

75. The word "pieces" in line 15 refers to
    (1) the fragmentation of modern life.
    (2) the sheets of paper on which the author writes.
    (3) people.
    (4) gadgets.

75. 1 2 3 4

XIII

1 Some are dinning in our ears that we Americans, and moderns
2 generally, are intellectual dwarfs compared with the ancients, or
3 even the Elizabethan men. But what is that to the purpose? A living
4 dog is better than a dead lion. Shall a man go and hang himself
5 because he belongs to the race of pygmies, and not be the biggest
6 pygmy that he can? Let every one mind his own business, and
7 endeavor to be what he was made.
8   Why should we be in such desperate haste to succeed and in
9 such desperate enterprises? If a man does not keep pace with his
10 companions, perhaps it is because he hears a different drummer.

76. "A living dog is better than a dead lion" (lines 3–4) is a(n)
    (1) proverb.   (3) personification.
    (2) oxymoron.   (4) simile.

77. In this passage, the author suggests how to
    (1) be better than the Elizabethans.
    (2) be better than the pygmies.
    (3) be an intellectual.
    (4) live.

78. The author of this passage is *not* a(n)
    (1) conformist.   (3) essayist.
    (2) individualist.   (4) philosopher.

79. The style of this passage is
    (1) aphoristic.   (3) stilted.
    (2) lyrical.   (4) mystical.

80. The author thinks that comparisons between modern men and intellectual
    giants of the past are
    (1) useful.   (3) irresponsible.
    (2) unfair.   (4) irrelevant.

81. The last sentence of the passage means
    (1) try to keep up with your companions.
    (2) tell others to follow your directions.
    (3) some men follow their own directions.
    (4) stay ahead of your companions.

XIV

Excerpt 1

1 Dad installed process and work charts in the bathrooms. Every
2 child old enough to write—and Dad expected his offspring to start
3 writing at a tender age—was required to initial the charts in the
4 morning after he had brushed his teeth, taken a bath, combed
5 his hair, and made his bed. At night, each child had to weigh
6 himself, plot the figure on a graph, and initial the process charts
7 again after he had done his homework, washed his hands and face,
8 and brushed his teeth.

82. Dad was efficient but somewhat
   (1) permissive.   (3) authoritarian.
   (2) cruel.   (4) disorganized.

82. 1 2 3 4
    ‖ ‖ ‖ ‖

Excerpt 2

1 My dream life does not seem as important as my waking life, if
2 only because there is far less of it, but to me it is important. . . .
3 It is as if there were at least two extra continents added to the
4 world, and lightning excursions running to them at any moment
5 between midnight and breakfast.

83. "Lightning excursions" (line 4) is a metaphor which represents
   (1) dreams in which the dead appear.
   (2) the mysterious fears which dreams may evoke.
   (3) passage into and out of the dreaming state.
   (4) the "trips" the author takes in his dreams.

83. 1 2 3 4
    ‖ ‖ ‖ ‖

Excerpt 3

1 There is nothing more tragic for a man who has been expecting
2 to die than a long convalescence. After that touch from the wing
3 of Death, what seemed important is so no longer; other things
4 become so which had at first seemed unimportant, or which one
5 did not even know existed. The miscellaneous mass of acquired
6 knowledge of every kind that has overlain the mind gets peeled off
7 in places like a mask of paint, exposing the bare skin—the very
8 flesh of the authentic creature that had lain hidden beneath it.

84. "Bare skin" (line 7) is a metaphor which represents
   (1) basic personality.
   (2) the sins of the flesh.
   (3) the nakedness of Adam before the Fall.
   (4) vulnerability.

84. 1 2 3 4
    ‖ ‖ ‖ ‖

ANSWERS AND EXPLANATIONS

I

"Sonnet 73," by WILLIAM SHAKESPEARE (1564–1616)

1   That time of year thou mayst in me behold
2   When yellow leaves, or none, or few, do hang
3   Upon those boughs which shake against the cold,
4   Bare ruin'd choirs, where late the sweet birds sang.
5   In me thou see'st the twilight of such day
6   As after sunset fadeth in the west;
7   Which by and by black night doth take away,
8   Death's second self, that seals up all in rest,
9   In me thou see'st the glowing of such fire,
10 That on the ashes of his youth doth lie,
11 As the deathbed whereon it must expire,
12 Consumed with that which it was nourish'd by.
13 This thou perceivest, which makes thy love more strong,
14 To love that well which thou must leave ere long.

Difficult Words Explained

LINE
1   **mayst:** you may
    behold: see
3   **boughs:** branches
4   **choirs:** gallery where members of a choir stand to sing. These choirs are, therefore, branches of a tree.
    late: recently
11 **whereon:** on which
    expire: die
12 **consumed:** burned up
    nourished: fed
13 **perceivest:** notice, understand
14 **ere:** before

Summary

The poet, addressing a friend, compares his old age with autumn, twilight, and a dying fire. He expresses his belief that the friend, understanding that the poet does not have many more years of life, loves him all the more strongly.

Answer Key

Inference

1. (4) This is suggested by the yellow leaves which remain on the branches. The branches "shake against the cold," empty of songbirds. If the season were winter, there would not be any yellow leaves.

Inference

2. (4) "Late" in this line is a shortened form of "lately," meaning recently or not long ago. We can guess this from the context. The choirs, or

branches, where "late the sweet birds sang" are now "bare" and "ruined"; the birds are gone. The first three lines tell us that it is now autumn. We assume that the birds sang on these branches during the summer, or just before autumn. Therefore, the birds sang recently.

3. **(2)** The phrase "Death's second self" follows after and describes "black night" (line 7). Night is "Death's second self," or brother, because both bring darkness. In addition, "Death's second self . . . seals up all in rest." Both death and night bring rest to us. We can conclude then, that "Death's second self" is a metaphor for "night."

Figures of Speech

4. **(1)** When a fire burns, it leaves ashes. As the flame dies, it becomes just a glow on top of those ashes. The poet compares his life to a fire. His fire (his life) is just a glow now. This means then, that his life is waning, or ending. He imagines this glow burning on the remains (the ashes) of his youth (line 10). The "glowing . . . fire," therefore, represents the poet's waning life.

Figures of Speech

5. **(4)** This is expressed by comparisons of the poet's life to autumn, nightfall, and a dying fire.

Inference

6. **(3)** The poet dwells on his advanced age, but concludes (in the last two lines) that the friend's love is strengthened by the knowledge that the poet does not have many more years of life.

Supporting Detail

7. **(3)** A *sonnet* is a fourteen-line poem written in iambic pentameter, with a definite rhyme scheme. You should be able to identify the meter of this poem as iambic pentameter, but the easiest way to identify it as a sonnet is to note that it has fourteen lines.

Literary Forms and Levels of Diction

8. **(2)** *Alliteration* is the repetition of a consonant sound, usually at the beginning of words that are close to each other. In line 8, the *s* sound is repeated: "Death's second self that seals . . ."

Rhythm and Sound Devices

II

"Fear," by HART CRANE (1899–1932)

1 The host, he says that all is well
2 And the fire-wood glow is bright;
3 The food has a warm and tempting smell,—
4 But on the window licks the night.

5 Pile on the logs . . . Give me your hands,
6 Friends! No,—it is not fright . . .
7 But hold me . . . somewhere I heard demands
8 And on the window licks the night.

Summary

The poem communicates a mood of foreboding and threat, with an evil, unknown presence lurking in the dark. Even while the poet is in a place of light, warmth, and hospitality, he cannot feel safe. From somewhere, something is summoning him, and the night is threatening to come in, "licking against the window" (like some animal, monster, or nightmare).

Answer Key

Inference

9. **(2)** Choice (1) contains unsuitably archaic language ("Methinks"), and the "funeral" image is out of place. Choice (3) uses the word "Alas" which is inconsistent with the poem's simple and modern usage. In addition, the "hell" image is inappropriate, just as the "funeral" image was in choice (1). In choices (2) and (4), the "food" imagery is consistent with the preceding imagery of hospitality and firelight, and the rhythm matches the rhythm of the rest of the poem. The use of the colloquialism, "swell" in choice (4), however, is inconsistent with the standard English usage of the poem, leaving choice (2) as the correct answer.

Style and Tone

Rhythm and Sound Devices

10. **(1)** In spite of warmth, light, and friends, the speaker is apprehensive (fearful). This mood is expressed by his sense of the night pressing in (lines 4 and 8), his desire to hold on to his friends, and his feeling of "demands" coming from "somewhere" (line 7).

Literary Forms and Levels of Diction

11. **(4)** In poetry and song, a *refrain* is a line or group of lines that are repeated, usually at the end of each stanza or verse.

12. **(2)** A *quatrain* is a four-line stanza, usually rhymed. Lines 1–4 and 5–8 form two quatrains.

Rhythm and Sound Devices

Figures of Speech

13. **(2)** *Inversion* refers to transposed (turned around) word order. Normally, we would say, "The night licks on the window." *Personification* is a figure of speech which attributes human characteristics to nonliving things or to ideas. "Licking" is a human (or animal) activity; the night cannot really lick the window. "On the window licks the night," therefore, is an example of both inversion and personification.

Rhythm and Sound Devices

14. **(2)** Find the rhyme scheme by giving a letter to the last word in each line (the "end words"). Words that rhyme get the same letter. The end words of the poem are: well, bright, smell, night; hands, fright, demands, night. Therefore, "well" equals *a*; "bright" equals *b*; "smell" equals *a* because it rhymes with "well"; and "night" equals *b* because it rhymes with "bright." In the second stanza, "hands" equals *c*; "fright" equals *b* because it rhymes with "bright"; "demands" equals *c* because it rhymes with "hands"; and "night" equals *b* because it rhymes with "bright." The rhyme scheme, then, is *abab cbcb.*

III

"War Is Kind," by STEPHEN CRANE (1871–1900)

1   Do not weep, maiden, for war is kind.
2   Because your lover threw wild hands toward the sky
3   And the affrighted steed ran on alone,

4   Do not weep.
5   War is kind.

6   Hoarse, booming drums of the regiment,
7   Little souls who thirst for fight,
8   These men were born to drill and die.
9   The unexplained glory flies above them,
10   Great is the battle-god, great, and his kingdom—
11   A field where a thousand corpses lie.

12   Do not weep, babe, for war is kind.
13   Because your father tumbled in the yellow trenches,
14   Raged at his breast, gulped and died,
15   Do not weep.
16   War is kind.

17   Swift blazing flag of the regiment,
18   Eagle with crest of red and gold,
19   These men were born to drill and die.
20   Point for them the virtue of slaughter,
21   Make plain to them the excellence of killing
22   And a field where a thousand corpses lie.

23   Mother whose heart hung humble as a button
24   On the bright splendid shroud of your son,
25   Do not weep.
26   War is kind.

Difficult Words Explained

LINE
1   **maiden:** a young girl
3   **affrighted:** frightened
    steed: horse
6   **regiment:** a large unit of soldiers
8   **drill:** practice marching
11 **corpses:** dead bodies
13 **trenches:** ditches on a battlefield
20 **virtue:** goodness
    slaughter: mass killing
24 **shroud:** burial sheet for a body

Summary

Most of the statements in this poem are *ironic;* that is, the poet wants us to conclude the *opposite* of what he is saying. Speaking to young girls, babies, and mothers, he first describes the violent deaths of the men they love, and then tells them not to cry, for "war is kind." To the reader, though,   :ths represent war's brutality, *not* kindness. The poet is being ironic. Addressing the drums and flags of war, he praises the "excellence of killing," stating that men were born to "drill and die" in battle. But the reader concludes that the men were born to be with the mothers, maidens, and children who love them. Again. the poet is using irony.

Answer Key

Style and Tone

15. (1) See SUMMARY.

Main Idea

16. (2) Stanzas 2 and 4 present an ironic glorification of war and killing. This is contrasted with a description of the agonies of dying young soldiers and the sorrowing of sweethearts, children, and mothers in stanzas 1, 3, and 5.

Inference

17. (4) As explained in the SUMMARY, the poet expresses the sentiment that war is cruel.

Inference

18. (1) The "lover" referred to in line 2 is a soldier. He "threw wild hands toward the sky" when he was killed in battle. The "steed ran on alone" (line 3) because the dead soldier could no longer ride him.

Rhythm and Sound Devices

19. (2) Line 23 contains the simile, "humble as a button." The poem has rhythm, with the short lines of the refrain having two stresses each, and the other lines having four. The poem consists of five stanzas. But the words which end the lines do not rhyme in a regular pattern.

Rhythm and Sound Devices

20. (3) The lines are a refrain because they are repeated at the end of each stanza.

IV

Excerpt 1   from "A Ballade of Suicide," by G. K. CHESTERTON (1874–1936)

1   The gallows in my garden, people say,
2   Is new and neat and adequately tall.
3   I tie the noose on in a knowing way
4   As one that knots his necktie for a ball;
5   But just as all the neighbours—on the wall—
6   Are drawing a long breath to shout "Hooray!"
7   The strangest whim has seized me. . . . After all
8   I think I will not hang myself to-day.

Difficult Words Explained

LINE
1   **gallows:**   the platform, scaffold, and noose used in an execution by hanging
2   **noose:**   the loop of rope placed around the neck of someone about to be hanged
3   **knowing:**   practiced; familiar
7   **fancy:**   whim, an original idea

Summary

While the spectators happily await his downfall, the speaker prepares to hang himself. Then, at the last moment, just as the onlookers are preparing to cheer his death, he changes his mind, deciding not to hang himself "to-day." We can infer that the speaker is "playing with" all those who wish him ill, first raising and then dashing their hopes that he will come to a bad end.

Answer Key

21. **(3)** The poet is not really pessimistic. He is making a gesture to those people who wish him ill. In response to their wishes, he goes through the motions of getting ready to hang himself, then changes his mind at the last minute. He has played a joke on his enemies. The little drama is intended ironically.

   Style and Tone

22. **(3)** The excerpt *does* illustrate extended metaphor (the "gallows" is intended to be understood figuratively, not literally, as a means of self-destruction). The excerpt *does* contain multiple meanings. The "surface meaning" is: "I decided to kill myself to gratify your desire, but on a sudden whim I changed my mind." The deeper meaning suggests: "You'd *love* to see me fall, wouldn't you! To get even, I'll pretend to be about to do myself in, but just as you're feeling triumphant, I'll disappoint you." The excerpt *is* written in iambic pentameter: /"The GAL-/ lows IN/ my GAR-/ den, PEO-/ ple SAY . . ."/ Blank verse is unrhymed iambic pentameter. This poem does rhyme; therefore, it is *not* written in blank verse.

   Figures of Speech

   Rhythm and Sound Devices

Excerpt 2   from "It Sifts from Leaden Sieves," by EMILY DICKINSON
            (1830–1886)

1   It sifts from leaden sieves,
2   It powders all the wood,
3   It fills with alabaster wool
4   The wrinkles of the road.

Difficult Words Explained

LINE
1   **sieves:**   literally, strainers; utensils with wire mesh bottoms, used for sifting ingredients such as flour
3   **alabaster:**   a white, marble-like stone

Summary

The poet describes a snowfall. As flour is sifted, so the snow sifts down from the gray, heavy sky, powdering the trees and filling the ruts of the road with a substance as white as alabaster and as fluffy and light as wool.

Answer Key

Figures of Speech

23. **(3)** "It" (line 1) is described as sifting from sieves (an image which suggests the sifting of flour from a sieve), "powdering" the wood, and filling the wrinkles (ruts) of the road with alabaster (pure white) wool. The imagery of something light, pure white, and powdery, which covers the trees and fills ruts, best describes a snowfall.

Figures of Speech

24. **(1)** The "leaden sieves" from which the snow falls can only be the heavy, lusterless skies from which the snow falls lightly down, like flour from a metal sifter.

Excerpt 3 from "my specialty is living," by E. E. CUMMINGS (1894–1962)

1 my specialty is living said
2 a man(who could not earn his bread
3 because he would not sell his head)

Summary

The speaker could not earn a living because he refused to sell his ideas for the profit of a corporation. (E. E. Cummings, the author of this excerpt, had once worked for an advertising firm, but left advertising to write poetry.)

Answer Key

Figures of Speech

25. **(2)** "His head" is a metaphor used to represent his mind, his creative ideas. The statement that he would not "sell" his head suggests that he would not let his mind be bought for the service of someone else (for example, a business firm).

Inference

26. **(1)** The speaker preferred to be poor (not earning his bread), but independent—free to think, speak, and act as he pleased. His refusal to "sell his head" (his thoughts and ideas) indicates the great value he placed on being independent.

V

from *The Corn is Green,* by EMLYN WILLIAMS (1905–   )

Difficult Words Explained

LINE

3   **incredulously:** unbelievingly
7   **subjunctive:**   a term used in grammar
10   **Ci bach yr ysgol:** "the dog of the schoolmistress"; Morgan is speaking Welsh, his native language
21   **mainspring:**   the chief motive or interest
28   **brusquely:** abruptly, harshly

Summary

The scene is a confrontation between Miss Moffat, an English schoolteacher, and Morgan Evans, her brilliant pupil and protégé (a gifted student whose career a teacher is furthering). Morgan finally rebels against Miss Moffat's direction and discipline, thinking that her formal and restrained manner is due to a lack of interest. Although talking about feelings is difficult for her, Miss Moffat tries to explain how much she does care, pointing out that for two years Morgan's education and future career have been her main interest and concern. But Morgan, not understanding the caring that lies behind the teacher's reserve, rejects her. Neither understands the other.

Answer Key

27. **(4)** Dialogue is a conversation between two or more speakers. A prologue, choice (1), is the introduction to a play. An epilogue, choice (2), is a concluding section at the end of a play or other literary work. A monologue, choice (3), is a dramatic speech spoken by one actor.

    Literary Forms and Levels of Diction

28. **(4)** This is evident from references to Morgan's studies, his career being the mainspring of the school, and Miss Moffat's statement, "If you want to go on, be at school tomorrow."

    Inference

29. **(1)** Choice (2) implies that the teacher is accusing her pupil of ingratitude and wants him to feel guilty. Choice (3) implies that Miss Moffat is angry and rejects Morgan. Choice (4) implies that she is angry and wants Morgan to pay her back. Only choice (1), indicating lack of understanding and communication, is consistent with the preceding speeches, in which Morgan expresses his feeling that Miss Moffat is not interested in him, and the teacher reveals how deeply she cares (but is not "understood" by Morgan).

    Inference

30. **(4)** This can be inferred from Miss Moffat's statement that Morgan's career has been the mainspring of the school for two years.

    Inference

31. **(3)** Miss Moffat has been tutoring Morgan in preparation for a brilliant career. The time she spends with him, and Morgan's being known as her "pet," indicate that he probably *is* a good student. We know, however, that it is difficult for the teacher to express deep emotion. She treats Morgan formally in spite of her concern for him, and says that she doesn't "like this sort of [emotional] conversation." Morgan makes it clear that he finds it hard to take direction from a woman by telling her to "mind her own business." It is clear from the dialogue that the two do *not* understand each other (choice 4).

    Inference

32. **(1)** Miss Moffat states that she doesn't mind the money she has spent on Morgan, but the two years of her life that she has spent on him, unlike money, can never be regained. Since she is past middle age, two years are very valuable to her.

    Inference

VI

from *The Importance of Being Earnest*, by OSCAR WILDE (1854–1900)

Difficult Words Explained

LINE

2	**utilitarian:**	useful, practical
5	**pray:**	please
9	**plain:**	not pretty, homely
10	**guardian:**	an adult other than a parent who is legally responsible for the welfare of a child
13	**lay stress on:**	emphasize, maintain the importance of
18	**gravity:**	seriousness
	demeanour:	manner, behavior
19	**commended:**	praised

Summary

The purpose of the play is to amuse us; the foolishness of the characters is to be laughed at rather than taken seriously. Miss Prism, Cecily's governess, suggests that Cecily shouldn't be doing anything useful, like watering flowers. Rather, she should delight in intellectual "pleasures," such as reviewing the German lesson she studied the day before. Cecily objects, claiming that studying German spoils her looks. Miss Prism insists that Cecily's guardian wishes her to study German, but Cecily thinks that her guardian is so serious that he must be ill. Miss Prism defends and admires Jack's seriousness.

Answer Key

Inference

33. (3) The absurd affectations of the characters make us laugh. For example, Miss Prism believes that reviewing a page of German grammar is an "intellectual pleasure"; and Cecily thinks that studying German spoils her looks.

Inference

34. (3) Miss Prism views the study of German as an "intellectual pleasure," but Cecily doesn't like German because it "makes her plain."

Inference

35. (2) A "frivolous" person is not interested in serious ideas or activities. In this passage, Cecily is mainly concerned with watering the flowers and maintaining her beauty. She equates seriousness in others with sickness (lines 15–16).

Inference

36. (2) "Gravity" means seriousness; "demeanour" means manner, or a person's outward behavior.

Inference

37. (4) Miss Prism refers to Uncle Jack as Cecily's "guardian"—a person, other than a parent, who is legally responsible for the welfare of a minor. The minor is known as the guardian's "ward."

Inference

38. (1) "Utilitarian" means useful.

VII

from *Julius Caesar*, by WILLIAM SHAKESPEARE (1564–1616)

Paraphrase: A modern translation

1   **Portia:** Brutus, my dear!
2   **Brutus:** Portia, what's this? Why are you up?
3   It's not good for you
4   In your weak state of health to be out in the damp, cold morning air.
5   **Portia:** And it's not good for you either. You've ungallantly
6   Slipped out of my bed. And last night at supper
7   You suddenly got up and walked around,
8   Thinking deeply and sighing with your arms folded,
9   And when I asked you what was the matter,
10   You stared at me with a hard expression.
11   When I repeated my question, you scratched your head
12   And stamped your foot impatiently.
13   When I insisted, you didn't answer me,
14   But, with an angry wave of your hand,
15   Gestured for me to leave you. My dear,
16   Tell me what's troubling you.
17 **Brutus:** I don't feel well, that's all.
18 **Portia:** You're a sensible man, and if you simply weren't feeling well,
19   You would be taking steps to feel better.

Difficult Words Explained

LINE
2   **wherefore:** why
3   **commit:** expose
5   **ungently:** rudely, ungraciously
6   **yesternight:** last night
8   **musing:** meditating, thinking
      your arms across: your arms folded
14   **wafture:** wave
19   **embrace the means:** find ways

Answer Key

39. (**2**) In lines 3–4, Portia states reasons why Brutus should *not* rise. We can assume then, that her question in line 2 is "*why* do you rise?"

Inference

40. (**1**) The double negative (the use of "nor" and "neither" in the same clause) was standard English in Elizabethan times. This diction (the choice of words) is now archaic because it is not accepted as standard English today.

Literary Forms and Levels of Diction

41. (**2**) The basic meter of the lines is iambic (da DA) pentameter (five feet to a line): da DA/ da DA/ da DA/ da DA/ da DA. (See line 7 for a perfect example of iambic pentameter.) If you are still unsure about how to determine the meter of a poem, review the section on METER in the "Reading Poetry" chapter.

Rhythm and Sound Devices

42. (**3**) It is evident from the loving concern Portia expresses, that she is primarily anxious (worried), not angry, injured, or teasing.

Inference

43. **(2)** Brutus' sleeplessness, pacing, and irritability indicate that he is worried about something. If he were really in poor health, he would probably have told Portia earlier, instead of behaving so strangely (lines 5–15). Portia notes too, that if Brutus were ill, he would do something about it (lines 18–19).

Inference

44. **(3)** Throughout the passage, Portia is loving, respectful, and concerned, eliminating choices (2) and (4) which express impatience and anger respectively. Choice (2), moreover, is a modern colloquial expression which is not appropriate to the Elizabethan English of the selection. Choice (1) does not conform to the meter of the passage.

Inference

VIII

from *Huckleberry Finn,* a novel by MARK TWAIN (SAMUEL CLEMENS) (1835–1910)

Difficult Words Explained

LINE

8   **victuals:**   food
10   **a barrel of odds and ends:**   a pot in which various foods are cooked together
13   **Moses and the Bulrushers:**   Moses and the Bulrushes, a story from the Bible. Pharaoh planned to kill all Jewish male babies. To save her son's life, Moses' mother placed the infant in a basket, which she set adrift on the Nile. Pharaoh's daughter found the basket among some bulrushes (water plants) and adopted little Moses, who grew up to be a great leader and prophet who delivered the Jewish people from their Egyptian captivity.
17   **take no stock in:**   not care about
21   **get down on:**   disapprove of
22   **kin:**   relative
23   **finding a power of fault:**   criticizing severely
25   **snuff:**   ground-up tobacco which is sniffed

Summary

Huck—apparently a boy who has been neglected—has been given a home by a widow. She is a religious woman, with definite ideas on how children should be raised. Huck is puzzled by the widow's behavior but submits to it, recognizing her good intentions. When she bows her head to say grace, he believes that she is muttering (complaining) about the food. She reads a Bible story to Huck, but he loses interest when he realizes that Moses is not a live boy. He can't understand why she doesn't approve of his smoking, when she herself takes snuff, and he decides it is because she is not familiar with cigarettes.

Answer Key

45. (1) Huck's speech is colloquial, non-standard English, as evidenced by such expressions as "the widow she," "never meant no harm," "I couldn't do nothing," and "go right to eating."

Style and Tone

46. (3) Huck says that the widow had to "grumble a little" [say grace] over the victuals before anyone could eat. He also tells us that the only thing wrong with them (the victuals) was that "everything was cooked by itself." From these clues we can assume that "victuals" means food.

Inference

47. (3) In lines 21–22 Huck states that the widow disapproved of smoking when she didn't "know nothing about it."

Supporting Detail

48. (4) Huck's pleasure in smoking, his dislike of new clothes, his colloquial speech, and his unfamiliarity with Bible stories indicate that he is not used to "polite" middle class behavior. His appreciation of the widow's good intentions does not suggest mistrust of adults; therefore, choice (1) is wrong. Huck's trust in his own judgment does not indicate an inferiority complex, eliminating choice (2). His taste in food is not elegant, making choice (3) incorrect.

Inference

49. (2) Huck obeys the widow, understanding her good intentions; but he thinks that much of her behavior is strange, and feels uncomfortable in the unfamiliar atmosphere. For example, he feels all "cramped up" in the new clothes (lines 3–4).

Inference

50. (3) The author is slyly satirizing (poking fun at) "civilized," middle class behavior by portraying it through the innocent, uneducated eyes of a child. The reader is invited to question the need for uncomfortable clothing, making a fuss over dead heroes, and "putting down" a habit just because we don't do it.

Style and Tone

51. (2) Huck has not been conditioned or moulded by middle class values. His values are "natural" ones: "good" to Huck is whatever tastes good, feels good, seems good, or seems right. In his uneducated opinion, many of the customs of civilization are plain silly (which represents the author's point of view).

Main Idea

IX

from "The Bear," a short story by WILLIAM FAULKNER (1897–1962)

Difficult Words Explained

LINE

2 **unaxed woods:** woods that have never been cut
3 **malevolent:** wishing evil, harmful
4 **to bay:** to chase by barking, to corner
6 **constricting:** confining, restraining
7 **divined:** predicted or foretold
8 **encompassed:** included

9   **punily:**   weakly
     gnawed: eaten away, picked at
10 **myriad:**   a large number; many
13 **anachronism:**   something which belongs to the past and is out of place in the present
     indomitable: unyielding
     invincible: unconquerable
14 **phantom:**   a ghost or spirit
     epitome: best representation of
     apotheosis: the perfect example of
15 **abhorrence:**   hatred
16 **pygmies:**   dwarfs
18 **absolved:**   freed or released from

Summary

The passage concerns man's attitude toward untamed nature and personal freedom. The author writes with respect for the bear and the wilderness through which he runs. Men fear the wildness of nature and try to destroy it. The bear symbolizes (represents) the free spirit—the wildness—of nature and of all living things which men cannot destroy.

Answer Key

Inference

52. (4) In lines 1–4, the author describes the object of the boy's dream as leaving a "crooked print" (a footprint), being "shaggy, huge, red-eyed," and "big." He is describing an animal, not the wilderness. Choice (1) is wrong. In line 11, the animal is referred to as "the old bear."

Supporting Detail

53. (1) See line 10: The men "... feared it because it was wilderness ..."

Style and Tone

54. (4) In lines 12–13, Faulkner describes the bear as "not even a mortal beast." The bear was "indomitable and invincible." It is considered not to be an ordinary animal—it is immortal and unconquerable. The writer's attitude, therefore, is one of respect.

Inference

55. (1) A clue to the meaning of "anachronism" is found in the phrase, "out of an old dead time," (lines 13–14) meaning, from a time which belongs to the past. Also note that, since the author respects the bear, he would not refer to it in any of the ways suggested by choices (2), (3), or (4).

Main Idea

56. (4) A *symbol* is something which represents something else. In this passage, the bear symbolizes wild, unconquerable nature which can never be tamed.

Figures of Speech

57. (1) The phrase is a comparison which uses the word "like." It is therefore a *simile*.

X

from "The Tell-Tale Heart," a short story by EDGAR ALLAN POE (1809–1849)

Difficult Words Explained

LINE

4   **acute:** sharp
5   **hearken:** listen
8   **conceived:** thought of
     object there was none: there was no hidden reason
12   **vulture:** an ugly bird that eats the flesh of dead animals

Summary

The narrator is explaining how he came to "take the life of" an old man. He didn't dislike his victim, but one of the old man's eyes was covered with a film. The narrator developed a feeling of horror for the eye and decided to destroy it by killing the old man. The narrator assures us that he is perfectly sane: in fact, his senses are even sharper than normal.

Answer Key

58. (1) At the beginning of the passage, the narrator says that he is nervous, but not mad.   **Supporting Detail**

59. (1) See lines 3–4: "Above all was the sense of hearing acute."   **Supporting Detail**

60. (4) In the second paragraph, the narrator admits that he wants to kill the old man because he hated the old man's "pale blue eye." He denies choices (1), (2), and (3).   **Inference**

61. (3) Generally, sane people do not hear things from hell. We can conclude, then, that he *probably was* mentally disturbed.   **Inference**

62. (4) This is the only meaning that follows logically from the first part of the sentence. The narrator speaks of an idea which "entered his brain." He then refers to the idea as having been "conceived." It is clear then, that "conceived" means thought of.   **Inference**

63. (1) The eagerness and excitement with which the narrator tells his story eliminate choices (2), (3), and (4). Both the subject—the plan to murder an old man—and the writing style—many short sentences—build up a mood of horror and suspense.   **Style and Tone**

XI

from "A Little Cloud," a short story by JAMES JOYCE (1882–1941)

Difficult Words Explained

LINE

4   **composure:** calmness
5   **repelled:** rejected
     defied: resisted

6   **rapture:**   ecstasy, joy
8   **voluptuous:**   sensuous
12   **hire system:**   paying for something on the installment plan
24   **keener:**   more intense

Summary

Little Chandler feels trapped by his marriage, his home, his life. Everything around him is confining and dull. He longs to be a poet, like Byron, and express himself, but he feels unable to escape from the circumstances which control his life.

Answer Key

Inference

64. **(3)** The word "keener" means more intense. Note that Little Chandler rocked the baby faster after "its wailing cry grew keener." He was trying to quiet the child, whose cries were growing more intense.

Supporting Detail

65. **(3)** In the first paragraph, Little Chandler notes the lack of passion and rapture in his wife's eyes. In the second paragraph, his "prim and pretty" furniture reminds him of his wife. He then feels "a dull resentment against his life." The picture of Little Chandler's wife, then, symbolizes (represents) the lack of excitement and rapture in his life.

Rhythm and Sound Devices

66. **(1)** In the preceding paragraphs, Little Chandler thinks about his life and grows more and more frustrated. His mind jumps from one thought to the next, without reaching a solution to his problem. In the same way, the last three lines of the passage are short and choppy. The short sentences reflect Little Chandler's impatience and frustration by forcing the reader to start and stop several times.

Inference

67. **(3)** Calmness.

Style and Tone

68. **(3)** Little Chandler repeatedly questions the meaning of his life and wishes he could change it. See lines 14–18. The last line provides the final clue to his trapped feeling. "He was a prisoner for life."

Inference

69. **(4)** Choice (4) is the only answer that is consistent with Little Chandler's impatience and frustration. It would be natural for him to take out some of his anger on the crying baby. The other choices reflect a mood of patience and calm.

XII

from "Departing Guests," an essay by J. B. PRIESTLEY (1894–   )

Difficult Words Explained

LINE

4   **business hospitality:**   feeling obligated to entertain business associates
5   **corruption:**   dishonesty, immorality
15   **animated:**   lively, very active

Summary

The author discusses his attitude toward having guests. He enjoys being a host for people whom he likes, but is happy when they leave. Then he feels freer and more relaxed. He no longer feels tied down to the solid world, and enjoys letting his thoughts roll around like a gas.

Answer Key

70. (4) An *essay* is a prose composition in which the author discusses a subject from his own point of view.

Literary Forms and Levels of Diction

71. (3) The author comments that when his guests leave, "they leave more room in which to live properly." The remainder of the passage adds to the feeling that he is more relaxed, or feels freer, without guests.

Supporting Detail

72. (2) This phrase is a *metaphor* because it makes a comparison without "as" or "like." The author suggests that his mind is relaxed. Instead of saying this directly, he says it metaphorically—comparing his mind to someone who "puts on [his] old clothes again," or relaxes.

Figures of Speech

73. (1) In the first half of the passage, Priestley comments that he refuses invitations because he doesn't like to be a guest, only entertains people he likes, and doesn't believe in "business hospitality." We can conclude then, that he behaves according to his own needs; that is, according to his own likes and desires. He does not feel obligated to do what other people expect him to do. Choices (2), (3), and (4) are, therefore, wrong.

Inference

74. (4) In the two preceding sentences, Priestley jokes that after his guests have gone, he turns into gas again. (This means that he feels free-spirited again.) The dashes and dots, and the incomplete good-by ("Good—"), jokingly suggest that he has risen into the air and disappeared the way a gas would.

Inference

75. (3) The words that come before and describe "pieces" are "animated and talkative." "Animated" means lively. "Pieces," then, must refer to "people," and not to the other choices.

Figures of Speech

XIII

from *Walden,* a book of essays by HENRY DAVID THOREAU (1817–1862)

Difficult Words Explained

LINE

1   **dinning:**   repeating persistently
5   **pygmies:**   dwarfs
7   **endeavor:**   try
8   **desperate haste:**   frantic hurry
9   **enterprises:**   activities, undertakings

Summary

Throughout the passage, Thoreau expresses the idea that all men should live according to their own needs and abilities. We shouldn't compare ourselves to men of the past, or even to our companions. Every man must make his own life-style.

Answer Key

Literary Forms and Levels of Diction

76. **(1)** A "proverb" is a wise saying written in figurative language. It is a metaphor because it makes comparisons. In this proverb, "a living dog" refers to modern man, whom many consider an "intellectual dwarf[s]." The "dead lion" represents the ancients, or intellectual giants. Thoreau's point is that modern man, even if he is only average (a "dog"), is more useful than the once brilliant, but now dead ancients (the "lions").

Main Idea

77. **(4)** The author stresses the idea that every man should "endeavor to be what he was made." This has nothing to do with being better than anyone else, which is what choices (1), (2), and (3) imply. Thoreau's concern for individuality is a suggestion for living.

Inference

78. **(1)** A conformist lives his life the way other people live theirs. He is afraid to develop his own life-style. This passage makes it clear that its author was *not* a conformist, because it stresses individuality—living in accord with one's own needs.

Style and Tone

79. **(1)** An *aphorism* is a proverb. ("Proverb" is defined in answer 76.) The style of this passage is aphoristic because it contains many aphorisms. In addition to the proverb quoted in question 76, others can be found in the third and last sentences of the passage.

Supporting Detail

80. **(4)** "Irrelevant" means having no relation to, or nothing to do with something else. A clue to the answer is in line 3: "But what is that to the purpose?" This means that comparisons between modern men and men of the past are irrelevant because they have nothing to do with "the purpose": each man fulfilling his own needs.

Figures of Speech

81. **(3)** The last sentence is a metaphor. The "drummer" represents each man's own needs and ideals. Thoreau means that if a man does not conform ("keep pace") to the life-style of the majority ("his companions"), it is because he lives the way his own thoughts tell him to ("he hears a different drummer").

XIV

Excerpt 1 from *Cheaper by the Dozen,* an autobiography by FRANK B. GILBRETH, JR. (1911–   ) and ERNESTINE GILBRETH CAREY (1908–   )

Difficult Words Explained

LINE

2   **offspring:** children
3   **a tender age:** a young age
6   **plot:** mark

Summary

Dad managed his children as an employer manages his employees, requiring them to carry out daily routines and to keep records of having done so.

Answer Key

82. (3) An authoritarian person is one who reserves all decision-making power for himself. Dad's strict rules for his children indicate that he is somewhat authoritarian.

Inference

Excerpt 2 from "Dreams," an essay by J. B. PRIESTLEY (1894–   )

Difficult Words Explained

LINE

4   **lightning:**   extremely fast
     excursions: short pleasure trips

Summary

The author values his dreams. The dimension that dreaming adds to everyday waking consciousness is compared to "extra continents"; entering and leaving the dream state is like a split-second trip to and from these "extra continents."

Answer Key

83. (3) The author represents the dream world as "two extra continents added to the world" (lines 3–4). The "lightning excursions" represent his passages to and from these "extra continents" when he dreams.

**Figures
of Speech**

Excerpt 3   from *The Immoralist*, a novel by ANDRÉ GIDE (1869–1951)

Difficult Words Explained

LINE

2   **convalescence:**   period of recovering from a serious illness
5   **miscellaneous:**   assorted, unrelated
8   **authentic:**   real

Summary

Recovery from near-death can be "tragic" because it can mean the "death" of one's old self. Values and behaviors that had been considered important are no longer so. The false person one was taught to be "gets peeled off," exposing one's real emotions and the truth of one's being.

Answer Key

84. (1) "Bare skin" represents the author's basic personality, the "flesh" of the real man buried under the "civilized" behavior he had been taught.

**Figures
of Speech**

QUESTION NUMBER	MAIN IDEA	SUPPORTING DETAILS	INFERENCE	STYLE AND TONE	FIGURES OF SPEECH	RHYTHM AND SOUND DEVICES	LITERARY FORMS AND LEVELS OF DICTION	CORRECT ANSWERS	SKILLS PAGE
1			✔						62–80, 108–119
2			✔						62–80, 108–119
3					✔				81–92
4					✔				81–92
5			✔						62–80, 108–119
6		✔							51–55
7							✔		120–129
8						✔			92–107
9			✔						62–80, 108–119
10				✔					69–80
11						✔			92–107
12							✔		120–129
13					✔	✔			81–92, 92–109
14						✔			81–92
15				✔					69–80
16	✔								26–51
17			✔						62–80, 108–119
18			✔						62–80, 108–119
19						✔			81–92
20						✔			81–92
21				✔					69–80
22					✔	✔			81–92
23					✔				81–92
24					✔				81–92
25					✔				81–92
26			✔						62–80, 108–119
27							✔		120–129
28			✔						62–80, 108–119
29			✔						62–80, 108–119
30			✔						62–80, 108–119
31			✔						62–80, 108–119
32			✔						62–80, 108–119
33			✔						62–80, 108–119
34			✔						62–80, 108–119
35			✔						62–80, 108–119
36			✔						62–80, 108–119
37			✔						62–80, 108–119
38			✔						62–80, 108–119
39			✔						62–80, 108–119
40							✔		120–129
41						✔			81–92
42			✔						62–80, 108–119

READING SKILLS EVALUATION CHART—SIMULATED TEST

QUESTION NUMBER	MAIN IDEA	SUPPORTING DETAILS	INFERENCE	STYLE AND TONE	FIGURES OF SPEECH	RHYTHM AND SOUND DEVICES	LITERARY FORMS AND LEVELS OF DICTION	CORRECT ANSWERS	SKILLS PAGE
43			✔						62–80, 108–119
44			✔						62–80, 108–119
45				✔					69–80
46			✔						62–80, 108–119
47		✔							51–55
48			✔						62–80, 108–119
49			✔						62–80, 108–119
50				✔					69–80
51	✔								26–51
52			✔						62–80, 108–119
53		✔							51–55
54				✔					69–80
55			✔						62–80, 108–119
56	✔								26–51
57					✔				81–92
58		✔							51–55
59		✔							51–55
60			✔						62–80, 108–119
61			✔						62–80, 108–119
62			✔						62–80, 108–119
63				✔					69–80
64			✔						62–80, 108–119
65		✔							51–55
66						✔			81–92
67			✔						62–80, 108–119
68				✔					69–80
69			✔						62–80, 108–119
70							✔		120–129
71		✔							51–55
72					✔				81–92
73			✔						62–80, 108–119
74			✔						62–80, 108–119
75					✔				81–92
76							✔		120–129
77	✔								26–51
78			✔						62–80, 108–119
79				✔					69–80
80		✔							51–55
81					✔				81–92
82			✔						62–80, 108–119
83					✔				81–92
84					✔				81–92

MY SCORE

BIOGRAPHIES

It is often said that writers write best about those things they know best. The experiences that a writer has, and the conclusions he draws from those experiences, may provide the theme, topic, or characters for a work of literature. Of course, not all writing is autobiographical; a writer's ability to create characters, settings, and experiences is one of his greatest talents. However, because so much of a writer's work is influenced by his experiences, it is interesting, and often enlightening, to know something about his life.

On the following pages are short biographies of many of the writers whose works appear in this book. All of the authors of the selections in the Diagnostic and Simulated Tests are included, as well as the authors of the longer passages used for practice tests and exercises. At the beginning of each biography is a list of the works by that author quoted in this book.

Although you will not be required to know biographical information about the authors of the reading selections on the High School Equivalency Examination, these biographies can be very helpful to you. It is greatly to your advantage to do extra reading in works of literature. You may have found some of the reading passages in this book particularly interesting or particularly difficult. Some knowledge of the author's life not only makes his writings more interesting, but also is helpful in understanding them. Additional works by the authors are mentioned, and sometimes described, in the biographies. Your local library will have many of these books on its shelves; most are available in inexpensive paperback editions. The poets are represented in anthologies of English and American poetry.

William Blake (1757–1827)

"The Sword and the Sickle," "Ah Sun-flower," "The Tyger," "The Lamb," "Auguries of Innocence," "The Echoing Green" William Blake was an English poet, engraver, and painter. He was also a mystic who, as a child, had visions of God, the prophet Ezekiel, and a tree full of angels. The visions he had throughout his life greatly influenced Blake's poetry. Blake received his only formal education in art and, at fourteen, he began a seven-year apprenticeship with an engraver. During that time he began writing poetry. Blake married Catherine Boucher when he was twenty-four. She was illiterate, but Blake taught her to read and write. She was very devoted to him although she once remarked, "I have very little of Mr. Blake's company; he is always in Paradise."

Beginning with *Songs of Innocence* (1789), Blake engraved his poems and illustrations, and then painted each page with watercolors. In *Songs of Innocence* Blake wrote for and about children. Later, in *Songs of Experience* (1794) he expressed his concern for the social ills of poverty, disease, prostitution, and war. The poems in *Songs of Experience* also reflect Blake's view that the root of all evil is repression—moral, institutional, and sexual. Like Shelley, Blake was a strong supporter of the French Revolution. He believed that political revolutions represented the violence predicted in the Book of Revelation, and were necessary before the world could be redeemed.

During his sixties, Blake devoted himself to painting and engraving. When he died, he was a little-known artist and poet. Since the mid-nineteenth century, however, he has been recognized as a highly original and brilliant artist and poet. His chief works include *Songs of Innocence* and *Songs of Experience, The Visions of the Daughters of Albion, Milton,* and *Jerusalem.*

Elizabeth Barrett Browning (1806–1861)

"How Do I Love Thee?"   Elizabeth Barrett Browning was an English poet and wife of Robert Browning, also a poet. Elizabeth became seriously ill at the age of 15 and was a partial invalid at the time she met Robert Browning. Her father disapproved of their marriage, but they ran off to Italy together and married. Their only child, Robert, was born there in 1849. Elizabeth is best remembered for her collection of love poems, *Sonnets from the Portuguese.* The story of the Brownings' love affair became the subject of a play, *The Barretts of Wimpole Street,* written by Rudolph Besier in 1931.

Willa Cather (1893–1947)

"The Sculptor's Funeral"   Willa Cather was thoroughly American. Her ancestors had farmed in Virginia for almost 100 years before her birth there, and her family later moved to Red Cloud, Nebraska, a pioneer settlement. Nebraska, however, was also the home of recent European immigrants, many of them German or Scandinavian. From them she learned about music and other cultures—information she later used in her novels and stories. Her Nebraskan friends and neighbors even became characters in those stories.

After attending the University of Nebraska, Miss Cather worked on a Pittsburgh newspaper and began publishing poetry and stories in *McClure's Magazine* and *Cosmopolitan.* Later she taught school there. Before joining the staff of *McClure's Magazine* in 1906, she had already published a book of poems, *April Twilights,* and a collection of short stories called *The Troll Garden,* which contains "The Sculptor's Funeral." "The Enchanted Bluff," published in 1909, was the first of her stories set in a Southwestern locale. Her novels include *O Pioneers!* (1913), *The Song of the Lark* (1915), *One of Ours* (1922), for which she was later awarded the Pulitzer Prize, *Death Comes for the Archbishop* (1927), and *My Mortal Enemy* (1926). Her later novels are each studies of one woman. *My Mortal Enemy* is the first novel stripped of all extraneous characters and situations to focus on one individual.

G. K. Chesterton (1874–1936)

"A Ballade of Suicide"   Gilbert Keith Chesterton was a versatile man. Born into an English Anglican family, he converted to Roman Catholicism in 1922. Much of his writing after that date indicates his concern for the spreading of Christian ideals. Although Chesterton tended to be conservative in his political as well as in his religious views, his sense of humor and his conversational talents brought him many admirers who did not always agree with him.

Chesterton viewed the "chief idea of his life" as the ability to see things in a new way, and much of his writing indicates that he was quite an original thinker. His critical works, *Robert Browning* (1903), *Charles Dickens* (1906), *George Bernard Shaw* (1909), *Robert Louis Stevenson* (1927), and *Chaucer* (1932), are considered brilliant. Chesterton's *St. Francis of Assisi* (1923) and *St. Thomas Aquinas* (1933) have also received great tribute from theologians for their originality and insight.

Chesterton is best known for his essays such as the humorous "On Running After One's Hat," and the Father Brown detective novels.

Hart Crane (1899–1932)

"Fear"   Hart Crane was an American poet whose short life ended violently. Born in Garrettsville, Ohio, as Harold Hart Crane, he was the son of a successful candy manufacturer who planned a business career for him. Crane had other ideas. He published his first poem at the age of 15 and planned a career as a writer. Shortly afterwards, his parents separated and Crane soon went off on his own. He worked as a mechanic, clerk, and reporter before moving to New York City in 1922. There he found work as a writer of advertising copy and slowly sold a few poems. His first volume, *White Buildings*, was published in 1926.

During this time, Crane lived in Brooklyn Heights, which gave him a good view of the Brooklyn Bridge. It came to symbolize for him the connection between the sea, the city, and its people, and was the subject of his poem, "The Bridge." This poem won the annual *Poetry* magazine award in 1930. In 1931, Crane received a Guggenheim Fellowship for use in Mexico, where he planned to write a long poem based on Mexican history. His failure to complete the project, combined with other disappointments, led him to commit suicide by jumping off the ship on which he was returning to New York City.

Stephen Crane (1871–1900)

"War Is Kind"   Stephen Crane (no relation to Hart Crane) was an American novelist and poet. The youngest of 14 children, Crane was born in Newark, New Jersey, and spent much of his life in New Jersey and New York City. After his father died in 1880, the Crane family lived on very little money, and Stephen's education ended after one year in college (1890–1891). He worked on his brother's newspaper and sold articles to the Detroit

Free Press and later to the New York *Tribune*. In 1893, unable to sell his story, "Maggie: A Girl of the Streets," Crane borrowed $700 and printed it himself. His private edition came to the attention of Hamlin Garland, also a novelist, who then introduced Crane to William Dean Howells. *The Red Badge of Courage* was published in 1894 in The Philadelphia *Press*, and then in 1895 in book form with Howells' help. Crane's five remaining years were spent as a correspondent for American and English newspapers. His stories about the Spanish-American and Graeco-Turkish wars led to books entitled *The Little Regiment, The Open Boat,* and *Wounds in the Rain: War Stories*. His volumes of poetry are *The Black Riders and Other Lines* and *War Is Kind*. Crane died of tuberculosis in Germany.

Crane's novels and short stories were unique in American literature, although similar themes were being used by writers in Europe. Crane used a technique he had learned as a journalist. He described events without comment or moralizing. His style was called "Naturalism," a belief that the fate of human beings is determined by factors completely out of their control. This idea became popular in later years with other American writers such as Theodore Dreiser.

E. E. Cummings (1894–1962)

"in Just-," "my specialty is living" Edward Estlin Cummings, who for most of his life insisted on signing his works "e. e. cummings," was born in Cambridge, Massachusetts. He received his M.A. from Harvard University in 1916. During World War I, before the United States entered the war, he joined the Norton Harjes Ambulance Corps. During his service in France he was falsely accused of sending treasonous letters, and was imprisoned in a French detention camp. This prison experience was recounted in his 1922 novel, *The Enormous Room*. After the war, Cummings studied painting in Paris.

Cummings' poetry has influenced a whole generation of poets. He ignored all the old rules about punctuation, capitalization and rhyme schemes. Cummings often ran many words together so that they appeared as a long string of letters. He also divided words in original ways, sometimes combining parts of several words to form a new one. As a result, Cummings' poems often look like word games which must be unscrambled by the reader. Through this method, though, he was able to convey ideas in new, and often humorous ways. Cummings' poems reflected his love of life and the workings of nature. He wrote freely about love and sex, always with respect for the human body and spirit. He also satirized those people whom he thought were anti-life, like advertisers and extreme patriots, and people who sacrificed their integrity and individuality in order to earn large sums of money. His collections of poetry include *Tulips and Chimneys* (1923), *ViVa* (1931), and *95 Poems* (1958). Other works by Cummings are *Eimi* (1933), an experiment in prose, *Tom* (1935), a poetic drama, and *CIOPW* (1931), a book of his paintings and drawings.

Emily Dickinson (1830–1886)

" 'Hope' is the thing with feathers," "It Sifts from Leaden Sieves," "The Lightning is a yellow Fork," "The Sea and the Brook," "There is No Frigate Like a Book"   Emily Dickinson was born in Amherst, Massachusetts, and spent most of her life there. Her father was a lawyer and treasurer of Amherst College. A strict Calvinist, he had a very strong influence on his daughter's life. She attended Mount Holyoke Female Seminary, but could not tolerate the strict academic regulations, and returned home in less than a year. She never left Amherst again, except for short trips to Boston, Philadelphia, and Washington, D.C. while still young. After returning from the Seminary, it is believed that she fell in love with Ben Newton, a young man who lived with her family as her father's law apprentice. He had a great influence on her thinking, and introduced her to the work of Ralph Waldo Emerson. Newton died of tuberculosis five years later. During later years, she dressed only in white and rarely left her room. From 1884 until her death in 1886, she was a semi-invalid.

Emily Dickinson wrote close to 2000 poems, but probably no more than seven were published during her lifetime. Her poems are short and contain many concentrated images. Although she lived a confined life, her ideas are witty, rebellious, and original. The definitive edition of Emily Dickinson's poetry is *The Poems of Emily Dickinson*, edited by Thomas H. Johnson.

William Faulkner (1897–1962)

"Speech on Receiving the Nobel Prize," "The Bear"   William Faulkner, considered one of America's greatest novelists, did not finish high school. In 1918, at the age of twenty-one, he enlisted in the Canadian Royal Flying Corps. He returned after a year, and attended the University of Mississippi for two years. Faulkner became interested in writing, and in 1924 he went to New Orleans. There he worked on an experimental magazine and published two novels. He returned to Oxford, Mississippi, in 1925, where he began his significant work.

Faulkner's major works take place in Yoknapatawpha County, an imaginary area in Mississippi based on Lafayette County, where Faulkner lived. Faulkner often wrote about the Southern social structure. He was concerned with the problems caused by the South's past; in particular, the relations between the races. He was also interested in the loneliness experienced by twentieth-century man.

The Sound and The Fury, which deals with the decay of an aristocratic Southern family, is one of Faulkner's finest novels. In *Light in August*, Faulkner tells the story of a black man, Joe Christmas. *Sanctuary* is among Faulkner's greatest works. It concerns the corruption of youth and criminal influence in a small town during the prohibition era. Among Faulkner's other works are *The Hamlet, Go Down, Moses, As I Lay Dying*, and *Old Man*. In 1950, he received the Nobel Prize.

Gustave Flaubert (1821–1880)

Madame Bovary   Although his father was a doctor and he himself studied law, Flaubert was most comfortable with literature. After his father's death in 1846, he lived at home with his mother in Rouen, France, and spent most of his time writing. His first novel, *Madame Bovary*, appeared in 1857.

Flaubert never married, but he did develop strong friendships with many women. One was George Sand, a female novelist. Another was Flaubert's niece, Caroline, whom Flaubert educated. His letters document his various love affairs and his attraction to a Mademoiselle Schlesinger, whom he met when he was 14. Whether any of these women served as a model for Emma Bovary remains a mystery. The heroine of Flaubert's most famous novel is a dreamer who hopes for a life of luxury, but instead marries a dull country doctor. After having several love affairs and accumulating huge debts, Emma takes arsenic to end her troubles. Flaubert and his editor were both brought to trial on obscenity charges for *Madame Bovary*, but were acquitted. Flaubert was an extremely careful writer who worked and reworked every sentence. Except for short visits to Paris and two trips to the Near East, he rarely left home. Nevertheless, he produced several books, including *Salammbo* (1862), *Sentimental Education* (1869), *The Temptation of St. Anthony* (1874), and *Three Tales* (1877).

Andre Gidé (1869–1951)

The Immoralist   Born in Paris, Gide lived a long and varied life. He wrote novels, essays, plays, and criticism, and he influenced a whole generation of French authors. Gide received the Nobel Prize in 1947. Gide's ideas, like his activities, were unconventional. Raised as a strict Protestant in a country where most people were Catholic, Gide grew up with a strong sense of guilt about sex and about his belief in science, which conflicted with his religion. Gide eventually believed that progress comes through new or odd ideas, not through the repetition of stale ones. His sympathy for unpopular causes led him to visit the Soviet Union, but he later rejected the Communist system.

In 1893, suffering from tuberculosis, Gide went to North Africa. Two years later, after another visit to Africa, he married his cousin Madeleine. During this time, he was writing novels which explored the themes of self-restraint and inhibition. *Fruits of the Earth* is a celebration of pleasure, while *The Immoralist* warns that excessive feeling may lead to madness. *Strait is the Gate*, written two years after *The Immoralist*, is the story of a woman who is so straitlaced that she can never be happy. The woman in this novel resembled Gide's own wife in this respect. Most of Gide's works retell his own life. In fact, Gide believed that all a man can really know is himself.

In his best-known work, *The Counterfeiters,* Gide again discusses the relationship between inhibition and free expression of emotion. He fears that men are blind to their own feelings—that they cannot face their problems or see their own good qualities. He suggests that they must follow their deepest feelings, no matter where they may lead.

Gide traveled widely and knew several languages. He was also a critic and began an important literary magazine, *Nouvelle Revue Française*. His last years were recorded in notebooks which were published the year after his death.

Frank B. Gilbreth, Jr. (1911–   ) and Ernestine Gilbreth Carey (1908–   )

Cheaper by the Dozen   Frank Gilbreth, Jr. and Ernestine Gilbreth Carey grew up in a family of twelve children. Both their parents were engineers and management consultants particularly interested in the efficient use of time in industry. *Cheaper by the Dozen* is a humorous account of life in the Gilbreth household.

Frank Gilbreth, Jr. has been a newspaper reporter, editor, and publisher in South Carolina. Among his other books, are *Belles on Their Toes* (with John Held, Jr.), *How To Be a Father*, and *He's My Boy*. Ernestine Gilbreth Carey is a lecturer and writer. Included in her writings are *Jumping Juniper, Ring Around Us*, and *Giddy Monument*.

Ernest Hemingway (1899–1961)

The Old Man and the Sea   Hemingway was born in Illinois. He worked as a reporter for the Kansas City *Star*, and during World War I joined a volunteer ambulance unit in France. His experiences in the war greatly influenced Hemingway's writing. *A Farewell to Arms* is the story of an English nurse and an American ambulance driver. After the war, he lived in Paris where he associated with many American writers and artists who did not wish to return to the United States.

Much of Hemingway's writing expresses the feelings of this "lost generation." They were greatly disillusioned by the war and could no longer accept their old values—they had discovered that war brings misery, not glory. In *The Sun Also Rises*, Hemingway wrote about a group of Americans living in Paris after the war. The characters, particularly Jake Barnes and Lady Brett, are spiritually empty. Hemingway was sympathetic to the Loyalists (the anti-Franco forces) during the Spanish Civil War, and in 1937 went to Spain as a reporter. His experiences during the war are reflected in a play, *The Fifth Column*, and a novel, *For Whom the Bell Tolls*.

In 1954, Hemingway won the Nobel Prize for *The Old Man and the Sea*, a novel about a man's struggle with nature. Some of his other works are *In Our Time, Men Without Women* (short stories), *Death in the Afternoon* (a novel about bullfighting), and *Across the River and Into the Trees* (about an aging colonel, thought to represent Hemingway). Two of his finest short stories are "The Short Happy Life of Francis Macomber" and "The Snows of Kilimanjaro." Hemingway published very little toward the end of his life, but wrote a great deal. His wife is currently organizing his last works into novels and stories. Hemingway died in 1961, shortly after shooting himself with his own gun.

Gerard Manley Hopkins (1844–1889)

"God's Grandeur," "Spring and Fall: To a Young Child"   Hopkins was an English poet and a Jesuit priest. As a student at Balliol College, Oxford, he was influenced by Robert Bridges (a poet) and Cardinal Newman. Hopkins converted to Roman Catholicism in 1866, and in May 1868 decided to become a Jesuit priest. He burned his poems during the following summer and vowed not to write poetry again. During that year, he entered the Jesuit Order.

Hopkins wrote nothing for the next seven years. In 1875, however, the death of five nuns by drowning affected him deeply. He broke his poetic silence with "The Wreck of the Deutschland," considered his first great poem. During the next two years he wrote some short stories and sonnets, including "The Windhover," a frequently quoted poem. Hopkins' poems reflect his love of nature and a deep faith in its creation by God. He also wrote of his experiences as a priest and expressed his concern over the effects of industrialization on society.

In 1884 Hopkins became professor of Greek at Dublin University. During the final years of his life, he experienced great torment and depression. This mood is reflected in his last poems, including the so-called "terrible sonnets," which express his feeling of alienation from God.

Even though he wrote during the Victorian period, Hopkins is considered a modern poet because of his original poetic techniques. He had a great influence on several twentieth-century British and American poets, including W. H. Auden and Dylan Thomas. Hopkins' best-known poems include "The Windhover," "Pied Beauty," "The Caged Skylark," "Felix Randall," and "The Leaden Echo and the Golden Echo."

Langston Hughes (1902–1967)

"Coffee Break"   Langston Hughes is among the best-known black American poets. His themes deal with the problems and joys of American blacks, and his poems often contain jazz rhythms and black dialect. Hughes began writing while he was a high school student in Cleveland. He supported himself by writing before his graduation from Lincoln University in 1929: *Weary Blues* was published in 1926. His other volumes of poetry include *The Dream Keeper* (1932) and *Ask Your Mama* (1961). At least one of his poems caused an uproar. When a young teacher, Jonathan Kozol, taught Hughes' poem "Ballad of a Landlord" to his fourth-grade class in Boston in 1965, school officials became angry and claimed that the poem was not on the curriculum. Kozol was fired from his job shortly afterward.

Hughes wrote in other forms besides poetry. Many of his humorous sketches about his character Jesse B. Simple were first published in a newspaper and later collected in two books, *Simple Speaks His Mind* (1950) and *The Best of Simple* (1961).

Ben Jonson (1572–1637)

Volpone   Ben Jonson is one of the few writers in the history of English literature lucky enough to have been equally popular during his lifetime and after his death. His poems and criticism influenced writers for 200 years.

Orphaned at an early age, Jonson was adopted by a bricklayer and educated at Westminster School. Although he later received honorary degrees from both Oxford and Cambridge, he never studied at either university. Instead, he worked as a bricklayer, soldier, and actor. He was also jailed a few times. Through his playwriting, Jonson became friendly with famous men who were in London at the time. Among them were John Donne, William Shakespeare, Francis Beaumont, and John Fletcher. Shakespeare, in fact, acted the leading role in Jonson's first play, *Every Man in his Humour*. After writing several more plays, including two very successful comedies, *Volpone* (1606) and *The Alchemist* (1610), Jonson staged some spectacles for King James I. He was made Poet Laureate in 1616.

Jonson marked a turning point in English literature. The language of the Elizabethan poets had contained many complex metaphors. Jonson and the poets who followed him used simpler, more specific language. Ben Jonson is buried in Westminster Abbey. His inscription reads: "O Rare Ben Jonson."

James Joyce (1882–1941)

"A Little Cloud"   James Joyce, one of the greatest writers of the twentieth century, was a rebel in both his personal and professional life and made radical changes in the art of the novel. His characters' thoughts often seem disconnected, flowing freely from one idea to another. Joyce's writing also contains made-up words and many complex puns and allusions to mythology, history, and literature. Joyce used these techniques extensively in *Ulysses*, which took seven years to complete, and *Finnegans Wake*, which took seventeen.

Joyce was born in Dublin, the eldest of ten children. His father drifted from job to job and the family grew continually poorer throughout Joyce's boyhood, always trying, however, to maintain middle-class respectability. From the age of six, Joyce attended Catholic schools, which contributed to his later rebellion against Catholicism.

He left Ireland in 1902, breaking away from her traditions and social conventions. Joyce met Nora Barnacle, an uneducated chambermaid, and ran off to Trieste, Italy, with her. Because he did not believe in the rules of the Church, Joyce and Nora did not marry until 1931. Before settling in Paris in 1920, he taught English in Trieste and Zürich, Switzerland, earning very little from his writing until late in life.

In his autobiographical novel, *A Portrait of the Artist as a Young Man*, Joyce wrote of his rebellion against his family background and Catholicism. The hero, Stephen Dedalus, refuses to serve anything in which he does not believe, be it his home, country, or church. Although he exiled himself from Ireland, Joyce's writing is always set in Dublin. One of his great talents, however, was the ability to write about Dubliners as though he were writing about people anywhere.

Both Joyce's literary career and personal life were difficult. Because of his original and complex writing style, his work was often misunderstood. Censors continually charged him with obscenity and banned his books. Joyce's sight grew progressively worse until he was almost blind, but he continued to write with the secretarial help of friends. Joyce died in Zürich in 1941.

Jean Kerr (1923–   )

Mary, Mary   Jean Kerr is an American writer known for her humorous fiction and plays. She was born in Scranton, Pennsylvania, and was educated at Catholic University of America. In 1943 she married the drama critic, Walter Kerr. The Kerrs have six children, whose mischievous activities Mrs. Kerr recalled in her novel, *Please Don't Eat the Daisies.* Her other works include *Jenny Kissed Me, Touch and Go, King of Hearts, The Snake Has All the Lines,* and *Poor Richard.*

Arthur Laurents (1918–   )

A Clearing in the Woods   Arthur Laurents is an American playwright. A native of New York City and graduate of Cornell University, Laurents has written scripts for radio, the stage, and films. He won an award from the American Academy of Arts and Letters for his play, *Home of the Brave* (1946). Later he wrote *Anastasia* and *I Can Get It For You Wholesale.* In *West Side Story*, Laurents adapted the Romeo and Juliet theme to Puerto Ricans living in New York City.

Edna St. Vincent Millay (1892–1950)

"Love Is Not All"   In her poetry and personal life Edna St. Vincent Millay expressed the rebellious spirit of the "jazz age." She began writing poetry as a child and published her first volume of poems before graduating from Vassar in 1917. She spent the next few years in Greenwich Village, New York, supporting herself by publishing poems and stories in magazines.

In her poems, Miss Millay often attacked the social rules that greatly limited the freedom of women. She wrote happily of going "back and forth all night on the ferry," and pretended to forget "what lips my lips have kissed." Miss Millay married Eugen Boissevain in 1923, and lived with him on a farm in the Berkshires. Toward the end of her life, she became very interested in social and political problems. Her major collections of poetry include *Renascence and Other Poems, The Harp-Weaver and Other Poems* (for which she won the Pulitzer Prize in 1923), *The Buck in the Snow and Other Poems,* and *Fatal Interview.*

Sean O'Casey (1880–1964)

"The Harp in the Air Still Sings" Sean O'Casey was born to a Protestant family in Dublin. Because his parents were poor and his eyesight weak, O'Casey received little formal education. Yet, he became one of the greatest of Irish dramatists. Among his best-known plays are *Shadow of a Gunman* (1923) and *Juno and the Paycock* (1924). Produced in Dublin's Abbey Theatre, these plays brought a new working-class audience to the theater. *The Plough and the Stars* (1926), another of O'Casey's best-known plays, is about the Easter Rebellion. Although the pacifist outlook of this play was not well-received at first, the play is now widely accepted. The language of O'Casey's dramas is often poetic. Many of his dramas contain elements of comedy along with their basically tragic themes.

Frank O'Connor (1903–1966)

"My Oedipus Complex" Frank O'Connor is the pen name of Michael O'Donovan, an Irish actor. After being educated by the Christian Brothers in Cork, Ireland, he worked as a librarian. O'Connor continued to train himself for a literary career, and was greatly encouraged by George Russell. He published over two dozen works, including *Three Old Brothers*, a book of poetry; *Leinster, Munster and Connaught*, local travel writing; and *The Saint and Mary Kate,* a novel. O'Connor is well known for his short stories from several collections including *Crab Apple Jelly* and *Travelers' Samples*. His autobiography, *An Only Child*, was published in 1961. O'Connor died in Dublin in 1966.

Eugene O'Neill (1888–1953)

A Moon for the Misbegotten Eugene O'Neill was born in New York City. His father, James O'Neill, was a famous actor, and O'Neill spent much of his early life touring theaters with his family. His real theater training began in 1914 under Professor George Pierce Baker of Harvard at the "47 Workshop."

O'Neill won the Pulitzer Prize for his first full-length play, *Beyond the Horizon* (1919). He also received Pulitzer Prizes for *Anna Christie* (1922) and *Strange Interlude* (1928). These plays and those that followed established O'Neill's reputation as one of America's best playwrights.

Two of O'Neill's best-known and most powerful works are *Mourning Becomes Electra,* a trilogy, and *A Long Day's Journey into Night. Mourning Becomes Electra,* which is often compared to Aeschylus's trilogy, *Oresteia,* is a powerful study of man trying to find the meaning of life and to understand his own destiny. Partly because of this trilogy O'Neill was awarded the Nobel Prize in literature in 1936. *A Long Day's Journey into Night* is a domestic drama based on O'Neill's early life. Written in 1941 and first produced on Broadway in 1956, this play was the first ever to receive a posthumous Pulitzer Prize.

Donald Culross Peattie (1898–1964)

An Almanac for Moderns An American botanist and writer, Peattie worked for the U. S. Department of Agriculture after graduating from Harvard University in 1922. He soon decided to be a writer, and often wrote about nature, combining scientific knowledge with his own impressions and philosophical insights, as in *An Almanac for Moderns*. Peattie's other works include *Flowering Earth, A Natural History of Trees of Eastern and Central America*, and *Sportsman's Country*. In *A Prairie Grove*, he discusses the history of a piece of land in Illinois. Peattie's interest in the influence of the forest on American history is reflected in *American Heartwood. The Road of a Naturalist* is Peattie's autobiography.

Edgar Allan Poe (1809–1849)

"The Bell," "The Tell-Tale Heart" Poe's life might almost have come from one of his own short stories. He was born in Boston, the son of traveling actors. After his father disappeared and his mother died, Poe was taken in by John Allan, a Scottish tobacco importer who lived in Virginia. Poe's extreme attachment to Mrs. Allan was the first in a series of unusual relationships he had with a variety of women. The crush he developed on the mother of one of his friends inspired the poem "To Helen." And in 1835 he secretly married his cousin, Virginia Clemm, who was then 13.

Poe's life was not a particularly happy one. He and John Allan were always arguing, partly because of Mrs. Allan's affection for Poe. Poe was also unstable. He piled up large gambling debts at the University of Virginia and then ran off to Boston when Allan refused to pay them. Later he joined the Army, entered West Point, but dropped out within a year. Even after his marriage to Virginia, Poe kept losing jobs on magazines and newspapers in New York and Philadelphia. From 1838 to 1844 he published many of his famous short stories, some of which won prizes, but his writing did not bring in enough money to keep him from poverty. In 1846 Virginia died of tuberculosis. A few years later, Poe himself was found unconscious on a street in Baltimore; he died a short time afterward.

Poe's work has survived, though, becoming more popular in the last 100 years. His most famous stories include "The Gold Bug," "The Fall of the House of Usher," and "The Pit and the Pendulum."

J. B. P. estley (1894–   )

"Departing Guests," "Dreams" John Boynton Priestley is an English novelist, essayist, and playwright. A strong believer in the goodness of man and in the joy of life, many of his works are humorous. He is also known for his criticism of social injustice.

Priestley and his family lived in Arizona for a few years. He recalled his experiences in America in his autobiography, *Midnight on the Desert*. Among his novels are *The Good Companions* and *Angel Pavement*. His plays include *Dangerous Corner, Laburnum Grove, Eden End, When We Were Married*, and *An Inspector Calls*.

William Shakespeare (1564–1616)

Hamlet, Macbeth, Romeo and Juliet, Julius Caesar, "Sonnet 94," "Sonnet 73" Shakespeare was an English dramatist and poet, considered by many to be the greatest writer in the English language. He was born in Stratford upon Avon. Not many facts about Shakespeare's life are known, but it is assumed that he attended grammar school in Stratford. He did not enter Oxford or Cambridge. Shakespeare married Anne Hathaway in 1582 and by 1585 they had three children. Nothing is known about Shakespeare's life during the next seven years, but by 1592 he was in London, where he acted and was a well-known playwright.

Shakespeare was a member of the Chamberlain's Company, which became the King's Men after 1603, a company of actors who eventually owned their own theater and attracted the patronage of Queen Elizabeth and King James I. He remained in London until some time after 1612, when he retired to Stratford.

Shakespeare's works consist of two long poems, *Venus and Adonis* and *The Rape of Lucrece,* written during his early years in London; a series of 154 sonnets published in 1609; a few miscellaneous poems; and some 37 plays, for which he is best known. Many of these plays were published in imperfect versions during his lifetime. They were collected and published together in 1623.

Many of Shakespeare's early plays (*Henry VI, Richard II, Richard III*) were based on English history. He also experimented with comedies and formal tragedy. In the late 1590's he wrote *Romeo and Juliet,* a romantic tragedy. He also wrote a number of comedies, including *A Midsummer Night's Dream* and *Much Ado About Nothing.*

Between 1600 and 1606 he wrote four tragedies on which his reputation is most firmly based. They are *Hamlet, Othello, King Lear,* and *Macbeth.* During this same period he wrote the "dark comedies," so-called because of their somber mood, such as *Measure for Measure.* His late plays, such as *The Winter's Tale* and *The Tempest,* are allegorical romances, neither really comic nor tragic.

Little is known about Shakespeare's own philosophical or political beliefs. The most universal of dramatists, he seems to blend his own views in those of his many characters.

Percy Bysshe Shelley (1792–1822)

"Ozymandias" Born into the British aristocracy, Shelley was known during his lifetime as a revolutionary who believed in the necessity for radical social reform. His first act of rebellion, a tract he wrote entitled "The Necessity of Atheism," resulted in his being expelled from Oxford.

Shelley's personal life was also unconventional. He eloped with Harriet Westbrook when he was 18 and she 16, but they drifted apart. Though still married to Harriet, he ran off with Mary Wollstonecraft Godwin, whom he married after Harriet committed suicide. Mary was the daughter of Shelley's teacher, William Godwin. In Italy, Shelley and Mary had three children, two of whom died. They developed friendships with Lord Byron and Edward Williams. Shelley and Williams died while sailing at sea during a violent storm. Shelley was 30.

Shelley's poetry also broke with tradition. He experimented with new forms and is considered a major Romantic poet. Influenced by ancient Greek poetry and Plato, Shelley wrote *Prometheus Unbound, The Cenci* (a tragic play), and a poem entitled "Adonais," an elegy on the death of John Keats. Shelley also wrote translations from four languages and original lyric poetry such as "Ode to the West Wind," "To a Skylark," and "Hymn to Intellectual Beauty." Mary, his wife, wrote *Frankenstein*, which has become famous as a movie.

Henry David Thoreau (1817–1862)

Walden   A quiet and simple man, Henry David Thoreau nevertheless was a prophet of trends that are just reaching fruition today. Thoreau did not care about money or a career. Life, he thought, was simply to be lived. So he spent much of his time by himself in the woods, on long walks, or among a few friends. He did odd jobs to support himself, tutored children, or kept house for Ralph Waldo Emerson.

The second son in a poor family, Thoreau graduated from Harvard University in 1837. There he began to write his *Journals*. These contained most of the ideas and sketches that were published by friends after his death, in volumes called *The Maine Woods, Cape Cod,* and *A Yankee in Canada.* During his life, he published poems in a magazine called *The Dial* and two books, *A Week on the Concord and Merrimack Rivers* (1849) and *Walden* (1854). *The Dial* was sponsored by the Transcendental Club, a group of men from Concord and Boston who shared similar philosophical views. Thoreau also became friendly with Walt Whitman and Bronson Alcott. Emerson and Thoreau were the first to recognize the greatness of Whitman's poetry.

Thoreau is most famous for his feelings about nature, as expressed in *Walden*. He believed that in this one place, Walden Pond, could be found all the different elements of the universe. He lived in the woods near Walden Pond for two years, growing his own food and watching the life around him. However, he was also deeply concerned about social issues. He believed in abolition, and spoke at anti-slavery rallies, once with John Brown. He also refused to pay unjust taxes, such as church taxes which were applied equally to all people, whether or not they were church members. His refusal to pay the poll tax in 1854 led to his being jailed for a day. Later he wrote his theory about passive resistance in an essay entitled "Civil Disobedience." This concept became the basis of resistance campaigns waged by Gandhi in India. Other volumes excerpted from Thoreau's *Journals* and published after his death are *Excursions, Early Spring in Massachusetts,* and *Poems of Nature.*

James Thurber (1894–1961)

"The Case Against Women" James Grover Thurber was born in Columbus, Ohio, which served as the source for many of his essays and drawings. Because a childhood accident had left him blind in one eye, Thurber was barred from military service during World War I. However, because of his exceptional ability to remember names and other details, he was able to work as a code clerk for the State Department.

Thurber's writing career developed slowly. He worked for various newspapers, such as the *Chicago Tribune* and the *New York Evening Post*. Eventually he was employed by *The New Yorker* magazine, for which he wrote many of his best pieces. As the number of his essays and drawings increased, so did Thurber's fame. His essays and drawings were published as books, the best-known of which are *The Owl in the Attic* (1931), *My World—And Welcome to It* (1942), and *The Thurber Carnival* (1945).

Mark Twain (1835–1910)

The Adventures of Huckleberry Finn This American writer of novels, humorous and satirical sketches, and travel books, was born Samuel Langhorne Clemens in Florida, Missouri. He spent most of his childhood in Hannibal, Missouri, the town that served as a model for St. Petersburg in Twain's most famous novel, *Tom Sawyer*. When his father died, Twain left school at age 12 to work as an apprentice printer on his brother Orion's paper, the *Journal*.

In 1857 he boarded a Mississippi riverboat at Cincinnati intending to go to South America to seek his fortune. But during the trip he changed his mind and persuaded the pilot of the boat to teach him his craft. Twain worked as a riverboat pilot until the outbreak of the Civil War in 1861 stopped all commercial traffic on the Mississippi River. In that year he accompanied his brother Orion to Nevada, where Orion had been appointed secretary of the Nevada Territory. There Twain tried gold mining; he failed, but his humorous accounts of his experiences earned him a job with the *Territorial Enterprise* in Virginia City. About this time he began to sign his articles "Mark Twain," a riverboating term meaning two fathoms (a depth of 12 feet).

In 1864 Twain went to San Francisco, where he continued writing, achieving his first national success with the story "The Celebrated Jumping Frog of Calaveras County." After a trip to Hawaii, he began his second career—as a lecturer and humorist, known for his homespun American view of foreign countries. As his reputation spread, he published accounts of his travels in Europe and the Holy Land in *The Innocents Abroad*.

In 1870 Twain married Olivia Langdon, of Elmira, New York, with whom he fell in love when he first saw her portrait in 1867. Their home in Hartford, Connecticut, was one of the most spectacular houses of the day, designed to suggest a Mississippi River steamboat. The cynicism that underlay Twain's humor took on a more bitter flavor in his later years. His wife and two daughters died. He disapproved of United States acquisition of territory through military power, and he gradually adopted a cynical attitude toward human nature. He died on April 21, 1910, and is buried in Elmira.

Walt Whitman (1819–1892)

"A Noiseless Patient Spider," "When Lilacs Last in the Dooryard Bloom'd" Whitman was an American poet, born in West Hills, Long Island, New York. As a young man he was employed in a variety of occupations, and from 1846 to 1848 he was editor of the Brooklyn *Eagle*. He also worked on a New Orleans newspaper and on the Brooklyn *Times* and served as a volunteer in military hospitals during the Civil War.

In 1855 Whitman published *Leaves of Grass*, a collection of poetry which he revised and expanded in several other editions published during his lifetime. *Leaves of Grass* caused great controversy and was labeled "obscene literature." A Massachusetts district attorney demanded that two of the poems in the collection, "A Woman Waits for Me" and "To A Common Prostitute," be removed. Whitman would not agree and found a new publisher in Philadelphia who published his works. Dominant themes in these poems are freedom, the self, and brotherhood. He viewed all of nature as miraculous and celebrated the beauty and sexuality of the human body.

Whitman was one of the first American poets to write in free verse. In 1865 he published a volume of Civil War poems, *Drum Taps*. Among his best-known individual poems are "Song of Myself," "O Captain, My Captain!," "Out of the Cradle Endlessly Rocking," and "Crossing Brooklyn Ferry." Whitman lived most of his life in poverty, but said that, in his lifetime he had "really arrived."

Oscar Wilde (1845–1900)

The Importance of Being Earnest, "The Ballad of Reading Gaol"   During his years as a writer, Oscar Wilde's reputation changed drastically. Once the most desired acquaintance and dinner guest in London, his life ended in disgrace.

Wilde was born into an upper-class family in Dublin. His father was a well-known eye and ear surgeon, his mother a poet. As a scholarship student at Oxford, he gained a reputation as a brilliant and witty conversationalist, known too for his unusual style of living and clothing. In 1878, already recognized for his literary talents, Wilde left Oxford for London. In London, both his personal and artistic reputations grew. He published many stories and poems, and his talent as a conversational wit brought him fame and a high social position. Wilde continued his habit of dressing unconventionally, often appearing in velvet knee pants, silk stockings, and a velvet coat.

Wilde's humorous plays, *Lady Windermere's Fan, A Woman of No Importance, An Ideal Husband,* and *The Importance of Being Earnest,* attracted large audiences and brought their author huge sums of money. He was at the height of his success when scandal broke. The Marquess of Queensberry, angered because his son was one of Wilde's admirers, accused Wilde of homosexuality. Wilde sued the Marquess for libel. The charge, however, was true, and Wilde was tried under an 1885 law which made homosexuality a crime. He was sentenced to two years at hard labor. Wilde's high social position was destroyed, and his former hosts and acquaintances worried about their own reputations.

Wilde was released from prison (Reading Gaol) in 1897 and lived the last three years of his life in France, where he wrote "The Ballad of Reading Gaol," a reaction to his harsh prison treatment. Wilde never recovered from the scandal and imprisonment. In *De Profundis*, his autobiography, he wrote: "The gods had given me almost everything. I had a genius, a distinguished name, high social position, brilliancy, intellectual daring . . . Tired of being on the heights, I deliberately went to the depths in search for new sensation. . . . I ended in horrible disgrace. There is only one thing for me now, absolute humility."

Additional works by Oscar Wilde include *The Picture of Dorian Gray* (a novel), *Salomé* (a play), and *Intentions* (a discussion of his artistic philosophy).

Emlyn Williams (1905–   )

The Corn Is Green   Emlyn Williams is a Welsh actor, director, and playwright. He grew up in a working-class home, and spoke only Welsh until he was eight years old. A scholarship student at Oxford, however, he eventually became fluent in five languages.

Although Williams began his acting career in London in 1927, he did not become famous until his 1931 appearance in Edgar Wallace's play, *The Case of the Frightened Lady*. He achieved even greater success acting the part of a psychopathic murderer in his own play, *Night Must Fall* (produced in 1935). Williams' best-known play is *The Corn Is Green*. In it, he recalled his own boyhood as a Welsh miner's son. The play centers on a poor Welsh boy, extremely bright but unaware of his own talents until he is encouraged and guided by a stern but dedicated teacher. The play was a great success in London and New York, where it won the New York Drama Critics Circle Award as the best foreign play of 1940–1941.

Since the end of World War II, Williams has been more active as an actor than as a playwright. He is well known for his readings from the works of Charles Dickens and Dylan Thomas. An autobiography, *George*, was published in 1961.

Thomas Wolfe (1900–1938)

"The Lost Boy"   Thomas Wolfe lived such a short time that an outline of his life seems meager. The best record of it was kept by Wolfe himself in his novels. Only two of them were published during his lifetime; two more were published after his death. All of his novels, however, focus on one main character, Wolfe himself. The books stand as his explanation of his life and his family, although the main characters in *Look Homeward, Angel* (1929), for example, are called Oliver, Eliza, and Eugene Gant.

Wolfe was born in Asheville, North Carolina. At 16 he began courses at the University of North Carolina, where he studied with Frederick Koch, founder of the Carolina Playmakers. After graduating in 1920, Wolfe went to Harvard for an M.A. At both schools he wrote plays. From 1922 to 1930 he taught at New York University and wrote his first novel, *Look Homeward, Angel*. Wolfe was so enthusiastic a writer that words poured out in huge quantities. He might never have had them published without the suggestions of Maxwell Perkins, an editor at Charles Scribner's Sons who helped Wolfe pare down his huge manuscripts. After the first one was published, Wolfe won a Guggenheim Fellowship for travel in Europe. In 1935 he published *Of Time and the River* and a book of short stories, *From Death to Morning*. He died of a cerebral disease in 1938. Later, two other novels he had written were published: *The Web and the Rock* and *You Can't Go Home Again*, as well as a collection of his shorter pieces, *The Hills Beyond*.

William Wordsworth (1770–1850)

"London 1802," "The World Is Too Much With Us," "Written in March" William Wordsworth was an English poet who lived in the English Lake District, where he spent much time exploring the countryside. Wordsworth read widely and was encouraged to write poetry at an early age. As a young man, Wordsworth was influenced by Jean Jacques Rousseau and William Godwin, and he strongly supported the French Revolution.

In 1791, while in France, Wordsworth had a love affair with Annette Vallon. They planned to marry, but after their daughter Caroline was born, Wordsworth's lack of money forced him to return to England. The war that broke out between England and France prevented Wordsworth from returning to Annette, and they eventually drifted too far apart to marry. Wordsworth became guilt-ridden about Annette and disillusioned about the French Revolution. He suffered greatly and was close to an emotional breakdown.

Wordsworth's recovery began when he and his sister Dorothy moved into a cottage in Dorsetshire. Wordsworth met the poet Samuel Taylor Coleridge, and soon moved to Alfoxden to be near him. The two became very close friends and worked together on *Lyrical Ballads*, published in 1798. In 1802, Wordsworth inherited some money, and after a settlement with Annette Vallon, he married Mary Hutchinson. Wordsworth experienced great unhappiness following his marriage. His brother John drowned in 1805 and two of his children died in 1812. He and Coleridge drifted apart, and his sister Dorothy suffered physical and mental decline from the 1830's on.

As he grew older, Wordsworth became more conservative politically. His reputation as a poet grew, and in 1843 he was made Poet Laureate (the official poet of England, appointed by the king or the queen). Wordsworth's best-known works include the *Lucy* poems, "Resolution and Independence," "The Prelude," "Tintern Abbey," and "Ode: Intimations of Immortality."

2620